# PROFESSOR BASEBALL

# Edwin Amenta

# PROFESSOR BASEBALL

SEARCHING FOR
**REDEMPTION**
AND THE
**PERFECT LINEUP**
ON THE
**SOFTBALL DIAMONDS**
OF
**CENTRAL PARK**

THE UNIVERSITY OF CHICAGO PRESS · CHICAGO AND LONDON

EDWIN AMENTA is professor in the Department of Sociology at New York University, and at the University of California, Irvine

The University of Chicago Press, Chicago 60637
The University of Chicago Press, Ltd., London
© 2007 by The University of Chicago
All rights reserved. Published 2007
Printed in the United States of America

16 15 14 13 12 11 10 09 08 07          1 2 3 4 5

ISBN-13: 978-0-226-01666-5 (cloth)
ISBN-10: 0-226-01666-8 (cloth)

Library of Congress Cataloging-in-Publication Data

Amenta, Edwin, 1957–
     Professor baseball : searching for redemption and the perfect
lineup on the softball diamonds of Central Park / Edwin Amenta
        p.   cm.
     Includes bibliographical references and index.
     ISBN-13: 978-0-226-01666-5 (cloth : alk. paper)
     ISBN-10: 0-226-01666-8 (cloth : alk. paper)
     1. Softball—New York (State)—New York.   2. Amenta, Edwin,
1957–   3. College teachers—Recreation—New York (State)—New
York.   4. Middle aged men—Recreation—New York (State)—New
York.   5. Central Park (New York).   I. Title.
     GV881.A47 2007
     796.357'8097471—dc22                          2006030305

*For my father*

# Contents

# *Preseason*

**CALL ME EDDY.** I'm not your average baseball-loving professor. Unlike the sweater-wearing talking heads who wax poetical in front of Ken Burns's cameras, I'm going to be playing ball in New York City this summer, probably on five softball teams. At this late date I am still trying to prove myself. My ball-playing career has been checkered at best. I had a great season as a nine-year-old at the lowest level of the local Little League in our Chicago suburb. I was the team's top hitter, threw a no-hitter, and played shortstop or catcher when I wasn't pitching. With the championship on the line, two outs in the bottom of the last inning, I hit a home run. My sterling performance earned me promotion to the major leagues of Little League.

In the majors I was overmatched. Between the ages of ten and twelve the other kids grew, but I held steady at four-foot-eight, sixty-five pounds. In my first season I got no hits whatsoever, waving hopelessly at heaters unleashed by kids with precocious pituitaries. For the good of the team I was relegated to the minimum three outs in the field or one plate appearance. I had plunged from superstar to mascot. I did only marginally better in Pony League, where I was the littlest guy on a losing outfit sponsored by the Optimist Club, whose manager expressed his confidence in my hitting by shouting from the bench for me to bunt.

I have a team photo from my Little League days that reveals my plight. I am, of course, in the front row, third from the right, wedged in with the other small kids. My neighbor Stevie, one of the starters, stands directly behind me. A year older and a head taller than me, he has just slapped my cap askew. This exposes my wiry hair, which older teammates would rub for luck, to bond with each other, or just to annoy me. As the shutter snaps Stevie is relating something rudely nonsensical to ensure that I will flash a stupid, metallic grin for posterity. I keep the photo in a frame on my dresser.

My change in status was more upsetting for me than it might have been for most. My love for and ability to play baseball were the only things that made

I FLASHED A STUPID GRIN FOR POSTERITY

me fit in with the other boys. At about the same time that I stopped growing I noticed that they didn't share my other interests. No boys I knew would
admit to liking to read, beyond the John R. Tunis baseball books. I was reading them, sure, but also the Little House on the Prairie series and the diary
of Anne Frank. And my love of baseball transported me into territory where
others dared not follow, such as devising a fantasy baseball game with a deck
of cards, playing entire seasons and compiling the team standings and player
stats. Even worse, I liked school and, once grades stopped measuring pen-
manship and comportment, began noticeably to outperform my classmates.
I had lost the respect accorded a baseball star and minor discipline problem
and was revealed to be a very little boy with strange hair and hobbies, and
even more suspect vocabulary and math skills. My physical appearance and
unorthodox interests made the other boys less likely to befriend me than to
separate me from my lunch money. I didn't reach a hundred pounds, or pu-
berty, until sophomore year.

After my baseball career fizzled, I tried softball. In Chicagoland we play a
"weird and wonderful game," as sabermetrician and baseball historian Bill
James has put it, swinging "a stick at something about the size of your head"—
the sixteen-inch softball. For me the game was not weird, being the only softball I knew, but it wasn't any kind of wonderful. A new sixteen-incher also
resembles a head in its hardness, and like their macho nineteenth-century

2

baseball forebears, Chicagoans field with bare hands. The one thing I could still do in baseball was to flash leather, and that too was gone.

So it was a revelation when I went away to college at Indiana University and learned that Americans across the fruited plain use the standard twelve-inch softball. Right away I sent home for my beloved glove, a USA-made Wilson A2000, and threw myself into intramural softball. I had filled out, at least for me. In full uniform, including plastic cleats and bat, I stood five-foot-six and weighed 150 pounds, my curly hair ballooning so far that it repelled the cap, a little like Oscar Gamble. With my elevation to almost standard size, my game returned. After my senior year, I was recruited by a Bloomington slow-pitch team, establishing myself at shortstop and batting .600. I always suspected that somewhere I had retained the ability to play, but it was only arc ball, and soon my time had run out. I was starting graduate school and had to return to Chicago, my hometown, the softball badlands.

Seven years later, when I became an assistant professor of sociology at New York University, I was excited about the possibility of playing twelve-inch softball regularly again. But I didn't know anybody in New York, much less anybody who played. On weekends I would sometimes set aside my research and make a pilgrimage to Central Park. There they played a type of ball that reminded me of Little League. The pitchers stood close to the batters and threw modified fast pitch. The fields were always booked by organized leagues stocked with excellent players. Hoping they would notice me, I would stand on the sidelines pounding my fist into the A2000 like a youngster at Yankee Stadium praying for a foul ball, but I might as well have been invisible.

I took an unlikely route to Central Park. After several softball-less seasons, some NYU graduate students invited me to a Saturday-night pickup game in the West Village, a leisurely, slow-pitch event played on a tiny Little League field enclosed by massive chain-link fences. For the next four years I treated this diversion as if it were the World Series and Super Bowl combined, playing a mean shortstop and hitting up a cyclone.

My play caught the attention of Jesús, a second-generation Dominican and a power-hitting infielder, who is usually referred to by the second syllable of his sacred name. Zeus's job with the Newark school board leaves him free for a lot of summer softball—his true calling. He plays in about a dozen leagues and the occasional pickup game. When the Performing Arts Softball League was facing the prospect of folding and needed teams, the commissioner turned to Zeus, who knew most of the players in the tristate area. The league is confined to actors, musicians, stagehands, playwrights, and the like, so the pitchers don't throw as hard as pitchers in other modified fast-pitch

3

leagues. But it was still a big step up in intensity from the pickup game. Zeus recruited several musicians, but he couldn't fill the roster. The league honchos let him know that it would be OK to add a few ringers, as long as they weren't the kind that could hit shots from one of Central Park's Heckscher Ballfields over another. So one day Zeus descended from the softball heavens and asked me if I wanted to play for "Jesús' Angels."

The name didn't last long. Zeus went to Sports Center in the Bronx and saw a set of grey Dodgers-style away jerseys that read "Sharkeys"—no apostrophe—which the company was eager to unload at a steep discount. The jerseys' selling point for me was that sewn in white on the swooshing tail of the blue tackle lettering was "Clifton, NJ"—a location that offered an air of menacing industrial decline. None of us had even heard of Sharkey's, which is apparently a sports bar, but we adopted the name on the jerseys, typo and all. Our opponents were not intimidated. During my three years on the Sharkeys we lost two-thirds of our games—a record of haplessness reminiscent of the early New York Mets. Though I played well, my non-power game is not the kind that earns much notice or credit. I had been quarantined to a desolate northern New Jersey of softball. I was playing so little that I had time most summers to train for the New York City Marathon.

But last season, despite having my best years well behind me and shrouded in a loser aura, I was discovered as a softball player. Getting onto an organized softball team in Manhattan is next to impossible. There are tens of thousands of potential players but only about five places to play. And anyone who is invited onto a team is, usually, in for life. It is less like a dugout pass than an appointment to the federal bench. Recruitment is based partly on merit but mainly on word of mouth, herd mentality, and serendipity. This is where Billy comes in. Billy plays guitar for a theme band but, like Zeus, is a softball impresario, a pitcher on four teams who devotes most of his waking summer hours to the game. When the Saturday pickup game was moved temporarily to the spacious East River fields, Billy learned that I could chase down fly balls. This was sheer luck. He had seen me play many times in the West Village, where there is no outfield to speak of, and had never considered recruiting me. But now, looking for versatile players that he could deploy at any position, he asked me to join a highly skilled Sunday men's team called the Nuclear Pencils, in the Lower Manhattan Softball League, and recommended me to the managers of two competitive coed teams: Thespian Aid, in the Broadway Show League, and d.b.a., the defending champion in the East Village Softball Association.

With the gates to New York softball at long last opening, I was ready to break out. I began the season leading off and playing third base for the Pencils. In the second game, our shortstop Mike—of the many softball-playing Mikes in New York, the only one I know who rates the honor of being called simply Mike—waved Billy over after I had made an error. He told Billy that I didn't "look comfortable" at third base—softball code for "Get him out of my infield." I was exiled to right field, and soon to the bottom of the batting order. Before I could play my way back into the team's good graces I injured myself. I had qualified for April's Boston Marathon and decided to run in it, but without the usual extensive training I cramped up badly on Heartbreak Hill and limped to the finish. Soon afterward, I popped my hamstring trying to stretch a single, then aggravated the injury trying to come back too quickly. Although I wasn't kicked off the team, I was now riding the pine.

It was like Little League all over again. I had made good with the Sharkeys in the less competitive weekday league, had been promoted to the weekend league, where the big kids—people with regular jobs—play, and had faltered. I feared that my new teammates would start rubbing my head.

Now it has again turned spring. With a new season of softball, I have a rare opportunity. How many of us have wanted to redo something we failed at as children? I also have a sense of urgency, like a baseball general manager in a small market with a roster of stars on the verge of free agency. I'm on the far side of forty, and despite a winter of rehab my hamstring still isn't right. The beautiful and brilliant Francesca has persuaded me that it's time for us to have a baby. My playing ball all summer is part of the deal—next year I will probably be pushing a stroller instead of swinging a bat. Like any GM who trades for known quantities and relinquishes prospects, I wonder if I've given up too much. On top of all that, Francesca is up for tenure at Columbia. If she doesn't get it, we may have to leave New York. And this winter I was elected chair of the NYU sociology department, a three-year term that starts in the fall. So this season I am going to play softball nearly every day and twice on Sundays. I will also get my first chance to run a team—the doormat Sharkeys. I'm looking forward to the challenge. This season may be my last chance to avenge my Little League humiliation.

## Jumping the Sharkeys

Last fall Zeus decided to quit as the Sharkeys' manager because he was fed up with complaints and hates to lose. When he asked some of the players about candidates to replace him, my name kept coming up. I had established a reputation as being friendly and dependable, and, I like to think, I'm seen as having good ideas and being well organized and responsible. Maybe that is why my sociology colleagues elected me chair. The fact that I would often dispense with the Sharkeys jersey in favor of one from my game-used collection might also have been a factor; I suspect my teammates sensed that I could afford to front the thousand-dollar league fee.

I'm no big fan of writing, usually by my humanist academic colleagues, that considers baseball as a metaphor for life. I am partial to the so-called sabermetricians—sometimes scientists but mainly self-taught former Strat-O-Matic players—who have reinterpreted baseball by applying sharp analytical thinking to the game's voluminous statistics. Between the Ken Burns expert who intones about how baseball recovers primordial memories of village greens and the one who relates how his boyhood worship of the Say Hey Kid and a passion to prove to chums that he was better than the Mick or the Duke revealed the magic of Markov chains, I'll take the math guy every time. I am also a big fan of baseball novels, the best of which aren't about baseball at all.

As I tell the students in my "Baseball and Society" seminar, the beauty of baseball—softball too—is that it is an almost perfect world, nothing like life. Life is messy, ambiguous, complicated. Baseball is neat, clear, elegant. In life, dramatic moments are rare and often difficult to identify when they happen. In baseball, drama is frequent, and everyone in the ballpark, even from the cheap seats, can identify a big situation. In baseball, pet theories can be tried out, and, in contrast to most areas of life, there are rapid and ruthlessly specific outcomes—reach base or make an out, win or lose, succeed or fail. After criticizing major league management from the outside for decades, the sabermetricians have in recent years used their powerful analyses to break into general managers' offices. Even the quintessential outsider, the sabermetrician Bill James, who holds down several positions on my syllabus, finally got his chance in the 2003 season, when he was hired as a senior adviser for the Boston Red Sox. In my own small way I hope to use some professor-baseball ideas to turn around the loser Sharkeys. Call it better softball through sabermetrics.

ZEUS FACED THE PITCHER
LIKE A SAMURAI

Revamping a softball team is in many ways different from drafting a fantasy league baseball team or running a major league franchise. In softball, there are no expensive free agents. In the Performing Arts Softball League, the only ones getting paid are the umpires and drink vendors. And although there are no contracts, there is a kind of reserve clause—only in reverse. Whereas baseball's reserve clause, before the advent of free agency, bound pro players to their teams in perpetuity, softball's binds the team to the players. There is an unspoken understanding that anyone who played for a team one season has the right to remain on the team the next season, and the longer the tenure, the stronger the right. What's more, because of friendships, if a manager decides to add or drop a player, it often means adding or dropping two or three players. In New York, ethnic ties further complicate roster moves.

My main obstacle, however, is the person who brought me into the league: Zeus. All winter he has been battling me over players. For Zeus is not only jumping the Sharkeys, but also joining our PM-division rival and perennial power the Friars Club. In this, he is like the nineteenth-century ballplayers known as "revolvers" or "shooting stars." Before the reserve clause, revolvers shifted allegiance from team to team, even in midseason, looking for more money. Unlike his mercenary predecessors, however, Zeus just wants to win. He had jumped to the Friars Club once before, two years ago, but failed to win a championship and returned to us last year. Zeus wants to keep his options open, so he doesn't want me to build a powerhouse that would make it impossible for him to return again as manager.

If I want the Sharkeys to win—and I am as tired of losing as Zeus is—I will have my work cut out for me. We didn't lose many players in the off-season, but the ones we did lose were valuable. Zeus, who was our best hitter, is not much taller than me but carries about fifty more pounds, mostly muscle. He intimidates pitchers by holding the bat high, the way a samurai holds the sword, with an extremely closed stance, his knees and toes pointing inward. His explosive power prompts opposing managers to wave to their outfielders to play deeper. I tried to convince him to stay with the Sharkeys. I would do all the dirty work, I promised; he could focus on playing the game, and we would win. He didn't go for it. With Zeus went Manny, a more recent Dominican immigrant and a spray hitter with some speed who can play anywhere.

The Sharkeys also lost Amanda, who is about my height but slight and gangly with a pageboy haircut, a crooked smile, a suntanned face, and a whip for an arm. She pitched softball in high school and was able to make the transition to the more restrained "modified" delivery required in our league. Pitchers can throw as hard as they can underhanded, but the rules forbid snapping their wrists or raising their arms above shoulder level. Women can play in the league if they are good enough—there is no rule. Amanda, our first and only woman player, compensated for her pitching dominance with comic sexual suggestiveness. She would pay exaggerated attention when any of us hitched up our shorts to minister to a strawberry and would facetiously volunteer to massage our strained muscles and others as yet unstrained. We staggered into the playoffs last year. From there Amanda carried us on her scrawny back, and we edged out the best three teams in the division before losing the championship. Zeus would've tried to take Amanda, but she suffers from chronic knee and relationship trouble, and the latter put her on the disabled list. During the off-season she didn't answer her phone or reply to e-mails. Word was that she had separated from her husband and moved away. Losing Amanda and Zeus was like the Yankees losing Clemens and Jeter or, more realistically, like the Bad News Bears losing the Tatum O'Neal character and the chain-smoking, Harley-riding little slugger who later turned up as Moocher in *Breaking Away*.

I tell my graduate students that one well-crafted two-by-two table can make a sociologist's career. This one, which breaks down the remaining Sharkeys according to their hitting and fielding performance, is not going to help mine, but it indicates what I was facing. Zeus left me with several guys who hit but don't field well and a few who field fine but don't hit. Several others were at best question marks.

After writing a check for the league fees, my next move was addition by subtraction, which wasn't easy under the reverse reserve clause. Charlie is a nice guy and an accomplished musician who had pitched the bulk of our

SHARKEYS PLAYERS, PAST HITTING AND FIELDING PERFORMANCE

| | | Hit? | |
|---|---|---|---|
| | | Yes | No |
| Field? | Yes | Cookie, Eddy | Dog (Swanny? Tanner? Q?) |
| | No | Mule, Roger, Papi, Nardo (Little Bobby?) | Charlie (Alan?) |

games for three years before Zeus found Amanda. But Charlie's repertoire consists solely of a nothing ball that he struggles to get over the plate, and his reaction time is so slow that Zeus, during his previous stint with the Friars Club, hit a shot that spun Charlie's old-timey cap off. He tumbled backward in the turbulence like Charlie Brown, though without being divested of his remaining clothing. I talked the issue over with some of the Sharkeys. They felt that Charlie walked too many, got hit too hard, and fielded too poorly to be reinstated as the number-one pitcher. And when he doesn't pitch, he's so unhappy that doesn't even root for us. I leaked the news to Zeus that Charlie was out. He worried that he would be blamed, but when I offered Charlie to the Friars Club, Zeus declined. Having heard the bad word from Zeus, Charlie called me. He said he didn't want to be a substitute, but he asked me to keep him on the roster and call him if I needed him to pitch. I agreed, but I won't ever need him.

Gone forever are the days when Whiteys, Sparkys, Mooses, and Pee Wees roamed baseball's majors. They have been replaced by Jonesies, Rods, Macs, and Gonzos, more respectful nicknames suitable for today's richly rewarded celebrities. But being neither rich nor famous nor young, the Sharkeys are flush with old-school nicknames. The guy sharing the hits well/fields well box with me has a moniker that might have come off a 1950s baseball card. Like most of the Sharkeys, Cookie is a musician, a trombonist from Sunset Park in Brooklyn. He is of Puerto Rican descent and, like many of the musical Sharkeys, has a regular job to pay the bills, troubleshooting computer problems at CUNY evenings, helping to support his mother. Cookie is talented enough to play any infield position but too self-effacing to play shortstop. He has a mild stammer that is more endearing than embarrassing. He is an excellent line-drive hitter and isn't too macho to take a walk. The last time Zeus left the Sharkeys, he turned the team over to Cookie, who crumples at the prospect of interpersonal conflict, but he agreed to help me run the team.

Our main trouble is the many Sharkey holdovers with no hope of playing their way into the hit-and-field box of the table. As is, this team promises to do no better than our record last season: 6–9. More likely, given our roster losses, we could revert to the 4–11 record of our inaugural season. In attempting to improve the team, we face several problems. I call them the batting-practice fallacy, faded-glory fielders, attitudes, and the perennial-loser syndrome. Actually, although Cookie and I both recognize these problems, I'm the only one facing them. He would rather reinstall an operating system than make a roster move.

Start with the batting-practice fallacy. Batting can be broken down into hitting for average, getting on base, and hitting for power. For the Sharkeys these qualities are easy to track. The Performing Arts Softball League Web site—maybe my favorite thing about our league—calculates not only the standard, overrated batting average, but on-base percentage (OBP) and slugging average (SLG). The last two are often added together to produce on-base plus slugging (OPS), the best quick-and-dirty summary stat of a batter's production and usefulness. Many of my teammates had compiled three seasons' worth of on-base plus slugging numbers in the .600s, unacceptable even for utility infielders in the big leagues, let alone higher-scoring competitive softball. Yet my underperforming teammates see themselves as hitters and can crush the ball before games in batting practice. The psychological footwork required to square the positive self-image with the negative record is not as tortuous as one might think. In softball games somewhere my teammates have hit, and they demonstrate during BP that they can hit. This works for their egos but leaves me with half a roster of guys who don't hit well in games and think walks are for pussies.

We do have a lot of guys whose specialty is producing at the plate, and they are valuable in competitive recreational softball, which is like the American League run amok. Not only is there a designated hitter, but two extra hitters can be placed in the batting order, and someone has to play catcher, a position of minor defensive importance. Unfortunately, most guys who can hit but can't field well believe they can field. I call them faded glories. At some point they were good fielders and they know about stances and positioning, but in many cases age-related losses in agility mean that they can field well only in their memories.

Papi, another musician of Puerto Rican background, a trumpeter, is a case in point. He has a broad body and a thin mustache. If you are going good, Papi will call you "Papi," which other players then started calling him. Papi takes a vicious, almost perfectly level cut that produces a lot of line drives to left field. When he gets a little under the ball, the visual force of his swing tips outfielders back on their heels, resulting in many Texas League safeties.

He knows how to field, but his chronically bad knees and back limit his mobility. Papi sees himself as a first baseman and will be upset unless he sees considerable action there. The same goes for Nardo and Alan, both of whom consider themselves third basemen.

Then there is Mule, an underemployed salesman grandfathered into the league. He is rotund on the Babe Ruth model and couldn't beat your grandmother in a race around the bases, even if the prize were a fistful of the funky cigars he is always brandishing. He can hit but not for much power, consistently shooting line drives to the opposite field with a dainty flick of the wrists. The problem is that Mule sees himself as a Ruthian hit-and-pitch threat. But on the mound—and there's nowhere else to put him—he'll walk one or more batters per inning, so he won't be pitching for us. And he literally cannot control his tongue, which, when he speaks, bunches up in his lower lip like a wad of Skoal. Over the winter, Mule would phone me with scenarios that all had him batting cleanup and pitching. "I'm an RBI guy; I'm a big-game pitcher," he'd insist in a voice half Mike Tyson, half Ratso Rizzo. I like his enthusiasm, and we need his bat, but I had to stop taking his calls. Much as I dread it, my only option is to play the faded glories where they should play, if anywhere, and be prepared to take the fallout.

In contrast there is Roger, a jazz saxophonist whom Zeus recruited for the team near the end of the last season. With his sturdy body, close-cropped blond hair, and aging boyish good looks Roger resembles Roger Maris in 1961, or '61*. He too falls into the hits well–only category, but otherwise he plays against type. As a hitter, Roger is a natural—with good power. His fielding deficits are not due to injury, immobility, or obesity. He is new to the game and still learning to catch and throw. Most players see playing catcher as beneath them. They are like Mike Piazza in reverse, ready to quit if shifted to catcher. In baseball, catcher is the most important defensive position aside from pitcher. But in softball, the catcher is only slightly more important to the defense than the designated hitter. Runners can't steal bases or advance on passed balls, so catchers get few opportunities, except the chance to take a foul tip off a shoulder, hand, or worse. But Roger finds catching a challenge and acts like a little kid offered a chance to play with the bigger kids. This attitude, in combination with his hitting, makes him worth a lot, and I argued with Zeus long, hard, and eventually successfully that Roger should stay a Sharkey.

Which brings me to attitude. In major league baseball team harmony is overrated. Winners produce good chemistry, not the other way around, and when pro players lose they can console themselves with their massive paychecks. But attitude and harmony are everything in softball. There is little worse than playing a sport to blow off steam and ending the game more up-set than you were when it started. The irascible, foul-mouthed blond kid in *The Bad News Bears* who was supposed to be so amusing—I would boot him off the team in a New York second. A lot comes down to a player's attitude toward winning. The more winning matters the more one sees what nine-teenth-century baseball writers like Henry Chadwick decried as "boyish" behavior, also known as being a poor sport or acting like a jerk. Not all can find the happy middle ground between caring and giving their best and not taking defeats too hard.

The late sociologist Pierre Bourdieu wrote that the further one goes down the social class scale, the greater the desire among children to win at all costs in competitive team sports, whereas among the higher classes team sports are valued for building character and teaching participants to win within the constraints of rules. What happens, then, when players from all backgrounds pursue team sports as adults—an increasingly common phenomenon that Bourdieu did not consider? Few of my teammates come from well-off families, most are single, many have work that is intermittent, and they pay to play.

After discussing it with several of the guys, who have been barraging me with suggestions, I'd informed Zeus that I am dropping Tanner, a Sharkey who wants to win too much. A percussionist, Tanner rose quickly in the music world and thinks of himself as unstoppable in any activity involving a stick, but he hasn't hit well for the Sharkeys. He has fielding skills but sees himself as the peer of Ozzie Guillen, the former great-glove–no-plate-sense shortstop of the Chicago White Sox, the hapless and historically tainted team that I've dissipated my life's fandom rooting for. Tanner is actually friends with Ozzie and—I'll admit, I was jealous—would occasionally sport one of Ozzie's game-used jerseys. Tanner's a music star and a good player, but he can be impossible when he doesn't get what he wants or when his teams lose—which the Sharkeys have done more often than not. He is the kind of player that other players, even those with large personal investments in winning, complain about. He has to go.

I began to realize that the off-season maneuvers of a softball team manager are less like those of a GM assembling a major league baseball team than a mid-dle-school girl planning a slumber party. Everything I considered was being gossiped about. Once word got around that Tanner was out, I fielded a call from my teammate Q, another percussionist and Tanner's childhood friend. Last year Q and Tanner formed their own team, P's & Q's, a name derived from the first initials of their surnames, which plays on Tuesdays. Q is short, trim, and as tightly coiled as his dark curly hair. His confrontational way of speaking and

BILLY LOOKED LIKE BUDDY HOLLY
REFRACTED THROUGH BILLY IDOL

wraparound mirror shades, worn even on the cloudiest days, give him an air of menace well out of proportion to his stature. "I didn't know you had a problem with Tanner," he said. I told Q that he knew managers sometimes had to make hard decisions—like when Tanner and Q didn't ask me to play for P's & Q's. I also told him that I liked Tanner and went on about how nice it was that Tanner got Ozzie to sign my glove, on the off chance that Tanner was listening on the other line.

My next, and most important, task was to plug holes. I could add fifty players to my roster if I wanted-ed, but I still faced the biggest obstacle of them all: perennial-loser syndrome. This is not something that can be overcome by dropping or shifting current players, as general managers in basketball know from experience. The loser Sharkeys were like the Chicago Bulls after they shed Michael Jordan, Scottie Pippen, and Dennis Rodman, only without the previous glory years. The Bulls had plenty of room under the salary cap, but no star free agent would sign for any amount of money because the team sucked. In softball too, no really good player wants to play on a hopeless team. So I went to work on some of the eligible players I had met last year, trying to convince them that the Sharkeys wouldn't be losers.

To do that, I needed a pitching ace. Pitchers are even more important in softball than in major league baseball, because in softball one pitcher can pitch every game. I turned to yet another softball magnate, Billy. With his blond hair, bleached an ironic Warhol shade, his lightly freckled face, and dark-framed glasses of the sort favored by certain architects, he looks like a postmodern Buddy Holly refracted through Billy Idol. Billy lacks the raw power of Amanda but is just as effective. He has encyclopedic knowledge of batters' tendencies and spends minutes each inning positioning outfielders. He can change speeds, hit locations, and take advantage of the count. His repertoire includes a knuck-

BIG ARTIE HAD A PRO BODY AND WAS A
GREAT TARGET AT FIRST BASE

leball and a curve—which he can get to break once the ball has been knocked around. His out pitch is a straight change that he sells by exaggerating the height of his arm. Billy was skeptical. He had played with the Sharkeys a few times over the years and was unimpressed. There would be major changes, I assured him. He would pitch, we would win—and have fun doing it. Billy said he wasn't sure how much time he could devote to the league, but I persuaded him to show up to the first game.

I also recruited teammates from d.b.a., which has been doing business as a championship team in the East Village Softball Association, a coed bar league. Arthur—called Big Artie to distinguish him from another Artie who plays for d.b.a.—is a playwright and daytime computer guy who looks like Bernie Kosar with glasses, but bigger. Big Artie is one of the few softball players with the body of a professional athlete. He's often used it to dominate the West Village pickup game, though he is too unassuming to do so all the time, as if he feels his strength gives him an unfair advantage. He can play a lot of positions, but there is no better target at first base. Another Mike, Pennebaker, called Penny, is a filmmaker and a child of academics with a little goatee, sad eyes, and a strong sense of responsibility. He tends to repeat himself, as if he were accustomed to being misunderstood. Penny hits the ball hard consistently, has soft hands, and, though he cannot run fast, is quick enough to handle any infield position. He is also very reliable, partly because he has worked only sporadically lately. Penny plays in as many leagues as Zeus, possibly just to help the teams. Krishy is a personal trainer and a talented outfielder and hitter who used to manage d.b.a. but handed the reins over to Billy. Krishy said that his playing would depend on his schedule, but with his poker face and deadpan delivery, I couldn't tell whether he even wanted to play. As a lure, I informed the new recruits that Billy "would be pitching

14

TREY WAS THE COOLEST GUY IN THE PARK

for us," though without specifying the number of games. It worked. They all agreed to show up to the first game.

One guy I really wanted was Trey, another personal trainer, who played for the Sunday-league Nuclear Pencils and had been on the Sharkeys roster during its first season. Trey is a smooth infielder who can hit with power and even pitch. I know he's played a lot of organized baseball, and he has the c'mon-you-can-do-it attitude of his occupation instead of the you'd-better-fucking-do-it attitude of many Sharkeys. Trey was out with an Achilles tendon injury most of last year but made a big impression on me during one of his few at bats at the end of the season. It was late in a close game, runners on, two strikes. The Pencils were giving him the usual anxiety-ridden patter—"you're big here," "show me something." The coolest guy in the park,

THIS SEASON'S SHARKEYS, EXPECTED HITTING AND FIELDING PERFORMANCE

|  |  | Hit? | |
|---|---|---|---|
|  |  | Yes | No |
| Field? | Yes | Cookie, Eddy, Penny, Billy, Krishy, Big Artie, Trey | Dog (Swanny? Q?) |
|  | No | Mule, Roger, Papi, Nardo (Little Bobby?) | (Alan?) |

he stepped out the box and addressed our bench: "Guys, I *have* played this game before." We all watched in silence as he stroked a base hit. Trey is also Hispanic and dark, another advantage. I'm dropping both white and Spanish-speaking guys from the team and don't want exclusively white replacements. Trey said he would try to clear his schedule, but he couldn't commit, even to the first game.

If I can get these guys to play this season, the Sharkeys will have an excellent chance of making a move in the PM division of the Performing Arts Softball League. That's my hope. But right now, I don't know if I've outmaneuvered Zeus or even if I'll be able to field a team beyond Opening Day, which is in less than two weeks against his team, the Friars Club.

TUESDAY, APRIL 8, 269 MERCER STREET

## *Big League Fun*

"Baseball and Society" is my most popular class ever and the one for which I have the least academic expertise. Today's subject is baseball in Japan. The journalist Robert Whiting says Japanese players embrace *wa*, which means harmony or teamwork. They engage in ruthless self-criticism, apologize effusively for errors, encourage teammates always, and cover talent deficiencies with hard work. If there is one thing I hope to achieve as Sharkeys manager it is to move the morale of the team more toward the Japanese model. We are grown-ups, so why do we have to get as worked up as a high school football team and bicker like teenagers? I'm not looking for anyone to make written apologies or take endless post-error grounders in atonement, as they do in Japan. But refraining from blaming teammates and complaining would be nice. A shift in the team's attitude might even turn around an underperforming player or two and help us win.

I'd like to think I'm above all this, but I like winning. It may not be everything or the only thing, but it is the thing the team is trying to achieve. It gives leisure a higher purpose. Winning is also a sign that the group is playing well together and so elevates the efforts of each player. And everyone wants a taste of what they've seen televised in World Series locker rooms and countless sports films. Also, it is a sad fact, but the best way for me to avoid catching flack from players who want to win even more than I do is to win games. When a team loses, the overcompetitive rarely point the finger at themselves. As manager I'll take the heat. Winning will keep my teammates from poisoning the air and getting on my back.

Winning also opens the possibility for a giddy sociability that might be called big league fun. This is a something that I know about only from books like Jim Bouton's *Ball Four* and Jim Brosnan's *The Long Season*. As I imagine it, this involves a lot of hard, irreverent, but good-natured teasing of teammates and yourself. No one can do that well when they're frustrated and angry about losing. Even in *Ball Four*, the winning Astros had more fun and were funnier than the losing Pilots. I want to win easily and quickly to reap the emotional benefits of garbage time. I want someone to say, "That's what I'm talking about"—the catchphrase of choice for the overserious player—only if it is meant ironically.

I also want to be a part of the magic that can happen in ball games. I'm not talking about hearing voices telling me that if I build it, he will come. I'm talking about the seemingly improbable situations that inevitably arise during the course of a season—when your team breaks out of a slump in the last inning and doesn't stop hitting until the game is won, when one of your weakest hitters launches one over the outfield, when your teammates make extraordinary plays that transform imminent disaster into triumph. I want to make the occasional magical play myself.

This probably goes without saying, but I want to be a star. Not the kind who hits homers—I don't have the power. But I can spark teams, relying on guile and plate sense, working walks, spraying to all fields, taking the extra base, and hitting in the clutch. Overrated as batting average is as a statistic, I would love to lead the league in it. It could happen. My first year in the Performing Arts Softball League I hit safely in every game and batted .550. Even though it was almost all singles, against fairly easy pitching, and, unfortunately, prior to the Web site, my average had to have been near the top of the league. It would be even more rewarding to me to lead in on-base percentage, which is far more important to scoring runs and winning games. I would like my teammates also to realize that getting on base is the most important thing they can do at bat—though that may be too much to hope for.

On defense, I want to lead the infield and be the one my teammates look to in tight spots. I want to do all the things it takes to win—handle routine chances flawlessly, head off bloop singles, convert fouls into outs, make lightning relays to cut down runners seeking extra bases, and turn lots of double plays. When the game is on the line I want everyone on my team, including me, to hope that the ball will come my way. Maybe I'll even pitch. I imagine goosing my lukewarm heater above fifty miles an hour and retooling my knuckleball—maybe with Bouton's help!—so that it dips and sails instead of just wobbling. I imagine baffling perennial champs Irving Plaza in the playoffs, striking out the last batter, and walking off the field into a line of triumphant fist punches from my adoring teammates. In the postseason get-together, my teammates unanimously vote me team MVP. I imagine Francesca calling me "Meat," like the old-time big-league hurlers in books, instead of "Poopyhead." Really, I do.

Young players have it drilled into them that it is better to play poorly and have the team win than to play well and have the team lose. I don't believe that. Anyone even slightly self-critical will feel useless being a poor player on a winning team. I did in Little League. Worse, underperformers are in danger of being benched. Playing well on a losing team provides some relief. The loss is somebody else's fault. But it's not that much fun, as I know from past seasons as a Sharkey. I don't see why I can't be a star on a winning team with guys who are fun to play with. And I want to prove myself in a more difficult league—Sunday's Lower Manhattan Softball League, where I bombed with the Nuclear Pencils last year. The pitchers there throw hard, and from right on top of you, just as in Little League. Most of the Sharkeys' opponents don't throw much harder than I can. I've never felt that this league is a true test of my skills.

I always have butterflies before the baseball class, probably because of my lack of expertise in the area. In my anxiety I'm inspired to e-mail Bouton. The former Yankee pitcher and author has been a longtime hero and seems just the guy to talk to my students about baseball's current problems and possible ways out. And like Bouton, I'm looking forward to writing about what happens in my season. In Ken Burns's *Baseball*, the writer George Plimpton recounts that when as a kid he saw professional baseball players he found that this was something he could imagine himself doing as an adult. When one of the older kids in the neighborhood took us down to his basement and read us passages from *Ball Four* it was as if he had got hold of a samizdat mimeograph, and I reacted as Plimpton did.

The kid read aloud Hall of Famer Joe Morgan's facetious interview, which presaged his illustrious career as an ESPN color commentator. Having just struck out and returned to the dugout, Morgan describes to an Astros teammate, who is pretending to be a broadcaster and using his fist for a microphone, the difference between a regular curve ball and the strikeout pitch he identifies as a "motherfucking" curve ball. Unlike your regular curve, which spins obviously and moves predictably, Morgan politely explains, the motherfucker looks like a fastball, then drops off the tabletop, and the next thing you know, it's motherfucking strike three.

Here were adults who were hilarious and who played baseball every day. Here was one big leaguer who had just struck out—which I had been spending most of Little League doing—and could joke about it. Here was another who was writing about all of it in a compelling way. I want to make it as a player and a manager, but I would also love to capture the world of New York softball the way that Bouton captured the major league locker room.

Beyond all that, I'm wondering if it is too much to hope for to make a friend or two. My softball teammates and I suffer no illusion that we have been gripping the ball and not the other way around, as Bouton famously put it. But for me this particular self-understanding hasn't served as a sound basis for friendship. In the past I've mainly seen my teammates on the ball field. Maybe if we win more, we'll be having so much fun that friendship will come as easily to us as it did to Bouton's Astros. Much to my excitement, Bouton e-mails right back, but he's booked for the semester.

# Early Season

**OPENING DAY** is a time of hope and a time of resolutions—like New Year's Day. No one has made an out. No one has made an error. No teams have lost. Everyone vows to make all the plays, hit a ton, and at long last win the championship. The first weeks of the season are also a time of trials. Managers will want to see how new players do and how veteran players fare in new positions. Managers distribute jerseys and find out in a more concrete way how their team is going to look—whether it is going to be competitive or need redesigning. For players, the first weeks can be unnerving. Veterans are hoping to keep their valuable places in the lineup. Newcomers are hoping to make good and displace veterans. Unlike baseball, softball has no spring training, exhibition games, or reporters documenting each move as rosters are whittled down. In softball, players often get bad news suddenly and unexpectedly. Disputes and hurt feelings are common. Seeing someone else playing your position on Opening Day is a little like seeing someone else, as the ball drops in Times Square, kissing your girlfriend.

**( MONDAY, APRIL 14, HECKSCHER #2 )**

## Opening Day Loss

I'm nervous again. My managerial debut with the Sharkeys is against the Friars Club, which roasted us in all nine regular-season games over the last three years. In between grading papers for tomorrow's class I am devising a lineup. I want to craft one that gives us the best chance to win, but in one way it's a no-win situation. I'm going to piss off somebody. If my recruits don't like where I'm playing them, don't like the team, or don't like its chances to win, they will just drift away. If the veterans don't like where I'm playing them, they will be quick to express anger and may quit, threatening my managerial status. Finally I decide on this lineup and head to the subway: Eddy ss;

Papi dh/Artie 1b; Penny 3b; Roger c; Krishy lcf; Mule eh; Cookie 2b; Q lf; Swanny rcf; Billy p; Bobby rf. Bench: Dog, Alan.

I'm planning to bat leadoff and play shortstop, the most crucial fielding position, not only because I'm in charge and can but because I think that it's best for the team. I believed in sabermetrics long before Billy Beane read his first edition of *The Bill James Baseball Abstract,* and I don't feel I place my manhood in jeopardy when I take a walk. In my last full season, I led the league with eleven free passes, as many walks as Ozzie Guillen accumulated in all of 1991, a year when he came to the plate over five hundred times. I was the Sharkeys' shortstop during our first year in the league, and now, with Zeus gone, I'm the only player with both the ability and personality for it. Also, playing short will give me a chance to show off my talents to Billy and Zeus, the managers of my other teams. Most of all, I figure that since I'm going to be held responsible for what happens, I might as well put myself in the thick of it.

My plans to put Papi at DH and add Mule as an extra hitter might not sit well with either of them. Both want to play the field, and, especially given his seniority, Papi is not likely to be mollified by his high place in the batting order. He'll be irked that he's not playing first base, and Mule will want to pitch. Alan, an infielder, and Dog, the substitute pitcher, are going to be sitting until we get a big lead or, more likely, blown out. Dog won't mind, but Alan will.

On the A train, partly because the class assignment was about the original baseball players, I can't help thinking of the parallels between them and my softball teams. The first known recorded game of baseball took place two blocks from my apartment near Washington Square Park in 1823. Twenty-two years later Alexander Cartwright devised the first standardized rules of the game for his Knickerbocker Base Ball Club. Antebellum baseball was played chiefly for fun and in the middle of the day, during working hours. Most players were neither poor nor rich but had steady incomes and flexible work schedules. It was a game dominated by the highest rung of blue-collar workers and the lowest rung of white-collar ones—skilled artisans and clerks.

At first, baseball was played largely by clubs in the old sense of the word. They had by-laws, collected dues, and met away from the field. Each club had enough players for a few teams, or "nines," and members played among themselves. But there was already a question whether the point of playing was to have fun or to win. The clubs soon began to compete among themselves to see which was best, and the secondary nines began to play less and cheer more. Spreading from the East after the Civil War, baseball had become a national pastime by 1870. The rules were constantly being modified to promote greater self-control and skill—more "manly" play, as observers called it at the time. For example, Cartwright declared in 1845 that fielders could no longer put out a runner by plugging or "soaking" him with the ball. And starting in the 1870s fielders had to catch the ball on the fly, rather than on one hop, to put out batters. The game of that era developed most of the standard plays of modern baseball, including the relay, the changeup, the sacrifice, tagging up, and sliding.

But as Bill James writes, the baseball of 1870 "resembled fast-pitch softball more than any other [ball game], including modern baseball." The pitcher stood forty-five feet from home plate and threw underhanded. Although pitchers tried to retire batters, they were prohibited from snapping their wrists, ruling out curve balls. Most pitchers pitched every game, about thirty a summer. The ball was handmade and resembled modern-day softballs in size and the softer ones in resistance. Fields were rarely enclosed. When players and their followers—"cranks" or "bugs"—referred to the long ball, they did not mean a shot over a fence but one driven past the outfielders. Many more runs scored on errors than on homers.

The National Association of Base Ball Players sought to prevent pay for play, but the antiprofessional forces found themselves in an uphill fight. As newspapers took an interest in club championships, the focus came to be more and more on skill and winning by fielding the best team possible. The entrepreneurially minded soon discovered that cranks would pay to watch a better brand of ball. They enclosed fields and charged admission, and paid players became the norm. When the National League of Professional Base Ball Clubs was formed in the mid-1870s, it was an organization of corporations, and the Knickerbocker Club disbanded. Baseball never looked back.

As the historian Warren Goldstein puts it, the descendants of the losers of that contest re-create themselves every season on softball fields across America. In the weekday New York City softball leagues, we historical also-rans still play ball in the original setting and at the original time. Like the first players, we play when most people work. There are leagues every weekday in Central Park, and most of them have more than one division with six or eight teams each. We are neither rich nor poor but have flexible working schedules or work at night. We are actors, musicians, writers, models, bartenders, cops, firemen, real estate brokers, small businessmen, salesmen, personal trainers, and teachers. We are men and women. We are white, black, Hispanic, and Asian. We are old and young. We do it for fun but also to prove we are the best in our little softball circles.

IT WAS THRILLING TO APPROACH THE HECKSCHER BALLFIELDS

It is thrilling to get off the subway at Columbus Circle, pass through Merchants' Gate, head north on the West Drive, and jog down the slope to the Heckscher Ballfields, where most of the Central Park softball leagues play. Falling between Tavern on the Green and Wollman Rink in an island defined by Park Drive and the Sixty-Sixth Street Transverse, the Heckscher Ballfields are five intersecting diamonds that fall out like points on a star. They define a sacred place that is wholly devoted to softball and its rituals and practices. Soccer players and sunbathers stay away. Trespassers looking for shortcuts to the Carousel, the Sheep Meadow, Columbus Circle, or the Central Park Zoo are barraged with profanity and ridicule. By springtime the ice has melted at Wollman Rink, but visitors to the south end of the park can ride the Carousel or horses that are slightly more alive, witness the feeding of sea lions or penguins—or watch softball. Each of the diamonds has green-painted bleachers where spectators sit with sodas, ice cream bars, or pretzels from the official green-and-white carts or beers from the unlicensed vendors under the nearby stands of silver maples.

Before the game we occupy field #1, which is not used by the PASL, to get in some practice. Everyone I had contacted shows up. And just before game time, a teammate whom I wasn't expecting also appears. Word was that Nardo had landed a day job and wouldn't be available until later in the season. Nardo is about my height but very stout. He must run about 210 pounds, and with his shaved head, powerful torso, boxcar ears, and almond eyes, he resembles Mr. Clean. Zeus had Nardo batting cleanup at the end of last year, and it was fitting. He's a two-year Sharkey who can hit for power, but he is uncertain in the field. With our American League–style rules, however, it's the more hitters the merrier. I slot him in as a second extra hitter at number five, between Roger and Krishy. We head over to field #2, which I face with some trepidation. Its base paths harbor little moats of loose sand, especially near first base and at shortstop. I tore my hamstring here last May.

As I'm correcting the scorecard, too much seems to be happening too quickly. At the last minute, to buy myself some mental parking space, I switch places in the batting order with Cookie. During the exchange of lineups with the Friars' manager, a sore loser named Sport, I receive my first managerial lesson. In this league, it transpires, teams can bat only eleven, not twelve as I had thought. Although he could allow an exception, Sport elects not to. Seeing me erase Nardo's name from the book, Q registers his displeasure that his P's & Q's teammate is being benched and lobbies me to reconsider. "We need Nardo's bat in the lineup," he says. But it's time to take the field, and I trot out to shortstop.

Adding to the atmosphere is our outfielder Swanny, a stagehand who immigrated to Staten Island from Jamaica as a boy. He is the Sharkey who most looks the part of the player—six-one, rangy, and sporting a full line of baseball accessories: knee pads, sanitary socks, stirrups, flip-down shades on the bill of his cap, batting gloves dangling from his waistband. He is all about team spirit, and patriotic too. Swanny joined the team near the end of last season; by then Zeus had added so many new Sharkeys lacking official jerseys that Swanny induced several of them to buy special playoff unis: 9/11 tourist T-shirts with a flag-and-Statue-of-Liberty motif. Most of all, Swanny's a champion chatterer. He starts the game with a stream of old-school patter that never lets up. Being Swanny's teammate is like playing for the Depression-era Dodgers of the John R. Tunis books. Every pitcher is a "shooter," every batter a "sticker." Before each pitch he will shout from the outfield something like "Whaddaya say, shooter," following up, if it's a strike or close, with "That's a honey shot." I myself use only one line. When an opponent takes a strike with a count of 3–0 or 3–1, I trot out my Chicago favorite—"Hey batter, what's the matter?"—hoping to shame the hitter into swinging.

Leading off for the Friars Club is Manny, who plays with Zeus on many teams and followed him when he left the Sharkeys. Unlike Zeus, who is coffee-colored, Manny is dark in complexion. He is no doubt over thirty but youthful in appearance and outlook, with a joyous approach to the game—

and an indifferent commitment to time. A bicycle messenger and jack-of-all-trades, Manny is often around Central Park, just not always when his team's game is starting. Zeus is Manny's self-appointed big brother, seeing Manny as in need of discipline, much like the prodigal youngsters Zeus works with in Newark. As manager Zeus constantly moves Manny in and out of games and positions based on inning-by-inning assessments of his performance, attitude, and level of concentration. Manny's mood blackens only after tough losses and when Zeus criticizes him. In their frequency and vehemence Zeus and Manny's disputes border on marital. Manny is all sunshine as he steps to the plate. Billy induces him to lift a fly to Q, which Swanny identifies as a "can o' corn." The season has begun!

Next up is Zeus, whose appearance is greeted by our team with Bronx cheers—the sort of rude treatment baseball fans give a former star who has recently defected for greener pastures. During the off-season Zeus slipped on a patch of ice and strained ligaments in his left knee, which required arthroscopic surgery. His mobility is limited, and he's switched from short to second; he probably shouldn't be playing the field at all. But he is a right-handed batter, pushing off his right knee, so he should be able to drive the ball.

I am shading him up the middle, because I know that's where he likes to hit, and glove his smash on one hop as it shoots past Billy behind second. I'm ready to convert his hit into an out, but my first throw of the year, though catchable, is low and skips under the bleachers—E-6, error on the shortstop. Zeus greets me with a grateful smile as he jogs to second base and tells me, "Nice stop." I am somehow not comforted by the sabermetric dictum that an infielder has to do something right—position himself well, get to the ball, snag a grounder—in order to make an error. Four hits and a couple of mishandled relays later the Friars are up 3–0. When a batter gets two strikes, Swanny is prone to say, "Hey shooter, throw him the squiggly one." That expression is one I'd never heard as a child, but Billy seems to catch his meaning and whiffs the next guy on a straight change.

Teddy the umpire is a bearish man with dark hair and a closely cropped salt-and-pepper beard and has the essential characteristic of all good umpires: the ability to project authority and control the game. More than that, he never anticipates a call and hustles to get a look at the close ones. Teddy is also the nicest of the umpires. He greets by name the regular players and even some scrubs. With his keen concern for our well-being he sometimes seems as much therapist as umpire. He often seems hurt when he's accused of blowing a call, which, since there is usually only one umpire per game in softball, happens almost every game, even for the best umpires. Because we like

him and know he's the best and doing his best, he usually gets the benefit of the doubt. When Billy runs a squiggly called strike three past the next batter, there is no argument.

Still, we are down by plenty before our first ups of the year, and we put nothing on the board through two innings. The third inning starts inauspiciously, as Swanny pops to short and Billy flies to right. But the outfielder won't accept delivery on Billy's can o' corn, depositing him on first. Little Bobby hits a grounder in the hole to Zeus at second. Zeus rushes the throw and sails it into the bleachers.

Our bench gets on Zeus, someone accusing him of alienating our already limited audience and endangering his own teammates, who've set up on the first-base side. At Heckscher, there are no dugouts. A team merely secures a section on one of the bleachers, usually the bottom rows near home plate. Our fan base, such as it is, usually consists of one or two friends, a few players from just-finished games, retirees, and European tourists with their tight trousers and sandals who aim their tiny digital cameras from respectful distances. Japanese visitors are too baseball-savvy to waste their vacation and virtual film on us.

Next Cookie sends home two runs with a grounder to the outfield that first passes between Zeus's legs. Our bench jockeys are all over Zeus now, and in less clever ways. Someone is shouting, "Zeus, you suck!" Papi grounds to third for the second out, and it looks as though the Friars Club will end the inning with its lead intact.

But then it happens—one of those improbable confluences of events that occur all the time in softball games and make them seem magical. Penny drills a single to left scoring Cookie and tying the game. Then one after another Roger, Krishy, and Mule also single. When I get to the plate, I repeat to myself one of Swanny's mantras—"right back through the originator." I succeed almost too well, ricocheting the ball off the thigh of Burnsides, the Friar's fireballer, who has muttonchops reminiscent of Abner Doubleday or

Richie Allen. It skitters past the spot the shortstop has just abandoned, as if the hit and run were on. By the time the inning ends, thirteen guys have batted and seven runs scored.

On the field things go quiet, but on our third-base bleachers I have a minor revolt on my hands. Nardo is now sitting among the spectators. I ask him to stick around: "We may need you later, and I will get you in the game." Nardo has nowhere in particular to go but is adamant about going. "I deserve better than this," he says, as much to the tourists as to me. For the first time they seem to be entertained. Nardo takes off his spikes and starts packing his gear.

In the top of the seventh, our defense starts to falter. A couple of infield hits, one on a ball that skips by me sideways on the loam, and a line drive to left bring the tying run to the plate. An out and a hit later, the tying run is at first. Their number-eleven batter, Sport, runs the count to 3-1, threatening to fill the bases and advance the tying run to second. Billy grooves him one, and Sport is taking all the way. From right center Swanny declares it a "honey shot," and I ask the batter "what's the matter?" On the next pitch, another cantaloupe, Sport takes off for first before Roger can glove the ball. Not so fast, Sport! It's the squiggly one, and Teddy rings him up for the second out. Sport complains loudly and at length that the pitch was high. Teddy seems a little doubtful, but he's not about to change a ball-and-strike call.

When play resumes, the Friars' leadoff batter stands in. Under the circumstances—the treacherous infield, one, maybe two, errors already—I cannot say that I'm hoping he will hit the ball to me. But he does. Thankfully the hop is true, and I flip to Cookie for the force. We win! The final is 7-5. Shaky though it is, the victory is sweet—not only because we beat a team that had dominated us for three years and not only because we beat Zeus. It is also that my moves seem to have been vindicated. All four of the new guys in the lineup played well. The game established Billy as the ace, and I'm sure he and the other newcomers will want to return.

The win makes it harder for anyone to complain, but in some ways it seems I've managed to pump defeat from the stomach of victory. I couldn't get Alan into the game, and I can tell he isn't happy. And Papi seems none too pleased with his nonfielding role. Both are keeping quiet but acting as though we had lost. Then there is Nardo. The controversy deflates for me the festive atmosphere. Yes, I had anticipated hurt feelings, but I couldn't do anything to avert them. We won, but we fell short of achieving anything like *wa*, much less big league fun. And I didn't make any friends here today. I stow the bases in the green bins—the task of the winning team—and head back to the subway by myself wondering how bad the dissension might have been had we lost.

On the way back to the subway I cross paths with Nardo, who apparently has been waiting for me, and we start talking at cross-purposes. Nardo makes his case that, as a two-year team member, he "deserved more consideration" than I gave him. His arms are folded across his chest—very much like Mr. Clean, but more intimidating than self-satisfied. I tell him that I'm sorry he didn't start, but I didn't know he was coming and not everyone is going to start every game. I also say, "No one should ever walk out during a game." But his view remains that I was at fault. He says, "Call me if you need me," meaning, I take it, if I need him to *start*. I invite him to show up next week, meaning we will see what happens if he does. Possibly the thought that I might reinstate him is the only thing keeping him from taking a swing at me. What am I going to do, fine him?

**WEDNESDAY, APRIL 16, 5 WASHINGTON SQUARE NORTH**

## *The Freshman*

It looks as though I am betting double or nothing on my softball season. I thought I was going to be running both the Sharkeys and a sociology department. A few years ago I served as acting chair, and at the end of February I was elected chair in a close vote. The election was advisory to the dean, but deans almost always appoint the department's choice, especially if the dean has agreed to the election procedure, as this one did. I thought it was only a matter of time until the dean contacted me to talk turkey, so instead of demanding a meeting, I waited. But instead of calling me in, the dean sent an e-mail message to my colleagues asking for their thoughts on the result, and some lobbied him not to appoint me. March came and went, and two weeks ago I finally heard from him. He sent an e-mail notifying me that he had chosen as chair someone just hired by the department. I felt a little like Sarah Jessica Parker's Carrie of *Sex in the City* after one of her boyfriends breaks up with her by way of a Post-It.

There was, not coincidentally, a departmental faculty meeting the next morning. My colleagues were incensed at the dean's fait accompli. But there was a divide between those who wanted the new chair-select to step aside and those who argued that as the dean's choice he could "leverage" resources for the department. Most feared that the small world that is sociology would find out about this and think that our department had fallen into a state of receivership—the term for when a department forfeits its right to self-determination. NYU sociology has been trying to ramp up its ranking from the low twenties—where *U.S. News and World Report* has had us since the mid-1990s—to the top ten. This wouldn't help. The outgoing chair convened a committee to draft a statement of protest.

Since receiving the dean's message, I've been waking up most mornings around three o'clock wondering why some of my colleagues, even friends, would go to such lengths to keep me from taking charge and why the dean wouldn't appoint me. Do they really think I can't handle a department of thirty people? What are they afraid of? I am responsible to a fault, having taken on thankless committee assignments that my colleagues dodge instinctively. And, frankly, I'm charming. I know I should feel lucky not to have to take on yet more responsibility, but it feels so embarrassing and insulting not to be appointed after having been elected.

I had been meeting regularly with my colleague Jeff, my best friend in the department and a pickup basketball mate, to see if we could devise a way to get the dean to reconsider. Jeff is my age but about a foot taller, with all-American good looks and glasses. We might as well be Mutt and Jeff, if Mutt hadn't been the taller one. Jeff has a soft baseline turnaround jump shot, superhuman range, and a manner so mild that his basketball nickname is Clark Kent. The only time I ever see him angry is when someone flagrantly fouls him. Then he is liable to punt the ball into the rafters. Too bad there was no ball at the faculty meeting. I have slowly, painfully, realized that even though the department has expressed outrage at the dean's move, there is no chance that I will become chair. Most of my colleagues who voted for my opponent are happy with the dean's choice. Most who voted for me weren't so much for, I've learned, as opposed to my opponent. The rest don't care much one way or another, and the departmental committee, split between the supporters of different candidates, isn't going to change things. When Jeff is wrestling with a conundrum, he looks thoughtfully off into the middle distance with his lower lip covering his upper one. Nowadays he does that all the time.

Since the softball season has started, I've been trying to use my extensive team-sport experience to help me deal with the debacle. I don't mean the high-school-coach chestnuts about the game fish swimming upstream or what the tough do when the going gets tough. I'm thinking about the lessons that pickup softball has taught me about narrative limitations and appropriate behavior. In these games, the winners stay on the field, while the losers sit down and wait their turn to play again.

There are only five story lines in pickup softball, and probably in life. There is comedy. A great team messes up—bobbling grounders, throwing the ball away, popping up—but holds it together enough to win anyway. All's well that ends well. The team goes on to play again and meet another team. Then there's tragedy. A team has the talent to win, but because of strategic mistakes, misplays, or failure to play as a team it loses and has to depart the field. The demise of the team is mourned along the sidelines in funereal silence as softball life goes on without it. In the third plotline, redemption, a team falls way behind, but given a second chance, it perceives and corrects its errors. Redemption is the most rewarding in the end, and can happen during the course of one game, but often requires at least one tragic loss. And in pickup softball there is no guarantee that the team will come back as a group, or that it will win if it does.

By far my favorite is a fourth scenario—total domination, in which the team wins, handily and repeatedly, dispatching one team after another. Francesca takes issue with this one. More than once she has patiently explained to me that total domination does not, strictly speaking, qualify as a narrative—a subject she is writing a book about—because there is no reversal of fortune. When she does this I'm reminded of a character in French new wave cinema. A script's worth of well-argued ideas flow from her mouth, though without the cigarette smoke. She is trapped in a model's body, remaining willowy, though she seems to subsist mainly on ice cream and chocolate. And she is so pretty—cobalt eyes, auburn hair, button nose, rosebud lips, dimples—that at first I found it unnerving to talk to her, as if I might be accused of gawking simply for looking her in the face. I imagined her pointing one of her elegant fingers and saying, "Look, pal, my breasts are down here." But I soon learned that she is practically blind without her contact lenses and anyway is usually too busy theorizing, while gesturing and looking off into space, to notice what her conversation partner might be staring at. I work a lot, but I play ball, fool around with a camera, train for marathons, and watch as many films as I can. Francesca has no hobbies. She is all sociologist all the time. Probably all our restaurant meals are tax-deductible. Most of her daytime hours are spent staring daggers at her video screen, as if irked that the computer isn't entirely getting what she is transmitting to it. In any case, I don't agree that total domination entails no reversal. What Francesca doesn't take into account is the epiphany of realizing you were mistaken after having anticipated a struggle. Chicago fans will think of the Bears in 1985 or the Bulls in 1991, but the examples are many: Clay versus Liston, Ali versus Foreman, Jets versus Colts, Mets versus Orioles, and so on.

Finally, there is the lost cause, which is something like the flip side of total domination. Here the team is overmatched, with no chance to prevail.

FRANCESCA WAS ALL SOCIOLOGIST
ALL THE TIME

There are several ways to play it. One is to deny that the cause is lost and act as though it is a tragedy in the making. Another is to give up, pout, absorb punishment, and sit down. A third is to fight to the finish with anyone who will join in—with no illusions about winning—and then sit down. If the lost cause is identified quickly and played properly, I don't mind it so much. Realizing that the story is going to end with your loving Big Brother or drinking the Kool-Aid can even be a little liberating.

These plotlines are useful for any amateur athlete needing to summarize numerous contests to someone only mildly interested, as, for instance, when I need to report on hour or two's worth of sporting activity to Francesca, who is usually tapping away at her keyboard. She will say, "How did it go?" I'll respond with something like "Lost cause" or "Tragedy." And she'll reply, "Oh, sorry to hear it, Poopy," without looking up from the screen. But the standard stories are can be even more helpful when one is in the middle of a situation in that they provide guidelines for one's actions and feelings. My problem is that I have been seeing the chair situation as a close game and a tragedy in the making. I have been trying to rally the squad to play tighter defense and scratch out a few runs. Really, though, my team is being blown out. The game's all but over, and my colleague-teammates are taking off their cleats and heading to the showers. So I've decided to swing for the fences—or, to change the sporting metaphor, to take it right at the dean and see what happens. I've e-mailed him to request an audience and plan to unload on him. Looking at the issue as a lost cause is far easier on the psyche. I have nothing more to lose.

This morning, ten weeks after being elected chair, I finally meet the dean in his Henry James building on Washington Square North. His office is a stately, high-ceilinged room looking out above street level over a children's playground. In the 1990 film *The Freshman*, a new NYU student played by

31

Matthew Broderick vaults out this window when he sees his car being stolen. The word is that the dean leaves visitors with the feeling that he agrees
with them. He is a picture of studied thoughtfulness, as he details the thinking that led to his overruling the election. The close vote indicated a divided
department, not the consensus he was expecting. As he carefully chooses
words, he gazes out the window. Unless there's a carjacking in process, I'm
facing a filibuster. When he solicited private opinions from the faculty, he
tells me, stroking his well-groomed salt-and-pepper beard, "not a few" colleagues thought that the chair-select's appointment would clear the way for
the department to advance. And he hadn't met with me out of concern for
my best interests. If we met and he then decided not to select me it might
appear to be a personal rejection. His eyes are so liquid that I fear he might
start to cry.

The dean's slow-down discursive offense burns twenty minutes off our
half-hour meeting, and I am at a disadvantage because I am afraid my sprin-
kler system might go off. Once he regains control of the conversation, I know
he will run out the clock, and so I start to rattle off as many points as possible as quickly as I can: I won the election, and he should have met with me.
He surely knew that our secret election process, which he had signed off on,
was likely to produce a close vote. The personal opinions he solicited did not
have the same legitimacy as a democratic election—and did not justify setting aside the election results. What's more, it was wrong to announce the
selection of a chair without consulting the department. And repudiating the
vote without meeting me could also be read as a personal rejection—which
is how my colleagues have interpreted it.

I start fast, but I am choked up and find my words leaking out increasingly
slowly. I occasionally peer out the window myself, though I don't have as fa-
vorable an angle on the playground. I find myself speaking so faux-thought-
fully as I'm making the point about his not meeting me that I have time to
think about how slowly I'm talking and how absurd and beside the point this
is. There is nothing I can say that will change the dean's decision, and my colleagues aren't going to try to override it. The dean is really good, I think, as
if he had done graduate work in charm school or the Method. Still talking,
I find myself wondering how he would have handled Nardo at the park yesterday. If I'd had the dean's skills, Nardo no doubt would have signed on as
our batboy. I'm sure people criticize the dean all the time, and I wonder how
he handles it. Because the gap between what I'm thinking and what I'm saying has expanded dangerously, I suddenly panic that I'm going to change the
movie and blurt out some highly inappropriate lines, a la Fredo Corleone in

*The Godfather, Part Two:* "I'm smart! I can handle things! I want respect! I was passed *ovah!*" To avoid that fate, I just shut up.

We both stand. So much for taking it right to the dean. He admits that, knowing what he knows now, "some things might have been done differently." We are all smiles as he shows me the door, inviting me to return and chat any time, but I think for a moment about exiting through the window because I know I've been robbed. The literary critic Hayden White, or maybe Francesca, notes that narratives always assume a point of view. I need to keep in mind, too, that for those who glimpse our games on their way to other parts of the park, they are all comedy.

( THURSDAY, APRIL 17, 269 MERCER STREET )

## *Shakedown Pitch*

When I think about it, and being dumped as chair has made me think about it a lot lately, my status as softball manager seems precarious. I was selected for the job rather than elected to it, selected by an opponent, no less, and largely because I would front the cash for the league fee. I decide to act. This afternoon I head over to Pamela's Cantina, a popular lunch spot on the NYU campus, looking to recruit a key teammate, one who doesn't know how to play softball. I want to make a pitch to Mickey, the owner, to sponsor the Sharkeys. Sponsors of softball teams nowadays are like the owners of the original U.S. professional baseball teams or today's Japanese ones. They bankroll teams not to make a direct profit but for advertising purposes and the public goodwill that flows from ostentatious civic involvement.

Mickey, whose given name is Mohammed, hails from Tunisia. I've known him since I joined NYU. Then he was making sandwiches for Pamela's, a takeout place, but before long he had taken over from Pamela and then opened a restaurant, which assumed the space of a former student hangout called the Cactus Café. Though this new venue serves mainly Mediterranean-influenced food, Mickey was reluctant to lose the Cactus Café's clientele, so he retained nachos and burritos on the menu. Thus was born Pamela's Cantina. I feel a certain kinship with Mickey. Over the years he's provided me as many meals as my mother. He is also the epitome of the American dream and an avid sports fan. In 2002, for instance, he opened his establishments at dawn for World Cup matches. And he chose the classic baseball name "Mickey." In terms of displaced identity, Sharkeys could have no better replacement than Pamela's Cantina—an eatery named after a previous woman owner run by a Americanized Tunisian man serving purportedly Mexican cuisine.

Running a softball team means being a general manager, manager, and player all at once. If I can drum up an outside sponsor, it will make me like an owner too. In addition to saving money, it will help me establish managerial authority and minimize complaints and backbiting. Zeus had a roster full of Sharkeys with specific ideas about when and where they should play. They were quick to complain when he moved them to less critical fielding positions, dropped them in the batting order, or, especially, sat them down altogether. Much of their beef was that they had paid eighty dollars. When players pay such hefty fees, they expect to play, regardless of whether they are helping the team. If the fees are taken care of, it eliminates these sorts of complaints, or at least simplifies the complainers' exits. Also, the better players gravitate to teams where they can play for free.

Outside sponsorship also makes the team seem less like a vanity project and removes the problems of divided authority that can arise when one of the players sponsors the team. Last year Billy's Sunday-league team, the Nuclear Pencils, was sponsored by the team's other pitcher, Dick, and named after his one-man graphics business. If anyone asked him if he carried the eponymous pencil with him, he would glance down at his crotch and say, "All the time." Though not the manager, Pencil Dick saw the team as his enterprise—giving him license for divalike pitching performances and incessant criticism. It was like having Steinbrenner on the mound. I could probably afford to sponsor the team myself, but player-sponsors can look pathetic, as if they might not be good enough to play otherwise or have to buy friends. Mickey, by contrast, seems the perfect prospect; there is no way he is going to want to play at all, much less pitch.

I approach Mickey with all my reasons at the ready: I know he loves sports. Other local businesses have teams in a league. He can write off the fee as a business expense. I'll add a "Pamela's Cantina" patch to our new jerseys. The cantina has a bar that is begging for a sporting clientele. I could take a photo of the team for the wall, and guys could show up in uniform postgame, talk sports, and blow some money. We might even win a trophy for him. Regular-season division winners in the Performing Arts Softball League take home massively garish hardware, and if we somehow won it all, Pamela's could display the coveted Heckscher Cup, the traveling trophy that has taken up permanent residence at Irving Plaza. I may have overthought the proposition, as Mickey agrees to it before I can use up all my talking points. He looks at me gravely and says, "So, what do you want?" Then he writes a check for a thousand dollars.

On my way out the door I have the unsettling thought that he might have seen my pitch as a shakedown. The United States is fighting a war in Iraq, and along comes some white guy demanding a four-figure check from an Arab running a small business during a weak economic recovery. I'm also asking him to pledge symbolic allegiance to our national pastime, a sport he has never played and, for all his game talk, probably doesn't follow, American sports being the only aspect of our beguiling pop culture that has failed to catch fire worldwide. In baseball there is a common behavior pattern I call the instant-redemption fallacy. An infielder misplays a grounder and then, no longer having a play at first, makes another ill-advised move in the false hope of undoing the first one. He unleashes his strongest throw, which often ends up in the stands or the dugout. It happens in basketball too, when a player takes a crucial but poorly chosen shot that clanks off the rim and into the hands of an opponent, then tries immediately to steal the ball back and inevitably fouls. Having recently had a chance at making a play does not in fact confer some future right to make another, and bids for instant redemption invariably backfire. I should have acted after I was elected chair, but I didn't. Now I tell myself that Mickey and I go back far enough that he could have turned me down if he'd wanted to, though maybe I should've eaten the ball.

[ SATURDAY, APRIL 19, EAST RIVER #2 ]

## *Cartwright and Me*

My chance to show that I can run things in softball goes beyond team Pamela's Cantina. I also hold a permit for Greenwich Village Adult Softball, a group that has been playing pickup ball since the 1980s on James J. Walker Field, a West Village Little League park a tape-measure home run away from the Hudson River. We call the field J. J. Walker, as if were named not for the Jazz Age mayor but for the *Good Times* star who bestowed upon our nation the catchphrase "Dy-no-*mite!*" J. J. is so tiny that balls lifted over the outfield fence are counted as outs. A makeover to artificial turf a few years ago put J. J. temporarily out of commission. Aside from Central Park, New York's parks are bucking the major leagues' ineluctable return to natural grass. (The Astrodome, once called the eighth wonder of the world, has been put out to pasture, and now only the ridiculous Hubert H. Humphrey Metrodome has artificial turf.) The pickup game moved to the afternoon and three miles away to East River Field #2, which spreads out below the Williamsburg Bridge at Grand Street. Since then, East River #1 and #2 have also been converted to artificial turf.

When our league's commissioner resigned, I had volunteered to pitch in, filing the application at the city's Department of Parks and Recreation on West Sixty-First Street and writing a check for twenty weeks' worth of field— from four to seven o'clock every Saturday afternoon until Labor Day. I also bought twenty new de Beer Clinchers, New York's soft softball of choice. A larger model of this ball is used by Chicagoans, who play with bare hands. If you ever roll out, even for batting practice, a Dudley, Worth, Red Dot, or any of the other hard softballs the rest of the country relies on, New Yorkers, tough guys all, will throw it aside and admonish you, "Are you crazy? Somebody could be killed with that rock!" All told, I was out of pocket more than eight hundred bucks.

The pickup game had been my only New York softball outlet for years. But more important, without this game I would never have been discovered by the players in the organized leagues. In the wide-open spaces of East River #2, Billy noticed that I could track down fly balls. And I would not have been playing at East River to be discovered, if not for something that happened several years earlier, when J. J. was a sandlot.

I had become a regular, but I didn't get along with all of the longtime regulars. Something about my style may have rubbed some of them the wrong way. I play hard and want to win, and I like to move the games along. When I first started to play, there was extensive batting practice, as many as fifty swings per batter. Once the game started, there would also be about five minutes of infield practice every half inning. I couldn't do much about BP but took aim at the between-inning delays. Local custom was that the batting team supplied an umpire, and I jumped at the chance. As soon as the defense was on the field, I would cry out, "Balls in, batter up!" In partial rebellion players began to mimic my trademark call, their voices cracking like teenagers, when they umpired.

For whatever reason, maybe an abiding attachment to infield practice, one longtime regular, Whitman, seemed to have it in for me. He ran about six-foot-two and 230 pounds, with long, dark hair, topped with a faded denim U.S. Postal Service cap, and an unkempt beard that grew best on his neck. A left-hander who had managed to harness his considerable power to keep his wicked liners within the confines of J. J., Whit seemed bottled up by the effort, and his frustration often seeped out in inappropriate base running. Whit was always a threat to do a Pete Rose into the catcher—whether man, woman, or child. But given his size and badass attitude, the most any of us ever did about it was commiserate. Several of us agreed that when reporters interviewed us after Whit had shot up the post office, we would dispense with the usual display of shock and tell them that we had seen it coming all the way.

One evening that summer, Whit was on first base, I was at shortstop, and the batter singled into center. Given the small dimensions of the field, I went to cover second in case there was a chance for a force play. The relay was slow, and Whit was going to be safe with ease. He might have gone in standing up, as the throw was late. He might have executed a pop-up slide, in case the throw got away. But instead he opted for a takeout slide—complete with roll. In a double-play situation, middle infielders know a takeout could be coming and prepare to jump or sidestep. But on this play, my back was to the infield and his move blindsided me like a football clip.

I got to my feet and looked for support, but either no one else saw it or, more likely, no one who did wanted to get involved. Whit glared at me and by way of apology offered, "If you can't take it, you shouldn't try to play." Taken together, my brush with injury, Whit's unsympathetic reply, and everyone else's resounding lack of response disengaged the car alarm that goes off in my head when I'm anywhere near placing myself in physical danger. I started screaming at him from my dangerously proximate shortstop position, "A takeout slide on a throw from the outfield? Do you have any idea how this game is played? Is there something wrong with you?" His only reply was a spurt of saliva.

I stayed upset for the entire week. As bad luck would have it—or maybe the captains picking the teams were entertained by the rivalry—we were opponents again the following Saturday night. This time I was playing second base. Whit was on first with nobody out when a grounder came my way. I stepped forward to tag him, hoping for a tag-out–throw-out double play. Trying to knock the ball free, Whit treated me to a forearm shiver—to my jaw. This belligerent play was way out of line and would earn a suspension in the Central Park leagues, and I would've got the double play too. But not here. I was holding my chin and trying to complain but could only squeeze out, "What the hell?" He gave me a dismissive look that all but called me a pussy. Since I had hung onto the ball, and, fortunately, my bicuspids, I was denied even the satisfaction of lecturing him on his primitive understanding of the game. I was starting to long for the more subtle abuse I had absorbed in Little League.

I tried to channel my anger into a plan of action. Picking a fight with him was, of course, out of the question. If I were going to get back at him, it would have to be in the flow of the game. And then I had it! In baseball, a runner who tries to break up a 4–6–3 double play stays down on the slide. The shortstop sidearms the relay to first, whizzing it right over the runner's head to enforce the custom. Everyone in baseball knows this, and runners seldom get hit. In softball, however, no matter how high the slide, short-stops try to avoid the runner. I knew that Whit tended to slide on the high side, and if he wanted to play hardball with me, well, two could play at it. The next time he is on first and a grounder comes to second, I thought, I will take the relay at short and, if he doesn't get way, way down, I will ricochet the scowl off his scraggly face. I fantasized about this frequently, rerunning this mental video clip, and was so satisfied with it that I could stand playing on the same field with Whit, almost always on the opposing team. "That's right—you'd better get down," I would say to myself and on occasion, dis-turbingly, aloud, as the weeks passed and I replayed the key footage. As with Whit's going postal, I was certain that it was just a matter of time before I would exact vengeance and win justice.

One day late in August, the game was unspooling just as in my internal highlight reel. Whit was on first. I was at short. There was one out. And then it happened, what I had been waiting for all summer—a sharp two-hopper into the glove of the second baseman. As I secured the relay, Whit came in sliding—high—and I was ready to sidearm the ball off his noggin. I don't know if it was instinct, habit, knowing that beaning him was wrong, or ab-ject fear of reprisal, but in the moment I couldn't do it. I sidestepped, fired, and jumped, just barely dodging bodily harm myself, as he rolled right at me with considerable malice and well outside the baseline.

I became resigned to my plight, and as summer turned to fall—with Whit still taking the occasional cheap shot at me—I decided that after the season I would quit. I wanted to play my game, but playing here was no longer any fun. Since I wasn't playing anywhere else—Zeus hadn't yet recruited me— that was going to be the end of my softball career.

One part of my game at J. J. Walker was a trick play. When a batter lined a base hit to left, I would take a few steps into the outfield to cut off the throw. But instead of tossing the ball to the second baseman, I would wheel and blindly throw to first, hoping to catch the runner off base. If I were to misfire, the nearby fence would prevent the runner from advancing. Runners often fell for this ruse—even after having seen me try it earlier in the season or, worse, earlier in the game. It seemed they were on such a natural high after getting a hit, rounding first base just like the big leaguers on TV, that their brains momentarily froze.

Near the end of the season, Whit came up to bat and, as usual, drilled a hit to center. I secured the relay, and mechanically turned and gunned to first. Despite the fact that Whit had witnessed this play countless times, he had to reverse course, desperately trying to beat the ball back to first. It was shaping up as a bang-bang play. My blind peg was going to beat him, though it was a little high. Then I noticed that Whit was not the only one caught napping. The first baseman, Snowdon, had struck up a conversation with the first-base coach and was out of position. Whit had decided, perhaps for maximum intimidation, to go in standing up. With no first baseman to stop it, the ball smacked off the back of his hairy neck.

I have a good arm, especially for someone my size, but it is no gun, and I was throwing a used Clincher from center field. Nonetheless, Whit dropped as if shot. There is a confusion that falls over the field when someone may have been injured. Stop the game or play on? My impulse was to urge Snow to pick up the ball and tag Whit since he had lost contact with the base and the soaking rule had been off the books since the Polk administration. But Whit wasn't getting up, and players on both teams started to check on him. I was trying to arrange my facial features into an appropriate show of concern, and although I was biting my lip, it was all I could do not to laugh. The big jerk had literally run into the ball. Which hadn't been thrown that hard. There was no way he could be injured. And he was acting like, what?

I cautiously approached the huddle that had formed around him, fearing that as soon as I got close enough Whit would quit playing possum and charge me. But I could soon see that his babyish performance was no ruse. He lay there for a couple more minutes and then got up slowly, nothing damaged but his pride. He walked off the field, collected his bag, and went home—never to return. I still look for him sometimes, in the *Times* Metro section.

Today I'm having a little of the feeling that Alexander Cartwright must have had when he drew up the rules in 1845 for the Knickerbockers, the social club that first played baseball as we have come to know it. Of Cartwright's twenty rules, six of the first seven had nothing to do with the number of outs, the distance between the bases, or fair balls. Instead they dealt with club matters: who was eligible to play, when games would be played, how sides should be chosen. Like me, Cartwright was forced to pay to secure something akin to a permit to play on the Elysian Fields. What's more, if the modified fast-pitch leagues are like baseball in the 1870s, our slow-pitch pickup game is like Cartwright's antebellum ball, with the pitcher acting as something like a "feeder," not trying to retire batters but just laying the ball in there to be hit. I want to make the game friendlier and more welcoming. Unlike in the leagues, the pickup-game players vary greatly in ability and demographics. Grade school kids sometimes play along with novice women and sexagenarians. If everyone tries his or her best, that's all anyone can ask for. But I want the game to be competitive too, an even distribution of experience and ability. Most of all, I don't want arguing—or rough play.

The bright sun is sending the temperature toward sixty degrees, and, with the shortage of pickup softball opportunities in New York, players are materializing, marching over the FDR Drive as if it were the cornfield in *Field of Dreams.* More than twenty people appear, many of them new to me, and most pay the thirty-dollar "regular" fee. Regulars, whose numbers are limited to twenty-five, buy a season's ticket to play, which makes them essentially members of the club. These latter-day Knickerbockers get first dibs on playing over "alternates," who pay three dollars per game and can play if there are not enough regulars to field two teams. Already I have defrayed half my down payment.

After a brief batting practice, we turn to Cartwright's practice of captains choosing sides. I pick teams against Weasel, one of the new players. An aspiring actor with a goatee, Weasel is short but with an outsize desire to win. He runs a team in the East Village Softball Association and brought some of his players here today. Weasel sees the world as a Manichaean struggle between his team, Josie's, and d.b.a., the champion team that I played for last year. I call him Weasel because that is what my d.b.a. teammates call him. Today he proposes to convert the game into a surrogate Josie's/d.b.a. contest. He wants to claim all the guys on Josie's for his side, giving me, the evil d.b.a. proxy, some of the more talented Saturday regulars. And from there we will pick the rest. Weasel's modification is OK with me. I want to move things along, the games are supposed to be fair matches, which is what Cartwright specified, and Weasel's way of choosing teams does produce even sides. We have a spirited, close, and cleanly contested game. Being responsible for the game for the first time, I don't mind very much when my team loses, though Weasel's postgame celebration, with all the whooping and high-fives, seems excessive. And I am happy that they want to play two, like a host whose guests stay a little longer than absolutely required. OK, maybe I want another chance, too, to kick Weasel's little weasel ass.

## *Spare Part*

Yesterday I called Billy, whose team's first game is today, to find out where I stand. His team, known in previous years as the Nuclear Pencils, plays in Central Park, in the Lower Manhattan Softball League, as its games used to be played at J. J. Walker. But this league is a quantum leap above the pickup games and is also well ahead of the weekday leagues. There are no occupational restrictions, and the teams are loaded with players with nine-to-five jobs, not just the nocturnally, flexibly, or equivocally employed weekday players.

I am in my second year on the team and still trying to make it in the more difficult league. Last season I played my way out of Billy's lineup early, got injured, and was unable to play my way back in. I spent a lot of time on the bench. Garry Templeton once famously said, about his prospective attendance at an All-Star game, "If I ain't startin', I ain't departin'." I feel something like the same way. It's not that I see myself as a star who requires pampering or even that I mind spending the time. It's that, because of typecasting, sitting here will reduce my chances of playing a bigger role elsewhere. Anyone playing the role of scrub will be treated like one. On the phone, Billy was refreshingly, if disturbingly, direct. He told me that he had "enough players" for game one—in this league, doubleheaders are the rule—but that he could use me in game two. A couple of teammates ahead of me on his depth chart can't stay for both.

So instead of heading right to Central Park, I am cleaning out closets. Francesca and I have the standard gender gap on this issue. She loves the streamlined life and purging belongings. I see my identity more wrapped up in things and fear divesting myself of totems from meaningful events. I have run four New York marathons, and no one can take that away from me, but just in case I want to keep the official T-shirts too. The New York apartment, always ludicrously undersized, is the sworn enemy of sentiment. We do spring cleanings every season.

It is also always an unstable situation when a man owns more clothing than the woman he loves and lives with, as is the case with Francesca and me. What puts me ahead is my store of game-used major league jerseys. Like many unthinking fans, several years ago I dropped a hundred dollars on a Rawlings, pro-cut jersey and was shocked when I later learned that on eBay it was actually cheaper to buy a jersey once donned by a major leaguer than a replica. Not only that, but the pro gamers do not lose value no matter how frequently amateur owners wear them, "extensive use" being a selling point in auctions. It was as if all recent major leaguers, at least the scrubs, were suddenly my brothers, forced to allow me to borrow their sacred garments. My closet was soon filled with the discarded laundry of utility infielders, fourth outfielders, long relievers, and bullpen catchers, whose striving I identify with. Billy doesn't have our team shirts yet but has asked us all to wear black. I pick a Sunday White Sox model once worn by Chris Singleton, a good-range–no-stick center fielder. Wearing the jersey of a marginal pro does not make a softball player look like a scrub, but instead like someone who possibly knows major leaguers.

It is another beautiful afternoon, sunny and in the sixties. Our opponents have a great name, On-Base Percentage. Their navy T-shirts sport old-school periods after the letters in the abbreviation. For some reason, however, the punctuation marks appear only after the *O* and *B*, stranding the *P*. The O.B.P team includes Cookie, Mule, and Swanny—my teammates on the Sharkeys turned Pamela's Cantina. We are winning the first game handily, with Dick, last year's sponsor, pitching. I can't say I'm pleased to see him. One of my formative experiences as a Nuclear Pencil was watching Dick stalk across the diamond to berate me in right field after a flare dropped in front of me, a ball even Chris Singleton could not have caught. I felt as though I were back in Little League facing one of the physically but not socially more mature kids who had terrorized me. Though Dick bats only when no one else is available, he was also always ready with an unsolicited hitting tip. Usually his advice would be offered after the fact in a public manner that made it all the more infuriating. If a teammate were walking back to the bench, say, after striking out looking at a pitch out of the strike zone, Dick would proclaim to anyone in earshot, "What ever happened to the idea of fouling off close pitches with two strikes?"

Billy has also had an eventful off-season as manager. His team has been on a downward trajectory. It won the championship three years ago; a year later narrowly lost in the finals to Rif Raf; and last year was swept in round one of the playoffs by Rif Raf, which went on to lose to the Hitmen for the championship. But Billy's main problem was Dick, who had alienated far more important teammates than me. Over the winter Billy sent an unusual e-mail to the team, asking the Pencils whether we wanted our pitcher/sponsor to remain on the roster. It was perhaps the nation's first softball recall election. I voted "no" on Proposition Dick, as did most of the Pencils, despite Dick's extensive lobbying campaign. But after all e-precincts had reported,

Billy couldn't pull the trigger. As a compromise, Billy put Dick on probation and removed him as team sponsor. Those steps were not enough to appease Zeus, who had plumped for the most radical ballot option, "I will not play if Dick remains on the team." So this season Zeus will be playing for Rif Raf. Escaping Dick's tyranny, however, means that the team has to cough up the league fee. Billy is collecting eighty dollars per person, as well as three dollars per game for the umpires. I can't help thinking that his need to defray costs accounts in part for his keeping me on the roster. After additional electronic debate, Billy was able to achieve consensus on a new name: the Machine, player-owned and -operated.

The guys on the Machine are all familiar, and I'm well aware of my role. I'm a spare part. Billy the front man and Dick the small businessman share duties on the firing line. The infield has Keith, a filmmaker, at first; the shortstop called Mike, a PhD candidate and teacher in communications; and at third the personal trainer Trey. Video producer Chad and Woody the dentist are vying for the second-base spot, and Frank, a photographer, can play there too. The outfield is full with writer and software guy Matt, emergency room MD Clooney, personal trainer Krishy, federal parole officer Tommy, and a Microsoft business systems analyst known as MikeHargrove, first and last names slurred together to distinguish him from Mike the shortstop. Walker, who runs a dog-walking business, is the DH. There is even competition at catcher, between Superman, an actor, writer, and apartment building superintendent, and Frank and Chad. Most of my teammates have positions and I don't, and so, despite our familiarity, it's as if there were an invisible wall between us.

Dick is subdued today, sitting off to the side by himself between innings and contesting only the occasional ball call. Despite the big lead our Machine teammates have granted him, he is, as he is prone to do, exhibiting control trouble. In the seventh, Billy, who is slated to pitch the second game, calls on himself for the save. Dick hands over the ball without complaint, and Billy gets his three outs. For game two Billy has plugged me into right field, batting tenth. Given license by our camaraderie, my Monday teammates on On-Base Percentage are really giving it to me when I come to bat in the third. I haven't had a haircut since last season. I'm using a headband to keep my thick, unruly, curly brown hair from obstructing my vision. Swanny is saying, "Hey, you can't hit with your hair, sticker." Mule seems to be snickering, "Snip, snip," while working his fingers like scissors. They have time for this because O.B.P has almost two complete teams, and my Pamela's teammates are sitting for game two. The bench jockeying and the fact that their pitcher is throwing nothing but junk make everything seem relaxed. Still, I am oh for two with a pop-up and a groundout when I come to bat in the seventh with our team down 8–7—and I pop up again. We have to settle for the split.

Billy takes the loss, but he isn't taking it well. He is complaining to all that this is the kind of game we need to win if we are going to win this league. This isn't the start I was hoping for. Guys drift toward the subway at Columbus Circle in little knots; I head there too, by myself. I am getting the old Little League feeling again, poor baseball performance making me feel like on outsider. Probably I will be available to clean closets again next Sunday.

MONDAY, APRIL 21, HECKSCHER #4

## A More Appealing Image

I wake up at three o'clock, just as in the days after being deposed as chair, with anxiety worse than what I go through before teaching class. For class I can reread the material until I have it down cold and gather supplementary items of interest. But there's not much a softball manager can do to prepare before a game. Looking at last week's scorecard and stats isn't going to help me deal with another confrontation with Nardo, nor are the insights I had while speaking with the dean. I'm hoping Nardo doesn't show up. I would feel obliged to sit him down, as I would look foolish starting him after he deserted us midgame last week. Also, I'm finding out that my teammates are too busy to practice before the game—Opening Day was an aberration. Mostly, though, I worry about how Pamela's will fare against the Gotham Comedy Club, a team that tied the Friars Club for the regular-season championship last year and that has had many softball laughs at our expense. In nine games over the last three regular seasons we lost each time. I write out several alternative lineups but don't feel any more ready.

My worries are mixed with excitement, though, because today I am distributing our uniforms. During the off-season, in a moment of enthusiasm, I splurged and bought outfits last worn by the Class A Columbus (Georgia) Red Stixx, a now-defunct farm team of the Cleveland Indians. The cream cotton flannel jerseys say "Foxes"—the red stick being a variety of fox—in red and midnight blue tackle twill. They are made by Mitchell and Ness and were used in turn-back-the-clock games. Although the jerseys were running about eighty dollars each on eBay, the dealer, Scott of On-Deck Circle, had flooded the market, and many had no bids. I e-mailed him to see if he would sell me the unsold remainder of his stock at a discount. He shipped me seventeen jerseys for

KRISHY HAD THE GOOD FACE

a thousand dollars and threw in twenty pairs of the old-time baggy knickers. On the left sleeve, in place of the comically offensive Chief Wahoo, the uniforms have a patch of a red fox; for the other sleeve, I'm ordering Pamela's Cantina iron-on patches of the sort sported by the restaurant's busboys. The new look not only provides a symbolic break with the old, loser Sharkeys. It's a more appealing image. We are no longer baby sharks, but wily foxes outthinking our opponents. Also, Francesca was thrilled to see the cartons exit the apartment this morning.

A few of the guys think the outfits are hokey, and someone says that Pamela's Foxes sounds a little like Charlie's Angels. But most really like them. Swanny, the spirited outfielder, suits up immediately, stripping down and even sporting the knickers, at which some of the guys were drawing the fashion line. Now Swanny has the old-school look to go with his old-school chatter. Penny, the third baseman, says how much better they are than the jerseys for any other team he has been on, and he has been on many teams. When he repeats the praise, I don't mind hearing it. Our former leader, Zeus, drops by and wants one of the jerseys too. He is keeping his options open for next year. I am wearing the jersey with the number one, but when Q asks for it I relinquish it. I'm trying to mollify him as I kicked one of his friends off the team before the season and have alienated another.

Between the jerseys, patches, and league fees, I'm down more than two grand. Mickey picked up about half, and if I can get sixty dollars from each of fifteen guys I'll nearly break even. A few of the guys are not so keen on the jerseys, put off by the up-front costs. One of them is Krishy, a newcomer to the team whom I'm hoping will stay. His family is from Guyana by way of South Asia. He identifies himself as "an Indian guy" but plays against type. He's no athletically challenged, nerdy grind in glasses. In fact, he has what scouts call the good face. Krishy is a personable personal trainer, a left field-er, and one of the few Foxes with all five tools—hit for average, hit for power, field, throw, run—but he suffers from lapses in concentration and motiva-tion. He sometimes drops fly balls that most other outfielders would never get to, as if he had lost interest after having accomplished the difficult part of the play.

Krishy wants to know how much it would cost to play without buying the jersey. I hadn't anticipated that contingency—having announced to my teammates only that Mickey had offered a partial sponsorship. So I make up a policy on the spot. I decide that the league fee will be twenty dollars and the jerseys forty. And if anyone doesn't want to keep the jersey, I will buy it back at the end of the year for twenty dollars. So playing this year is going to cost at most forty dollars—quite the entertainment bargain at less than three bucks per game. All the same, Krishy decides to hold off on the jersey, making his commitment to the team more tenuous. Now I am wondering if my enthusiasm for these retro outfits may have hindered my chances of retaining good new players, muffing the advantage I had gained in strong-arming an absentee sponsor.

I have fewer players this week, and that might be for the best. Alan, who sat down last week, says he can't make it, and Nardo, thankfully, doesn't show. I'd heard from Cookie that Papi was irked that he didn't play the field last game, and today I'm trying him out in right field. Otherwise the lineup is the same. I am leading off today, in part because I will go deep in the count.

Working the count, though, is a difficult chore on Heckscher #4—Klem's World. Klem is highly talented, the most authoritative and vocal of the Cen-tral Park umpires, and puts his personal stamp on every game he calls. He has the perpetual tan that comes with the territory and a barrel chest that sticks out so far that he looks as though he might pitch forward. The only safety equipment he is sporting today is a cup. He complains that the mask irritates his skin, so he doesn't wear it in modified fast-pitch softball, boast-ing that he is too quick to be hit. Many players reject the dermatological ex-planation and believe he just doesn't want to muss his flowing blond hair. To avoid inadvertent facial reconstruction, on the high ones, balls in the dirt, and whenever a batter swings, Klem ducks behind the catcher. For all his bobbing and braggadocio, he is suspiciously short in the tooth depart-ment. Having only one umpire ensures that calls will be missed, forcing umpires to devise a way to deal with it. Teddy's approach is to do his best, sometimes admit failure, and make it up later. Klem's approach is modeled on the pope's: infallibility.

Klem's voice is so reedy that it sounds as though it too might be sun-damaged, but without much prompting he will expand on the finer points of allowable substitutions, courtesy runners, and the ground rules of #4, which harbors numerous obstacles. In deep left field there is a stand of maples that serves as Heckscher's own version of the Green Monster. To the left of the trees is a footpath that strays into fair territory. If anyone skies one into the trees or skips a ball onto the footpath everyone is treated to Klem's screeching catchphrase: "*Two bases!*" Klem likes a fast game. Like most softball umpires, he is paid by the game—usually forty to fifty dollars—and is often scheduled to call several games a day, including better-paying high school baseball games, sometimes in far-flung locations like Sunset Park or Bensonhurst. Klem's strike zone varies according to his estimated time of the current game's completion, the starting time of his next game, and the travel time between them. Today Klem's dance card is full. We know because he tells us so.

Klem is going to have to be on his toes today, because Gotham's pitcher seems to take as his role model the surefire Hall of Famer Rocket Roger Clemens. He is large, throws hard, scowls, and sports Yankees apparel. He is the fastest pitcher in this league, but in modified fast-pitch softball pitchers can't wind up the way they do in windmill or even fast-pitch softball, so pitches rarely rise above the high sixties. Still, starting from only forty-five feet away, the ball reaches the plate quickly, adding at least twenty miles per hour to the effect. Underhanded fastballs also often have a natural rise to them that induces a lot of pop-ups and fly balls. Rocketman Jr. starts me off by missing badly with two risers. Then, with me taking all the way, he lays one down the middle for a strike. He tries the same thing on the next pitch, and I take ball three, low and outside. But Klem calls it strike two.

I step out of the box and, with my eyes trained on the spot on the ground where the ball hit, say with genuine pique, "Oh, Klem, that wasn't a strike." Not looking back at him is important, because if Klem thinks he's being shown up, he is liable to retaliate. He is not shy about ringing up batters looking and, unlike most softball umpires, seems to relish the confrontation that might ensue. Though definitive in his calls, he can be sensitive about them. Somewhere inside—not too far inside because with Klem what you see is what you get—he no doubt knows he calls strikes on a lot of pitches that are really balls. "Close enough to swing at," he probably tells himself, all the while wondering why he is working this rinky-dink league. But being infallible, he can't say that and counters quickly with "It caught the corner." I am thinking, the corner of what—Fifty-Ninth Street and Fifth Avenue? But I don't say anything.

You may be asking, What's one ball or strike more or less? "It only takes one" pitch to get a hit, as Swanny is now reminding me. But the bad call changes the complexion of my plate appearance. If the count were three and one, as it should be, I would be anticipating a specific pitch: down the middle, low, and with little on it, suitable for drilling back up the middle and testing the pitcher's reflexes. If I get that pitch, I hit it. If not, I let it go. Either I walk or I absorb a strike and take my chances with the next pitch—which would also have to be over the plate to prevent me from walking. But at two and two I have to contend with his best pitch—a rising fastball that I am not likely to hit safely even if I do catch up with it.

For all his glowering and speed, this pitcher, like all others in modified softball, is not intimidating in the standard baseball way. If he were to plug me, it would sting only briefly. The situation is more reminiscent of my Little League days—a much bigger guy standing right on top of the plate trying to blow heat past me. What's most menacing about the situation is that with two strikes I face the potential embarrassment of striking out. Aside from the bad memories it evokes, going down on strikes is stigmatized, like being dunked on in basketball. It shouldn't be, as an out is an out, but the dramaturgy of failure surrounding the strikeout is powerful. Striking out can harm a player's reputation, especially in softball, where strikeouts are supposed to be rare. Players who strike out occasionally are often viewed as lesser players than those who fly out almost all the time. So it is something to think about, and given my tenuous status as manager, I'm thinking about it now.

Sure enough, the Clemens wannabe's next pitch is a fastball, rising to neck level. I start to offer at it but stop as there is no way I can hit it well. Klem thankfully calls it the ball that it is, perhaps because he has already made one hurry-up bad call that drew a protest. Now the pitcher steps down from the rubber to complain. I have to hand it to him. He has even a passable imitation of 'roid rage. Klem turns him around with "The batter checked his swing." With the count full, the pitcher tries to lay one in to avoid walking me, but the pitch tails a little outside and low, like pitch four. At the last moment I decide to offer and foul it off. While the ball is being retrieved, Klem uses the baseball past subjunctive to inform me that had I not swung I would have had to take a seat: "That was strike three."

With the ball back on the field I'm looking for the same thing—another easy one, this time catching more of the plate. Pocket Rocket, deciding he wants the punch out, crosses me up with the rising fastball. It looks like ball four, but I'm not certain enough to risk taking it. I swing late and lift it softly to right center—a can o' corn, as Swanny would announce if he weren't on my team. In the scorebook, the out is marked F-9, but credit it to Klem, or to me, for being too afraid not to swing.

But my out does not deter my team, and even Klem can't rein in Rockito's wildness, which is producing free passes each inning. With the new uniforms and new faces in the lineup, we start acting like a new ball club. We have four runs by the fourth, and it would've been more if Krishy hadn't been called out for leaving first base before the pitcher released the ball. For the same reason that Klem calls more strikes than expected, he also gives an edge to the defense on close plays in the field. Billy is baffling the Gotham hitters with his junk, changes of speed, and control, and is exploiting the wide strike zone. I get a lot of action at shortstop and make all the plays.

I lead off the fifth and continue my personal battle with Clemens Jr. In the third, my guess was that after my first at bat he would be more worried about walking me than my hitting him and would opt to get the first one over. I was planning to drill one down the left-field line for a cheap ground-rule double. I got an easy one, low and inner half, and laced it safely but not quite to the footpath. Now he adjusts for this latest at bat and starts me off with the hard rising fastball, which—fuck!—he gets in and over for a strike. He misses with the same pitch, but then returns to it. It's a little high, but Klem gives him the call—fuck! fuck! Now it is one and two, and at his mercy I shorten up on the bat. He wants to blow me away with an inside riser, but it stays low and I fist it out to right for a bloop double. On his best sequence of pitches to me, he gets his worst outcome. Maybe it's the uniform, but this time we have the last laugh, and I can finally relax. With the new unis, new lineup, and new winning outlook, I declare the Sharkeys officially dead. Long live Pamela's Foxes!

## Of Men, Boys, and Babies

Francesca and I turned yesterday to our other spring project: conceiving a child. For relative oldsters like us, this is less fun than it sounds. Despite the fact that Francesca has one of her fallopian tubes blocked, we were able to get pregnant last fall, using timed sex and Clomid, a drug that stimulates ovulation, as well as being employed by major league cheaters hoping to bulk up. But over the winter, to mark her fortieth birthday, she had a miscarriage.

After that we began to see a fertility specialist, a tiny fashion plate who was extremely aggressive in her approach. She sat us down in her Central Park East office, a skimpy black cocktail dress peeking out from her open white jacket, and discussed options. We could continue with Clomid or use a drug that stimulates the release of multiple eggs, combining that with either timed sex or artificial insemination. Or, she pointed out, there was in vitro fertilization. IVF is high-stakes reproductive gambling; it costs about ten grand per try and succeeds about 30 percent of the time, and there are no good studies about the fates of the resulting children. (Of course, none of this is covered by our insurance.) In her pitch, the fertility specialist kept repeating that Francesca had "one tube down," as if we might have to dispatch a special-ops rescue team. Her mantra was that it was "all odds," though she declined to estimate the probabilities of pregnancies or live births for any line of action other than IVF. Unprompted she offered that she "couldn't argue" with us if we wanted to "go with IVF right way."

I found this hard sell unnerving because I think our prognosis for conception is good. We were able to conceive on the sixth try last time, and we have been examined up and down. Francesca has a lot of healthy eggs left, my sperm are still numerous, correctly shaped, motile. My estimate is with a similar level of Clomid and more meticulous attention to timing, the odds of it not happening after ten tries are almost zero. I showed Francesca the math on a pocket calculator, but she was not persuaded, and we have been arguing on and off about it ever since.

We both want a child, but it turns out that we are at different places in thinking about conceiving one versus adopting one. In couples' counseling, Francesca said that she wanted our child to have my sense of humor and benefit from my outlook on life. But apparently she wants the kid to have the hair too. She feels we should do everything we can to increase our chances of having our own baby and wants us to try Clomid plus artificial insemination this cycle, to the tune of $750. I'm unconvinced that this process will help much—the evidence is scanty—and conclude that it isn't worth the cost.

More than that, I fear a loss of control over the process. It seems to me that we are moving too rapidly down a track that ends at the expensive and chancy IVF. I dislike how the specialist is promoting a crisis atmosphere. She is used to treating chronic infertility cases, and her Upper East Side patients have incomes as elevated as their anxiety levels. I also have to admit that I find all this discussion and all these processes to be more than a little humiliating and definitely unmanly. I wish we could just have a baby the way younger people do. To make matters worse, when Francesca and I finish another round of heated discussion over this, we are unable to make up in the usual way because the timing is inappropriate. The right time was yesterday at midnight, which is usually past my bedtime. For foreplay Francesca was to give herself a subcutaneous shot of human chorionic gonadotropin—hCG—to induce ovulation. But we were groggy and had a difficult time getting the hCG to dissolve and had to page the doctor for help. Then Francesca almost fainted when she stuck the needle in her stomach. It was all pretty hot.

I face two manhood tests today. First I'm heading to the fertility specialist's Central Park East office for the postcoital results. This may determine how far down the road of assisted reproductive technology we will have to travel. Or whether Francesca will call for a reproductive pinch hitter. After that, I am seeking to upgrade my low status on the Machine. Billy is short of players again this week.

The first set of results is not promising. As I peer through the microscope, I can't identify anything, but the specialist says there are no motile sperm in the cervical mucus. The problem may stem less from my end than from the mucus, which is low, a standard side effect of Clomid, though probably not one that has bothered Jason Giambi. Anyway, so much for my happy conception calculations. Still, we have a chance this cycle. The hCG shot doesn't induce ovulation for thirty-six hours, and we can bypass the problem with an *intrauterine* insemination, as the specialist corrected me. "Artificial" is a bad word around these parts; the ingredients are all natural. So we will be undergoing "IUI," after all, tomorrow morning. In the meantime, my job is to generate sufficient sperm. I get no instructions about how to do that, but what better place to try than at a softball game?

I walk from the office in the upper Sixties and cross Fifth Avenue into Central Park. After a week of rain, cherry trees, forsythia, and daffodils galore are in bloom as I head west to the Heckscher fields to join my Machine teammates. Billy tells me he needs me to play the infield, tossing me my Machine jersey—a charcoal T-shirt with red-and-white screened letters. The team name appears in a black letter, AC/DC-style logo and features an umlaut over the *a*. Billy, whose metal-parody band is named Sküm, was going for an ersatz goth look. Frank, a teammate with far more seniority, had already chosen my favorite number, one, so I settle for thirteen. It is not a problem because I'm antisuperstitious. And thirteen was Ozzie Guillen's number.

Billy starts me at third base in game one, and I play as if plagued by a personal storm cloud, a big-city version of the *Li'l Abner* character Joe Btfsplk, the human jinx. On my second at bat, the umpire rings me up on a pitch that was not even ankle high. I'm quietly fuming on my way back to the bench.

Our pitcher Dick suggests that I got my just deserts because I left for first base "too early," thus "forcing" the umpire to call a strike. Now I'm angry. I didn't leave too soon. And in any case, I think that this analysis is wrong. A batter's actions rarely influence calls, and leaving slightly early probably has some small net positive benefit. Not all umpires are seeking to provoke confrontations, which inevitably ensue when they call a batter back to the box, or ring him up.

As a child I learned that on-field transgressions discredit a player's sideline observations, no matter how insightful, whereas a successful player's utterances are held in high regard, no matter how idiotic. I thought this state of affairs would change when I reached adulthood, but somehow it hasn't. My poor play makes it impossible for me to say anything, so I have to settle for seething. The walk/strikeout turns out to be my best plate appearance of the game. Although I have been in denial about it—denial being my first line of defense against physical ailments and denial of physical ailments being my first line of defense against recognizing and acknowledging scarier feelings—my right knee has been sore, possibly from the weight lifting I've been doing to rehab my hamstring. I've been having trouble moving laterally, digging into the batter's box, and pushing off.

If I am falling short in my day's manly activities, our opponents, the Pitt Bulls, are too. Yet another Sunday team that can't correctly spell its name, the Bulls are losing game one. Although they aren't putting up a big struggle with their gloves and bats, they are refusing to go quietly, engaging in what nineteenth-century baseball observers would call "boyish" behavior. Back then, baseball was thought by Victorian Americans to be a useful means to teach boys how to become men. Players would gain skills, strength, and a measure of essential self-control, playing the game for itself and accepting defeat graciously.

On base in the fifth, I find myself in the eye of a controversy when our next batter loops one into center. I advance from first and am already standing on second when the outfielder throws the ball there. But on the recommendation of the Pitt Bull pitcher, the umpire, who wasn't watching, calls me forced out at second. After a few minutes of Billy's complaining, the umpire realizes he's been buffaloed and reverses his judgment. The Pitt Bulls know I'm safe but remain adamant. "You called him out!" the pitcher and a few others keep reiterating, until the umpire reverses his corrected call. Later in the game, a throw home beats our runner Tommy, but the tag is high, and Tommy is called safe. Another fifteen minutes of rhubarb ensues. The call stands, and with my jinxing effect localized to me, we hang on for a 5–2 win.

The Bulls are not alone in their boyishness. At the beginning of the game, Billy asked us to place our hands in a circle and shout in unison "win," as if we were a high school football team, and throughout the game batters have received than the usual amount of useless advice. For instance, when one of our batters has two strikes, Billy invariably calls out, "You've got to protect"—the catch-22 of softball. "To protect" means that the batter should swing if the pitch is close to being a strike, to avoid being rung up, but not too hard, to avoid striking out. But a batter who swings at bad pitches or defensively will make the out that he was supposed to be protecting against.

Why all the needless advice? The player-fan defies Bourdieu's dictum that children play team sports and adults follow them, not only by pursuing team sports as an adult but by caring deeply about the team he plays for. The sociologist Gary Alan Fine argues that leisure organizations provide fun but are also in the business of providing meaning. Adults playing an organized team sport seriously are in it far less for sociability or sheer animal exuberance than for the affirmation of their self-images. In terms of maintaining their identities, they are playing for keeps. Their identities are also bound up with the team, to which they have an intense emotional attachment. But despite their excellent seats, despite being the team's biggest fans, they can't do anything about their teammates' plate appearances. To assuage their feelings of helplessness—to protect themselves—nonbatting teammates are compelled to say something to the batter, even if it is self-defeating. Usually all they can accomplish is to transmit their anxiety. If I ever start playing well here, I may share this observation.

In the nightcap, Mike the shortstop has returned. Given the infield pecking order, Billy shifts me from third base to second base. We score early and often, and I work the count and get good pitches to hit, but pop them up or bounce them harmlessly. I finish with a scratch hit in six at bats. On the brink of a double win, looseness breaks out on our bench. It centers on Woody, a dentist with old-fashioned horn-rimmed glasses who resembles Woody Allen with an even bigger attitude. Woody has been an excellent player but is now past fifty and watching in horror as his skills decline. He had complained about someone placing a sleeve on his bat. He had to bang his bat handle on the ground repeatedly to dislodge the weight and warned our entire bench that the culprit had better not do it again. Such a display of inappropriate anger cries out for just retribution, and near the end of the game someone of course replaces the sleeve. Woody, predictably, goes bananas. I overhear one of the guys advising Woody that he "shouldn't hold in" so much anger. "It could cause cancer or something." There may be hope for this team yet.

I go back to the train by myself wondering how playing ball as an adult relates to being a man. Fine argues that Little League coaches try to teach boys to become men. Ball playing can help growing boys and girls alike learn to control aggression, expressing it in appropriate and patterned ways, while developing skills and learning to use them under pressure. For middle-aged men playing softball, controlling aggression may not be something that can be settled forever, but it is a constant struggle. Some guys find it elusive. Others aren't even trying. No one presumes to be teaching it. At the same time, growing older and playing softball is a matter not of harnessing physical talent but of watching skills and strength inevitably fade, while staying in shape and compensating with savvy. But is there still something to learn about becoming a man here? If there is, it has to be coming to terms with almost unending physical taunts and insults with some measure of grace—or at least not being such a baby about it.

## MONDAY, APRIL 28, HECKSCHER #6

### *Production*

The modern-day technological wonder of intrauterine insemination requires a certain age-old, prescientific preliminary event. It need not be as degrading as countless movies and TV shows have suggested; it's even possible to skip the doctor's office and "collect the sample," as they put it, in the privacy of one's own home. Still, the act is humiliating. Then there is the specimen cup, which is so wide that it would take an impossibly wet dream to cover even the bottom of it. But I'm trying hard not to be a baby about it, and anyway, I can't dwell on debasements. Time is of the essence in getting the goods to the office. I dash out of the apartment unshaven and scruffily dressed, as if maybe I had produced the sample in the Astor Place station where I await the number 6 train. The cup is supposed to stay close to the body to keep it warm and its millions of microscopic passengers alive. I feel as though I were harboring contraband or had hijacked a miniature subway train, and I can't help reaching into my trousers pocket to check on the cup, the way that criminals inadvertently tip off their concealed handguns.

At eight o'clock, the number 6 is a cattle car, but I'm waiting near the front of the platform and manage to secure a seat. In my new position the enormous cup is outlined against my outer thigh as if I had stolen a mug from an espresso bar. At Union Square my car starts to fill and people squeeze in around me. I can't help noticing that the bulge is touching the leg of an un-

54

suspecting older woman dressed for work on the Upper East Side, who is inadvertently aiding me in keeping my pocket cargo stable and warm. Welcome to the new MTA. I get off at Hunter College and head east to the doctor's office on Central Park. Maybe I'm not wrong about the undercover nature of this expedition. The office manager asks me if I'm there for "the drop-off," secures the contraband, and summarily dismisses me.

The intrauterine insemination is a major production. First the semen is lowered into a chemical bath to induce the most motile sperm to "swim up" to the top, separating the quick from the dead and the merely tardy. The survivors are then scooped out like tadpoles, washed, and placed in a centrifuge to remove all excess fluid. I can't help imagining them pouring the mixture back and forth between two smoking test tubes like mad scientists in old B movies. But in fact the remainder, concentrated sperm, is injected directly into the uterus, cutting out the middlemen—the cervical mucus and me. I retrace my steps to the subway and home and pass the reproductive baton—the subway MetroCard—to Francesca. Despite the fact that she is heading uptown to embark on what could be one of the biggest moments of our lives, there is no reason for me to be there. In fact, my presence is discouraged, much as men of my father's generation were steered away from delivery rooms. I know exactly where my father was when I was born—on the golf course. Someday I hope to have a similarly winning story to tell my child about where I was during her conception.

Back at home and with nothing better to do, I toy with lineups before today's Performing Arts game and field phone calls. I learn that Trey pulled his hamstring during yesterday's Machine games—he can still bat but can't play the field or run. Penny also calls, saying that he has strained his back, having played five games on Sunday, and would prefer not to play. With his strong sense of responsibility, he would never just say he wasn't showing. As I work through the possibilities, Francesca calls from her office with a fun fact to pump me up for the game. Normally the technicians hope to capture a million viable sperm in the swim-up, but from my sample they netted eighty million.

I know I should feel somehow proud, but it all seems a little remote. Also, I'm not sure whether the credit is mine or theirs, as is often the case with situational counting stats, like runs batted in or wins in baseball. Maybe my sample was the biological equivalent of an in-between hop that they saved with a nice scoop. I reject the deep analogy between baseball and life, and here is one instance in which baseball seems much more important. It is far easier to assess the prospective professional trajectories of college baseball players than the life chances of babies born through IVF or other new reproductive technologies. And this imbalance in research findings will doubtless persist, at least until assisted reproduction becomes a spectator sport or someone devises fantasy leagues for families, with scoring categories for height, weight, GPA, and the SAT exam. Anyway, I suppose I should write a thank-you note to the woman on the train—or maybe to the Pitt Bulls, or Dick.

When I get to the field I notice that a few of the guys are not wearing the Foxes jerseys. Myself, I almost never wear any team-issued softball T-shirt or jersey if I can avoid it and instead sport something in team colors from my game-used collection. I'm irked at the defectors, but I'm not sure why. It's not that it's a slap in the face to our sponsor Mickey. The Pamela's Cantina patches won't be ready until next week. Is it because this is my team and the sartorial defiance seems antiteam? Or is it that the coolest jerseys by far in any Central Park league are being displaced by tank tops? Sporting this look are Krishy and Q. It is flattering on them. Krishy's upper body has been chiseled through his work as a personal trainer, and Q's shoulders are wiry as well as lavishly illustrated. Maybe they just want to enjoy the sun. It is an unusually warm day for late April, sunny and in the high seventies.

In any case, they are in the minority. Little Bobby wants a pair of the baggy, 1940s-style knickers that go with the jerseys. He says he can wear size 30—the smallest I have in stock. "I'm just a little bitch," he says by way of explanation, emphasizing the "little." I see an opportunity to amuse Q, the percussionist and outfielder, whose good side I am still trying to get on, and to josh the good-natured Bobby. So I make a mock issue of his apparent breach of our softball players' standard macho attitude and high self-regard. "Repeat after me," I say, emphasizing each word: "I . . . am . . . not . . . a . . . little . . ."—big pause—"*bitch!*" Bobby smiles uncertainly, while Q smirks. This is not the effect I'm trying for. Can't anybody have a little big league fun around here? Q lets me know that his friend Tanner, whom I had drummed off the team before the season, is still available if I need him.

Today Pamela's plays Production, a team that changes its name every season. Each version has pounded the Sharkeys up and down over the last three years. Is it possible that sabermetrics has so infiltrated daytime softball that this team has named itself after a synonym for the most illuminating of all simple batting statistics—on-base percentage plus slugging average? As they break out their new uniforms I wonder if they will include statistical formulae. Instead, out of the box come uniforms with the lowest production values possible, crimson T-shirts with no printing at all.

Before the game I call the guys together and try to make a statement about yesterday's pregame cheer. Contrary to the old baseball saying, the best softball teams can potentially win them all, not just 65 percent like the best baseball teams of recent years—so softball players often act as though each game is a big game. But a generic pumping-up of the team, which might be appropriate in sports like football, is deadly for baseball and softball, which call for a more thoughtful approach to performance. Overaggressiveness and adrenalin surges can backfire. Batters can't just swing as hard as they can and expect to succeed. Fielders need to think ahead and always be alert. It's useless to get pumped up as if to make one big play because no one knows when or if it is going to happen.

The novelist John Updike's dictum about baseball also holds for softball. It is essentially lonely. You bat or pitch by yourself. The ball is hit nearby, or it isn't. Impassioned pleas by teammates don't help. And acting like every game is critical is—how to put it?—so not big league, where one game bleeds into the next. If one goes badly, no need to dwell; another is coming soon. The cumulative result is what counts.

I was considering holding an ironic pregame huddle. I want to say, in the style of Walter Matthau, "Today we're playing Production. And what does that mean?" But I'm afraid not enough of my teammates would catch the dated film reference and reply, "It means *bad news* for Production!" So I read out the lineup and finish with, "On the count of three, don't say a thing." After a moment of silence, Krishy picks up the vibe and shouts, "Let's go, you foxy Foxes!" OK—that's what I'm talking about!

Billy is tenser than usual, perhaps irked that I mocked his pregame ritual. He yells at the infield in the first inning for not instructing Cookie, who is playing third, to throw to first on a slow grounder; instead he threw to second, where he had no play. I find it particularly annoying, because it is the kind of thing that I pride myself on doing. Billy also complains to me about Papi, who is making his debut at first base, for his inability to scoop a catchable throw out of the dirt. The guys in the plain red shirts take a 1–0 lead. In the bottom of the second, we load the bases on a couple of walks. Q , unburdened by his jersey, singles in two runs. In the third, Trey, the injured infielder and personal trainer who has showed only minor interest in playing for us, shows up for the first time and smashes a pinch hit for two more runs.

With Production threatening in the fourth, it happens—another bit of softball magic. Their speedy and powerful left fielder hits a shot up the middle, and I'm heading to my left to cut it off. But Billy gets a glove on it and deflects it right. I stop, change direction, barehand the ball, and throw all in one motion to nip the runner. He grouses that he can't believe he was gunned down by "Sideshow Bob." Though meant to be humiliating, I like being compared to the evil genius with the flowing dreadlocks from *The Simpsons*. It beats a lot of the things I was called as a kid and sounds a little like Shoeless Joe. We Foxes have beaten the three best teams in this league in consecutive weeks. Who can stop us?

## Professor Baseball

In my weekly e-mail newsletter to team Pamela's Cantina, I promote a set of principles I like to think of as Eddy Ball. It is essentially sabermetrics as applied to softball, with a little sociology added to the mix, and revolves around one core idea: outs are really precious. In softball, a team has only twenty-one outs per game, six fewer than in baseball, and scores are higher. I am, accordingly, the sworn enemy of small ball and its apostle Gene Mauch—who advocated playing for one run at a time—and worship Earl Weaver, the patron saint of the big inning.

The writer Michael Lewis argues in *Moneyball* that Major League Baseball is mired in something like a religious war. On one side are the insiders, adherents to the so-called Book of received baseball wisdom passed down through the generations. On the other side are the outsiders, sabermetricians who have questioned the Book, subjected it to systematic empirical evaluation, and slowly forced their way inside, based on the strength of their analyses and the value of their recommendations. The former major leaguers and their fellow travelers who have dominated big league front offices may want to continue to run an old boys' club and find the approach of the baseball analysts threatening, but they are facing extreme pressure to win, and the genie is out of the bottle.

In competitive adult softball, much of the value in the activity derives from players' imagining themselves to be something akin to big league ballplayers. If the distance cannot be made up through professional-quality play, one can still seek to identify with the big leaguers by aping their attitudes. So my teammates tend to be truer believers of the Book than baseball insiders. And like most fans my teammates make judgments based almost entirely on what they see. Someone who blasts a home run or makes a good catch earns much credit, no matter how many pop flies or missed chances in his past. A player who routinely reaches on errors is considered to have benefited from dumb luck rather than to have done something valuable.

I am skeptical of the Book, and although I trust my eyes as far as they go, I am far more attuned to making judgments based on a record of performances than on sheer appearances. Most of my academic research is on people long dead, and I employ techniques ranging from multiple regression to imaginary experiments to make inferences about causality. Because stat-heads are rare in softball and my views are so different from my teammates', I often feel as if I were a spy on my own team. I never make any reference to "Eddy Ball" or, for that matter, to "sabermetrics." The last thing I need is for one of my teammates to ask, "Who do you think you are, 'Professor Baseball?'" The ridicule would be ruthless. So I don't set out tenets but instead advance my views by example and by praising acts that are consistent with Eddy Ball on the field and, especially, in the newsletter.

But there are, of course, tenets. Two Eddy Ball precepts are to avoid outs on the base paths and never sacrifice. Since stealing and bunting are illegal in most softball, this means that runners should avoid taking chances that are not extremely high-percentage ones and that batters should never make an out to advance a runner, unless, maybe, the game is tied with a runner on third with one out in the bottom of the final inning. My teammates and I are most at odds over the sacrifice fly. To me, if there is anything worse than making an out, it is making an out on purpose. The name itself is Orwellian. It imbues the act with an air of nobility, as if the player were doing something at great personal expense to benefit the team. But the cost is to the team, not the player. The player doesn't get charged with an at bat and gets a free shot at picking up an RBI, a situational counting statistic that is less than worthless because it seduces players into hitting cans o' corn. These premeditated pop-ups are sacrifices only in sense of slaying a team's chance to win at the altar of conventional baseball wisdom. One reason that on-base percentage is so superior to batting average as a statistic is that OBP counts these team victimizations against the perpetrator. Yet my teammates see the sacrifice as not only noble but smart, having had its value drilled into them by Little League coaches and the *Gil Thorp* comic strip.

Eddy Ball does incorporate some small-ball ideas. Another one of my key injunctions is Don't be afraid to walk. On good softball teams a high percentage of base runners will score, so taking the free pass is also a sign of confidence in one's teammates. I see speed as highly valuable too. With the short distances between bases, speed exerts tremendous pressure on infielders, leading to the greatly underappreciated softball play—reached on an error. Speed also converts medium-percentage base-running moves into high-percentage ones. And another injunction, based mainly on logistics, is decidedly anti–Earl Weaver: Don't try to hit home runs. In Central Park these efforts will usually be fly outs, because the New York softball is very soft and the outfielders can play as deep as they want, having no fences to contend with. A player who hits line drives and grounders, given the well-below-major-league quality of the infields and infielders, has a far better chance of reaching base and scoring than a player who routinely launches balls in the air. A big inning in Central Park softball is more likely to develop from a couple of singles sandwiched between an error and a walk or two than from Weaver's three-run homer.

In the field, the central tenet of Eddy Ball is essentially the obverse of the offensive injunctions: Avoid the big inning. In the best case the pitcher would throw strikeout after strikeout. Within the usual circumstances it means that pitchers should have decent stuff, develop a better command of the strike zone, and only rarely give free passes—which open the door to big innings and take the fielders' heads out of the game. Fielders should accept outs when they present themselves. Outfielders should hit their cutoff men and always keep the force at second base alive. Heads-up playing is key.

But defense is still not well understood among sabermetricians, as the data are not as good. It is probably underrated in the majors, and even more so in softball. Routine plays in baseball often become adventures in softball, so fielding talent is crucial. I want maximum defensive flexibility—preferably an entire team of shortstops and left-center fielders (though without the usual accompanying attitudes), because I want players who can make plays and can assume different positions as the need arises. Everyone else—the few guys who can hit but can't field—I want to shunt to the far left, or undemanding, side of the softball defensive spectrum—catcher, designated hitter, extra hitter. And flexibility may yield larger benefits. George Herbert Mead, the only famous early sociologist to discuss baseball, thought that its fielding positions and rules promoted self-development and social awareness. In learning the game, children are induced to put themselves in someone else's shoes and, in the process, to gain a greater appreciation for the roles played by others and a greater orientation to and respect for the group.

In terms of player attitude and outlook, Eddy Ball provides a plea to remain calm and alert rather than getting worked up. Batting requires being relaxed. Most hitters are anxious but have batted many times before and almost always know the count, so it's unnecessary to instruct or remind them at the plate. It's better to try to crack them up with a joke than to tell them how "big" they are in a clutch situation or that they should "protect" with two strikes. I like fielders to rehearse to themselves beforehand what they are going to do if the ball is hit to them. During the many boring moments in a game fielders can while away the time by entertaining the possibilities, which are usually limited to a ground ball, fly ball, or line drive. I often wonder how it is possible that players can find themselves with the ball, yet have no clue where to throw it.

Sociologists may see the clash between the views of me and my players as resembling the one between rational and traditional authority, two types of legitimate domination identified by the early German sociologist Max Weber. I am applying science, logic, and evidence in seeking efficient ways to achieve our common goal—winning. The players, by contrast, are traditionalists, suspicious of any deviation from the Book's conventional wisdom. But it's not that simple. My teammates see themselves as rational and the Book as less a holy book than a textbook based on scientific thinking and a century and a half of baseball experience. A synonym for small ball when Weber visited the Saint Louis World's Fair in 1904—but as far as I know did not catch a ballgame—was "scientific baseball." Thus my teammates view new sabermetric ideas as crackpot, the softball equivalent of cold fusion in a jar.

It is becoming clear to me that the only way to establish my authority and legitimate my approach is through Weber's third basis of authority—charisma. This does not mean, as my colleagues know, having a magnetic personality or a hot body so much as being seen as magical, with extraordinary, inexplicable powers. My teammates want to win, and during my tenure we are undefeated, having beaten the three teams that have for years dominated us. They would not accede to my ideas if I presented them directly, but they'll go along with me as long as my magic remains powerful—as long, that is, as we keep winning.

Our streak is making me bold, and today I have an Eddy Ball lesson in mind. There has been considerable pressure from my teammates for me to name starters for each position and a set lineup. Players think this is how it ought to be because that is how it is in professional baseball. More than that, everyone wants to have an assured place on the field and in the batting order, one that corresponds to his self-image as a player and what he thinks batting orders should look like. I'm unwilling to do this. Sabermetric research shows that batting orders are insignificant. The most productive ones simply line up the players in descending order of on-base percentage, but the optimal order isn't much more productive than a random one. More important, once starters are named, it becomes difficult to move a player to a different position, however much it might benefit the team. Once positions are set, players are inclined to regard the positions as their property and to see a change as both a theft and an insult. As social scientists know, other things being equal, people tend to react more negatively to loss than positively to gain.

To prepare guys to be able to play different positions—to do whatever the team needs, and to undermine the sense of position as property—my plan for this afternoon is for our infielders and outfielders to rotate every inning, as in volleyball. My teammates may not become better people, but at least they will be better prepared to help the team win if called upon later in the season to play another position. One reason I think I can get away with this is that we are facing a team originally called the New Guys, which joined the league two years ago. The New Guys lost their first twenty or so games but could not have had more fun, cheering each other on in ways that I had not seen since grade school. When they finally won a game, near the end of last season, they were delirious. The New Guys enjoyed their one win far more than we did our half dozen.

Their low reputation is evening the odds today, however, because some of our more tightly scheduled players have decided that playing them is a waste of time. Billy, our star pitcher and a front man for a theme metal band, explained to me that he has been playing too much softball and wants to show only for "serious" games. Other guys are jaking too. With Billy away, the pitching start goes to Dog, our second-string hurler. Dog is a retired teacher, who defers to Billy and seems thrilled when he gets the opportunity to get in the game. Dog is on the small side, with rheumy basset hound eyes—though his nickname is simply short for Doug—and what little hair he has left on his head is shaved off. For a retiree, Dog is in excellent shape, riding his racing bike around Central Park a few times a week. Most of all, Dog has the arm and the pitching profile of a much younger man. Dog is a little like Nuke LaLoosh, Tim Robbins's character in *Bull Durham*. Dog throws a hard, heavy ball that is difficult to hit, but he exhibits only a modest command of the strike zone. I ask him to experiment with laying in first-pitch strikes and using his rising fastball as his out pitch, instead of relying on it for every pitch. I also warn him that I will yank him if he walks three batters. At catcher I slot the good-natured Big Artie, who can play anywhere on the field. Perhaps he can guide Dog through the game, as Kevin Costner's wise Crash Davis guided Nuke.

I was counting on the outfielder and personal trainer Krishy to be the tenth player. But he calls to tell me that his dog has shit all over his apartment. He is reluctant to leave her and asks me to call our teammate Q to see if he would give them a lift. But Q informs me that dogs, even those without diarrhea, are unwelcome in his ride, a new Mercedes SLK convertible. So there will be no Krishy today, we will be short a player, and so much for my volleyball rotation scheme.

Even more disconcerting is that the New Guys, who have changed their name to the Cornelia Street All Stars, have undergone a shift in attitude. This team wants to win. They practice religiously and in their first three games already have an upset to their credit. Last year, the New Guys could be counted on to have at least two women in their lineup—women can play in the league, but rarely do—and several player/fans in the stands. This year's All Stars have only eleven players, including just one woman. And she is the odd woman out, deployed as an extra hitter and visibly irked about not getting to play the field. When they perform the pregame hands-in-circle group shout—"Win!"—I have a flash of recognition. With their newfound seriousness and their improved but not-quite-talented-enough-to-contend roster, the New Guys remind me of our team last season.

Our chatterbox outfielder Swanny, who is like both a Little League player and a coach on the field, pulls our team together to respond in ceremonial kind. In our understaffed state, we must apparently fight seriousness with seriousness. Or maybe since I failed to field a complete team, the absentminded professor unable to take care of business, Swanny feels the need to take charge. He gathers the team to put its hands together, and everyone joins in but me. Sheesh—I thought I had put this children's routine to rest last week. It is the antithesis of Eddy Ball. We bat first but cannot convert our adrenalin surge into runs. Through four we produce nothing but goose eggs.

But that is all the New Guys/All Stars have to cheer about. Even with only three outfielders—the result of having only nine players instead of the standard ten—we are steady on defense. In part this is because of our outfielder Bobby, a blues drummer. He is short and rail thin, and is still often called Little Bobby, even though Big Bobby left the team two years ago. Little Bobby has long, stringy brown hair, held in place by a bandana, and a soul patch. I like the fact that he is both slighter than me and has longer hair. He is a young man of few words—midthirties still counting as youthful here—and spits a lot, like the "doomded" catcher played by the young, too-small, baseball-challenged Bobby De Niro in *Bang the Drum Slowly*. Little Bobby is a left-handed hitter with middling power but excellent speed. By drilling grounders and getting a quick jump out of the box, he pressures infielders, a little like Ichiro. I think that Bobby has the potential to be a great outfielder too. He has the speed and agility, and his father's vintage Wilson A2000. But our ex-manager Zeus considered Bobby too unschooled and mainly used him as a DH. Bobby is self-effacing to a fault, clearly hasn't played organized ball, and doesn't act the part.

THE UNDERVALUED PLAYER
WAS LITTLE BOBBY

Whenever I ask him if he minds batting last or as DH, he will look down and say, "That's fine. I'm not a baby." If I ask him to avoid hitting a fly ball and to try to hit the ball down and hard, he will not question me. He will do it.

In *Moneyball*, Lewis shows how the Oakland A's outfox better financed opponents by drafting and trading for players who perform well but don't look like what ballplayers are supposed to look like, don't impress scouts with their physical tools, and don't have the good face. For the A's that meant picking up slow pudgy guys with some pop and even better plate sense. In softball, however, the overweight slugger is overvalued. The undervalued player is someone who hits a lot of singles, reaches on errors, is fast and skilled enough to make more plays than most, and doesn't act much like how softball players think major league players act and thus has no entrenched attitudes about the game. That player is Little Bobby. Today he is covering a lot of territory in right, proving his value to all.

And Dog is pitching well, but in the bottom of fourth with one out, he falters, walking the bases loaded. There is, as TV baseball announcers say, nowhere to put the next batter, but Dog serves him four balls anyway, and the base runners seem happy to make room. The New Guys now have a 1–0 lead. A liner into one of the big gaps between the outfielders will break open the game. As Dog paces around, rubbing his neck, from left field Q yells, "Eddy!" His look of irritation is evident even through his wraparounds, and he is holding his arms out with his palms up and thrusting his face forward, the international signal for "Will you yank this wild man?" Needless to say, Dog's pitching has run well outside the bounds of Eddy Ball precepts, but I'm reluctant to replace him with the next pitcher on the depth chart—me. I haven't pitched since last fall, and with my minimal repertoire of pitches, I am definitely the last option.

Compelled to act on my principles, I send Dog behind the plate. I move Artie to second base, Cookie from second to third, and Penny from third to shortshop, replacing me, and take the ball. My plan is to force the New Guys to hit the ball and hope my teammates can field it. I wave Q, Swanny, and Bobby to play deeper in the outfield, and to calm myself I repeat under my breath, "Voros McCracken, Voros McCracken," invoking the hypnotically named sabermetrician who became famous for arguing that pitchers have little influence over whether balls put in play are hit safely. The idea has currency for the majors, where both the average pitcher and the average fielder are excellent, way out on the tail of the normal curve of talent. In weekday New York softball leagues, however, the pitchers vary from college level to tee ball, and fielding is all over the place too. All the same, my prayer is answered, as the first batter turns on a nothing ball and lines it right at Cookie, who gloves it and fires to first for an inning-ending double play.

We fail to score in the fifth, but I'm getting my "fastball" over the plate and thus can sell my changeup and upset the New Guys' timing. I retire them one, two, three. In the sixth, Penny leads off with a triple, and, trying to show by example that there is no need for a sac fly or a suicidal grounder to the right side, I work a walk. Dog does the same, and a couple of bleeders later we take a 3–1 lead, with a display of softball right from my unwritten textbook. I set them down again, and we pour it on in the seventh. In the team e-mail I send around after the game, I praise our guys for their patience in the big inning and Little Bobby for his play in right.

To anyone who wasn't there it reads like another easy victory, but I wonder if I made some key miscalculation. I began the season thinking that if I retained players who could hit, show or learn patience at the plate, field, and keep a good attitude, and added a few more such players, allocating them all to fielding positions they could handle, we would have an excellent chance to win and have a lot of fun doing it. I think I have this team, but I hadn't reckoned with the possibility that it wouldn't show up to play.

**SUNDAY, MAY 11, GLENVIEW, ILLINOIS**

## *Little League Redux*

On Mother's Day there are never games scheduled in the Lower Manhattan Softball League. Francesca was invited to give a talk at Northwestern University, and I've taken the opportunity to fly with her to Chicagoland, where everyone in my family still lives. Yesterday we went to my sister Kerry's home in Mundelein to attend my nephew Kyle's Little League game. He is sprouting up quickly—at least a half a foot taller than I was at his age. Although he's closing in on twelve, Kyle is only eleven in Little League years because his birthday is in August, just after the cutoff point. I feel as though this may be some cosmic compensation for my own July birthday (which got me counted as ten when I was really nine, eleven when I was ten, and so on) and for my delayed physical development. Kyle tried out for and made a highly competitive "traveling" team. Before the game, the coach gathered Kyle's team of eleven- and twelve-year-olds; under his direction, they placed their hands in a circle and shouted out, "Win!" Kyle looked impressive. He lashed a single and looked sharp in the field. After the game, the teams lined up to shake hands, just as my teams in New York do.

This morning, my sister Marybeth, Francesca, and I go jogging. The streets of the suburb are littered with tree branches snapped off by tornadolike winds the previous evening. We aim for Roosevelt Park, the site of my first Little League games. There are four fields that face each other, much like the Heckscher Ballfields, though bordered by evergreens instead of maples. They are unoccupied this Sunday morning. As a nine-year-old, I came to bat with the championship on the line for a team made up of kids from our Glenview subdivision. It was the bottom of the sixth, two outs, with a runner on first and my team down 3–1. I turned on an inside pitch and blasted it past the left fielder, the ball rolling almost onto the next diamond. My home run tied a game that looked like a lost cause, and I accepted the rapturous congratulations of my teammates. A walk and three passed balls later, we were champions.

I remember being especially excited because it was one of the first of my games that my father attended. After the game we returned in triumph to Tall Trees, a new tract-housing development conspicuously lacking in the arboreal area, in a caravan of convertibles, all the players sitting on the backs of the seats and waving. As our impromptu parade went from shade-free Blackthorn Drive to sapling-lined Sequoia Trail, the car horns honked as if it were the Fourth of July. When we return to the condo after the jog, I remind my mom that on the big day she, Marybeth, and Kerry waved towels at us from our front yard in salute. That day I thought that big things were in store for me in baseball, but that home run turned out to be the highlight of my career.

For Mother's Day, Francesca got her period. Conception didn't happen this round—so much for the pricey and humiliating intrauterine insemination process. Apparently eighty million wasn't enough. But having anticipated this unhappy possibility, we're getting right back up on the horse. When we return to New York, Francesca shoots her stomach full of Follistin, a fertility drug, the first of several such treatments to induce follicle, or egg, production.

( MONDAY, MAY 12, HECKSCHER #6 )

## *Traveling Secretary*

Running a softball team entails more than serving as general manager, manager, player, owner, and sometime beat reporter. As the season goes on, the main duties, I am realizing, are those of a traveling secretary—ensuring that the team makes it to the park each week. Tracking the schedules of fourteen guys is the part of the job that holds the least appeal to me. I don't like to talk on the telephone and remain a holdout on the cell-phone market. I prefer the time-saving group e-mail. My weekly electronic newsletter to the team asks everyone to get back to me only if they aren't going to make it.

But this system works imperfectly. Today I thought that I would avoid last week's personnel problems. It's a big game—the first "position" game, with our first-place, undefeated Foxes matched against the second-place team, Production, the red-shirted team we beat two weeks ago for their only loss. Billy sees the game as sufficiently compelling to warrant his presence on the mound, and Mule and Roger are back in town. But Penny has canceled, having agreed to help a friend move in Jersey City. And on Sunday I learned through one of Mule's calls to my answering machine that Swanny had found a few day's worth of stagehand work on *The Sweet Smell of Success*. Trey, still nursing his injured hamstring, sees this league as a low priority in his rehab schedule. Alan seems to be out for good, no longer returning messages. And this afternoon Krishy simply fails to show up—no explanation—leaving another hole in our outfield.

So I have ten guys to start the game, but they are far from the optimal ten. I am forced to station infielders in the outfield, and I have the second-string pitcher Dog and the defensively challenged Mule playing in the infield. It is no comfort to think that Mule may become better socialized and more appreciative of others when he fails to take even one step to charge a roller to second base, then drops a relay when I move him to first. The Foxes pop up ball after ball in their haste to get at the Production pitcher's soft servings. Swanny, who'd returned from his job to watch the last couple of innings in his street clothes, says at the end, "You guys looked like a bunch of Sharkeys out there." We played poorly, but most likely I lost the game before it started by mishandling the traveling secretary job.

After the game, after everyone has left, I am jogging back to the subway. It is always a little thrilling to run on the West Drive. I can't help associating this stretch with the New York City Marathon, where the Circle to Tavern on the Green constitutes the last five hundred yards of a 26.2-mile journey through five boroughs. Thousands of people would be screaming encouragement, and many of them would be calling out my name—not because they knew me but because I had written in Magic Marker on my shirt: "Ed DEE, Ed DEE." My primitive calligraphy often would touch off a wave of chanting along the race route, much to the annoyance of anyone running alongside me. By the time I reached Central Park, I usually found it annoying too. By that point I was suffering from exhaustion, and whatever goal I had set for my time was out of reach. But with all this softball I'm getting out of shape and have to exploit any minor exercise opportunity. As I dash along, I hear someone saying, "Eddy, Eddy." And then, as I am ignoring these cries as if it were the marathon, I hear someone shout, "Professor!" It's Big Artie, my teammate.

Artie's day job is as a computer systems troubleshooter at an Internet business that provides horse racing information for bettors. Of all my new teammates he seems like the best candidate for becoming a friend. He is interesting to talk to and, unlike most of my teammates, regularly reads the newspaper. He is also almost always online. He lives on Barrow Street in the West Village, and sometimes I ride the A train back with him, as we have the same West Fourth Street stop. I like it more than I can say that Artie is calling me "Professor." He is not using it respectfully or dismissively but with the needling tone that ballplayers of yesteryear used to slap the label on teammates with college degrees, published diaries, or prescription eyeglasses. He says it the way that Henry Wiggen's fictional New York Mammoth teammates in *Bang the Drum Slowly* call him "Author."

I worry that Artie is going to complain about the game, but he wants my consolation. With his new eyeglass prescription—maybe I should be calling him Professor—he has been having trouble in the outfield, having misjudged a fly ball last week and another one in today's loss. It is starting to bother him. He tells a tale of thrashing around in bed, chasing fly ball after fly ball as if underwater, only to have them disappear at the last second. He is thinking about wearing his old glasses. I tell him not to worry about it and that I will try to keep him in the infield.

# Getting Late Early

I have not played for the Machine for three weeks and have been thinking that maybe the team and Lower Manhattan Softball League aren't for me. I have one hit in nine tries, and no walks—stupid Ozzie Guillen number thirteen. I was trying to beg off the last Machine doubleheader, two weeks ago, in part because I didn't want my knee trouble to dig an even bigger hole for me. Billy cut me short, telling me that he didn't need me. But my stellar performance on Mondays is keeping my reputation afloat with him. Last night Billy e-mailed to say that many guys, including the pitcher Dick, would miss today's doubleheader against the defending champion Hitmen. He's taking no chances with my arm in this important matchup and plans to pitch both games himself, but he wants me to play second base. This Machine team is so serious that I know I can't afford to blow many more chances to make good.

By early afternoon the clouds and chill of the morning have blown away, and the temperature is lifting into the upper sixties on the Great Lawn, where many early-season games are scheduled. The park is filling up. Unlike Heckscher, the Great Lawn is mainly not about softball. It is where Simon and Garfunkel had their reunion concert. It is where John Paul II held mass. On summer days it is where all of Manhattan converges to celebrate the outdoors. Softball is wedged in, and we will be jostling for space on the bluegrass, ryegrass, and fescue. The orange cones that demarcate general-use territory from the deep outfield are reminiscent of the days when major league ballparks would siphon their spectator overspill into roped-off areas on the playing field. The main differences here are that nobody outside the cones watches the games and that balls hit beyond them remain in play. Since it's a nice day, the game is certain to be delayed numerous times by people unclear on the boundary concept cutting across the field or by Frisbee tosses gone astray. Since this is the peoples' part of the park, no players complain. The diamonds are haphazardly strewn around the lawn, and the parting of the clouds uncovers a wicked sun in left. As Yogi Berra once said about a similar sun hazard in Yankee Stadium, "It gets late early here."

Before the game I talk to Mike the shortstop. He is rangy and powerful, with longish, thinning hair and an expressive face. He is a fine fielder, and at the plate he is always a threat to go deep. Despite his lack of confidence in my game—his recommendation sent me to the outfield last year—I can't help liking him. He is pursuing a PhD in communications at Rutgers and teach-

THE GREAT LAWN WAS NOT MAINLY ABOUT SOFTBALL

ing to make ends meet. He is about my age and took time off to write a book for which he interviewed professionals who care for dying cancer patients. He was moved to do it by his father's loss to that scourge. For a graduate student, it was a daring thing to do. Graduate programs force students to move in lockstep through coursework, exams, papers, and a dissertation. That is what I did at Chicago. Even with tunnel vision the process takes seven years, and veering off the approved course can make it difficult to finish. But Mike is someone who does things his way.

Last season Mike traded me a copy of his book for a copy of mine, and now he serves up an account of epic academic pettiness and backstabbing. If we were playing upset one-upsmanship, the New York pastime in which friends and strangers alike compete to prove themselves worse off, he would win hands down. He had a minor disagreement with the chair of the communications department at Nassau Community College, where he is teaching six courses this semester, a thankless and underpaid job. Although the chair told him that he would teach this summer—"She just last week put

MIKE WAS ALWAYS A THREAT
TO GO DEEP

my courses on the schedule," he tells me as he steps into the batter's box in the first—she subsequently found a way to induce the college's promotions committee not to reappoint him. In most instances, the loser of upset one-upsmanship is disgruntled. It is a badge of honor to win these battles, and if you lose your lesser pain goes unacknowledged. But I feel sorry for Mike, and his situation helps to put mine in perspective. I didn't get to be chair, but it is not as if I were fired. And if I had to teach six courses a semester I would never have written a word, much less a book.

We go down in order, but our defense is playing well and the game settles into a pitcher's duel. Krishy, my occasional Foxes and d.b.a. teammate, adds excitement to routine fly balls to left, using his glove as an eyeshade and backing up a little just before he snatches them. Like me, Krishy joined the team last season. Unlike me, he is now a starter, having played well in his rookie year. Despite recent rain, the infield is as hard as asphalt. In the second, I make a sliding stop of a grounder at second base and throw out the runner from my back. In the process I scour my knee and elbow and am freshly reminded why I avoid sliding. But we don't hit, and late in the game they rally and beat us, 6–2.

Still, the atmosphere, like the weather, is not unpleasant. The sunshine and surroundings have conspired to build our fan base. The catcher Superman's wife Lois, who plays in coed leagues, is here with their two rambunctious grade-school daughters. Our outfielder Matt, who is out of action with a sprained knee, shows up with his girlfriend Nathalie, a beautiful dark-eyed dancer, just to lie in the sun. He is blonde, lanky, left-handed, quick and quick-witted, always ready to crack wise. As someone once said of Willie Mays, Matt's glove is where triples go to die. He's a writer who works in software, and like most of my Machine teammates, his day job relegates him to weekend softball only. For fun he runs a quiz game, called Quizo, on Monday nights in an Upper West Side bar, where teams of friends—rarely softball players—square off for nominal amounts of cash.

The first baseman Keith's girlfriend Jaely, a school psychologist, is here too. Keith is thirtysomething, clean-cut, with all-American looks. He's a serious guy, all about focus. No doubt he and Jaely have many serious conversations about serious issues. Like Matt, Keith is left-handed and extremely fast out of the box. He is also the sort of first baseman that baseball writers call stylish, like Don Mattingly, or Keith Hernandez minus the drug problem and silly mustache. Our Keith has great range, and his glove is where throwing errors go to die. If it were up to me, I would have him at shortstop, but since he's a lefty this is not something Billy can imagine. Between games, Keith tells me he is still looking for a distributor for his feature film, a tale of redemption for a drunken hit-and-run driver. Worse, the New Jersey Film Commission, the source of his day job, remains unfunded this fiscal year. He is facing the threat of being laid off.

There are no player-related controversies today. In game two, Billy takes the ball and, as in game one, puts in a DH for himself, meaning that no one's riding the bench—the standard source of softball discontent. With Dick missing, we're also spared his drama machine. When our teammate Chad shows up for the second game, Superman good-naturedly turns the mask over to him, then hangs out with his family when we are on the field and coaches when we are at bat. When I pop up in the second inning, Superman's older daughter razzes me: "Nice try. It was better than I could do, anyway." Her tone, however, suggests that she may think otherwise.

In the third Krishy pops up to the catcher and in frustration whips the bat against the backstop. Upon being thrown out of the game, the automatic punishment for this offense, he repeats the gesture. Casey, the manager, pitcher, and star player of the Hitmen, argues that Krishy should be suspended for future games. "Right, I get it—he's not suspended because he's on your team," Casey says sarcastically to Billy, who is also the league's commissioner. Once the controversy subsides, Keith lifts one among the nonfans in right, giving us a 2–1 lead. A toy terrier runs onto the field, starring in its own dodging game, energized by all the newfound attention, and ten minutes pass before it is coaxed off.

We are hoping that Billy and the defense can hold them, though it will be difficult. The late-spring sun is now terrorizing the right side of the field, and two of our best outfielders, Matt and now Krishy, are on the sidelines. In the fifth I bobble an easy chance. It doesn't cost us, but whatever I have seems to be catching. In the sixth inning the sure-handed Keith drops a routine throw to first, our third baseman Trey throws to the wrong base, and shortstop Mike forgets to cover second. The bases are loaded with two outs, but it looks as though we are going to get out of it when Mike makes a nice stop deep in the hole and sends a relay to Trey for the force. But Trey, who also broke for the grounder, has to backtrack to third base. He gropes for the bag with his foot, then decides to tag the runner. In getting into position, Trey inadvertently backs his heel into the base, forcing out the runner, whom he then tags out for good measure. Out of position, the umpire forgets about the force play and blows the tag call. Instead of the side being retired with our lead intact, the game is tied and the bases are loaded. We argue—but not nearly as long as our opponents would have had the call gone the other way. When the game resumes, the next batter loses one to right among the nonfans beyond the cones.

Almost as a group the team cuts back past Delacorte Theater to catch the C train at 81st street. On the train, we break up into knots based on the availability of seats. I am sitting with Billy, who gets off at Forty-Second Street, and Chad, who gets off at Twenty-Third Street. The rest of the guys are heading to Tribeca, Battery Park, or Brooklyn. Mike is explaining how he was fired to Woody. Keith is talking hopefully about the budgetary prospects of the New Jersey Film Commission to Walker and Tommy. And although I feel for Mike and Keith, I find myself sitting alone and worrying about the game. No one hit much today. But everyone else on the team had already proved himself, and my one-for-four performance isn't going to win over anyone. When I get off at West Fourth, I know they could easily be talking next about how to retool the Machine. It could be getting late early for me.

## Bang the Drum for the Kid from Greenwich Village

On Wednesday Francesca and I were squabbling again over assisted—not to be confused with artificial—reproductive technology. Our martinet clothes-horse of a doctor wanted us to do two intrauterine inseminations, at $750 a pop, instead of one. The double insemination is apparently standard operating procedure, which, until Wednesday, no one had bothered to tell me. That night as Francesca prepared her injection of hCG, which induces ovulation so that we can time the inseminations, she realized that this hCG was a different prescription from the last one—Pregnyl instead of Ovidrel—and must be taken intramuscularly rather than subcutaneously. Unfortunately, Francesca didn't have the right needle. She hailed a taxi up to Central Park East, and soon I was doing the same, with the prescription she had forgotten. It took less than a minute for the doctor, clomping in on Manolos from some uptown charity function, to explain the procedure—hit all butt, while avoiding the sciatic nerve and veins. Watching it, I felt a little voyeuristic, as if it were Oakland in the eighties and I had happened upon on a bathroom tryst of the Bash Brothers.

The next morning it was time for the first intrauterine insemination. I have come to grips with the counterintuitive drill: sex for recreation, jerk off for procreation. I had to come and go, though, as the specimen needed to be uptown and in the hands of trained experts for washing and winnowing by eight o'clock. But when Francesca went for her ten-thirty appointment, she learned that she had already ovulated. That meant that the previous night's crisis was for nothing. So was the argument about the number of inseminations. An egg lasts less than twenty-four hours; a second IUI would be useless. I was again planning to play softball while she was at the doctor's office trying to conceive, but the weather didn't cooperate, so I cleaned up some journal entries instead. This time they didn't give me a total. Maybe they agree that sperm count is a useless situational stat, or maybe my numbers are dropping everywhere and they didn't want to discourage me.

Yesterday Francesca and I took the Metro North to Poughkeepsie and met up with our friends Robb and Joey, who drove us to their home in Dutchess County's Hudson Valley horse country. All the rain has worked its fecund magic up here. Lilac, dogwood, and redbud are in bloom. Robb is getting to know the local birds. Grosbeaks, red-breasted woodpeckers, red-winged blackbirds, and catbirds dive for snacks at their seed and suet feeders, and there's a special feeder for goldfinches, who are coordinated enough to eat upside down. I can identify cardinals and blue jays and am on the lookout for orioles, which Robb claims to have seen.

The gloomy weather forces us indoors, and I prevail upon Francesca to read a few entries of this account. She says she likes it, "especially the part about my being brilliant and beautiful." Her mother was a colorist, however, so she fine-tunes my renderings of her eyes and hair, which I had described as "blue" and "reddish brown." She also has ideas for how to fill in the blanks. She suggests I get down as much as I can, see what turns out to be important, and then cut out the rest. Mainly, though, Francesca thinks the book should have a more of a focus.

"I've read several entries, and I've heard about Zeus and Manny, Charlie and Amanda, sabermetrics, two-by-two tables, ringers, perennial-loser syndrome, slumber parties, big league fun, and who knows what else, but there isn't enough about you," she says. "Shouldn't it be more about you?" She also notes that there are images of Zeus and several other players, though not one of me.

"Wait until you read more," I say. "Pretty soon all that stuff drops out of the picture, and it's all about me." But I decide to add the bit about the Little League team photo and make a mental note to have someone take a photo of me.

"It has to be about you and how you are triumphant, which in the end is what we all are—anyway, at least since *Rocky*. Stick to you and triumph! Isn't that right, Joey?" He nods, but barely looks up from the notebook computer on which he is writing his own story.

I agree that she is right—about baseball *movies*. If they remade *Bang the Drum Slowly* today, it would turn out that the diagnosis was all a mistake. The De Niro character wouldn't have Hodgkin's after all, only adult-onset diabetes. It was a miracle that *Eight Men Out* didn't finish by reinstating Buck Weaver and Shoeless Joe and sending the White Sox back to the Series. But in baseball *books*, the hero isn't always triumphant. Robert Coover's J. Henry Waugh goes schizo. Bingo Long's team folds. Bernard Malamud's Natural, whom I can't help thinking of now as Robert Redford, doesn't hit a sayonara home run and live happily ever after with a backlit Glenn Close. His team loses, and he is disgraced and broken. Even *The Kid from Tomkinsville* ends with the Kid crashing against the outfield wall. I know that I'm getting way ahead of myself, but if they were ever to make a movie of this book and wanted to change the ending, I would just as soon see them go all out—*Adaptation*-style. The screenwriter could expose me as a steroids dealer, kill off Mule, add himself and a fake twin brother to the team, and have them take over as the keystone combination and lead the Foxes to the championship.

In any case, I'm wondering what would it mean to triumph here. I want so much. I want to lead Pamela's to victory, I want to play shortstop, I want to make it in the harder softball leagues, and I want to be a star. I want to retrieve my ball-playing career, lost since Little League, and after this debacle in the sociology department I want to prove that I can run something. But I also want to have fun and make new friends. On top of that I want softball to take my mind off academic politics, assisted reproductive technology, and other worldly concerns but not to take over my life. I don't know if all of these things, or even a few of them, are possible. There have to be tradeoffs, but I am not sure what they will be.

With Francesca's encouragement, I can't help speculating about what sort of story it should be. It's a little daunting. Anyone writing about baseball has to contend with shelves of fine literature. It's no longer the most popular American sport, but baseball remains number one with writers. I don't want *Bang the Drum Slowly*, where someone dies. If I'm even halfway successful the story's going to tramp down the extensively limed baselines of the triumph of the little guy/human spirit, but I don't want it to be as sappy as *Rocky* or *The Rookie*. I'd prefer something like *Ball Four*, where the Pilots or, even better, the integrated Astros win. The protagonist leads the way, as the worthiness of his unconventional game and anti-Book ideas is recognized, and the team cracks wise all the way to the championship. Maybe that's asking too much. I would settle for *The Kid from Tomkinsville*, provided the Kid learns to stop running into walls.

This is all too difficult, and anyway, I don't know how things are going to turn out, so my mind turns to the simpler task of dreaming up a title. I could try takeoffs on the some of the great nonfiction baseball books: *The Real Summer Game, Softball's Great Experiment, Bouton and Me, The Shortstop Was a Spy, Only the Ball Had English on It*. Or I could play off first-person accounts by players: *The Central Park Zoo, or Strike Three (Looking): My Life and Hard Times Practicing Plate Discipline in Recreational Softball*. Then there are the great works of baseball fiction: *The Pamela's Cantina Foxes, Inc., T. Edwin Amenta, Prop.; Alibi Ed; The Studied; The Last Chosen; Bang the Drum, Tanner;* or *The Kid from Greenwich Village*. One thing I vow—if it happens for me I will not to foist upon the world another book that has in its title the word "season."

# *Midseason and Dog Days*

**MIDSEASON** is a time of assessment and decisions. By now, it's obvious whether teams are going to be competitive. Softball managers don't have the luxury of major league executives to wait until summer to revise their rosters. In the shortened softball season, Memorial Day is analogous to Independence Day in baseball. Softball managers wanting to make improvements need to take action. Conversely, by midseason softball players usually have a sense of where they stand with the team—whether they're starters, their positions in the field, their places in the batting order. Marginal players still have time to play themselves into the lineup—which I'm hoping to do with the Machine—or out of it.

With no game Monday, I have time to take stock. Pamela's Foxes are doing even better than I had hoped. We've won five and lost one. The three teams that pounded us the last three years are looking up at us. Our only loss might have been a win if we hadn't been shorthanded. My teammates seem fine with my leading them. With our record and my numbers, they couldn't complain much if they weren't. All the new players—Billy, Penny, Big Artie, Krishy, and Trey—seem to have been accepted by the old-line Sharkeys. Billy has been central to our success. Penny has hit and fielded well, and aside from his eyewear-related outfield difficulties, Big Artie has been steady. The other two are question marks. Trey has played when he can but remains injured, and Krishy seems unsure whether he wants to play. Most of the veterans seem OK, if not overjoyed, with their new, nonspecific roles. Papi remains upset that he is not a fixture at first, but we have so many good infielders it is difficult for him to say much—especially as he hasn't been hitting well. Little Bobby would have been satisfied not playing the field, but he has been impressive in right. I let Mule pitch against division doormat Mickey Mantle's. He got the W, but his performance was so shaky that he may stop asking to start. No one is making a fuss about players no longer with the team. It's a little sad, in a way, almost as if they had never existed. Overall, the atmosphere around the team has noticeably changed. Everyone is pretty loose. I would like to think that this is due to my unorthodox, irreverent approach and that my team-mates have become adherents of Eddy Ball. But I still haven't been so foolish as to propound my system as such.

I am constrained in making any moves, as compared to my rival Zeus. Knowing softball players is the equivalent of having millions to spend to make waiver deals at the major league trade deadline. Zeus seems to have met every player and is continually augmenting the Friars Club roster. The only moves I have in mind are picking up the outfielder Matt or the first baseman Keith from Billy's Sunday team. But they will be available only if Matt quits his job or if the New Jersey Film Commission is zeroed out and Keith loses his. I don't know what the story line will be for Pamela's, but I think the one that can be ruled out for sure is the lost cause.

Although I still don't feel completely comfortable at the plate, my knee feels better, and my numbers are excellent in the Monday league. I am second in the league in on-base percentage, reaching base almost 70 percent of the time. My on-base-plus-slugging figure is a Bonds-esque 1.350. I am one walk and one run scored behind the leaders in those categories, and I am leading the league in an unexpected but meaningless category: my ten RBI, a stupid situational counting stat, are two more than anybody else has. My schoolyard averages are no doubt too high to sustain all season long. Still, as my knee improves and the weather warms up, I'm hoping to hit better.

And I'm going to have to step it up if I hope to play a major role in the more difficult Sunday league. The only thing keeping me in contention for a regular spot on the Machine is that Billy has been watching me tear up the competition on Mondays. Even so, I will eventually have to impress the Machine team to prevent its key players from souring on me.

SUNDAY, JUNE 1, HECKSCHER #1

## Open to Suggestions

A player doing poorly at the plate will receive lots of unsolicited batting tips. With absences among the Machine outfielders giving me another chance to make good, and with Mule, whom I pound, getting the start for our opponents, On-Base Percentage, I'm thinking today I may break out of my Sunday slump. But with a chance to do damage in the second, I pop up. On the bench, shortstop Mike sidles over to me and asks, "Can I tell you something?" Without waiting for an answer, he continues: "I've been watching you, and I notice you aren't shifting your weight. You need to bend your knees more." He demonstrates, swiveling and striding toward an imaginary pitch. I'm irked, but not at his tip, which seems insightful. I probably have fallen into bad habits favoring my sore right knee. It's not so much that Mike has offered advice without my asking, though that does bother me a little, as that I have batted myself into a situation that elicits this sort of commentary. The humiliation seems to have no end. In my next at bat, with a 2–0 count, Billy shouts from the bleachers, "Take." It's not as bad as having a coach screaming, "Bunt," but it's a little too close for comfort. My dead bat has left me open to suggestions.

Matt the human flytrap is still out. To treat a case of poison ivy, he self-prescribed Clorox, and his leg responded with great irritation. So Billy has me in left field today. There is a lot of wide-open space here at field #1, much better than at #4. Apparently Manny, the Dominican bicycle messenger, is looking for new sources of income, and Billy has hired him to officiate. Manny looks professional in his navy umpire's shirt and is doing a nice job. In the third, I make a diving play on a sinking liner to left, and Manny correctly rules it a trap. Late in the game, though, he gets his first taste of softball controversy. Trying to advance on a fly ball, our outfielder Tommy dodges a tag, but the O.B.P bench argues that Tommy went out of the baseline—and won't let it go. They appeal to Billy, in his capacity as the league's commissioner. Billy decides to let them have it, overruling Manny and waving Tommy off second.

Taking to heart Mike's batting tip and trying to concentrate on the weight shift, I single sharply to drive in a run. We are rocking Mule, taking a 10–1 lead. With no margin too large to make Dick throw strikes, he walks two in the seventh, sparking a rally. On a fielder's choice the O.B.P players argue that Frank, playing second, took his foot off the bag too early. Mule comes out to argue, despite the fact that he is not the manager, saying something to Manny that is unintelligible from left field and probably to Manny too. Perhaps having seen too many ESPN Classic videotapes of Billy Martin, Mule starts kicking dirt on Manny's shoes, making comically small sweeps of his feet, as if trying to coax cookie crumbs off the kitchen floor into a dustpan. He looks like nothing so much as a cartoon character, and at first I think he must be joking. But he isn't. Manny throws Mule out of the game, and Billy suspends him.

For game two, Billy is Mr. Serious. He is on edge because of the Mule incident and because the Machine seems always to blow out its opponent in game one, when Dick is pitching, but to struggle offensively in game two, when it's Billy turn on the slab. It's as if our opponents were employing the softball equivalent of rope-a-dope. Before we take the field, Billy calls a huddle and reminds us what happened the last time we played this team. We had a chance to sweep but dropped the nightcap 8–7, with Billy taking the loss. Since then I have apparently moved up in Billy's estimation. A couple more teammates have shown for the second game, but Billy starts me at second base and sits Frank—a steady, longtime player. It has to be for fielding purposes; even after hitting Mule my average remains below the Mendoza line. We jump out to a 5–1 lead, well on our way to victory, but Billy won't let up. O.B.P's tenth batter is a new player, one whom Billy has no book on. He announces without irony that he doesn't know how the outfield should play the batter. Mike shouts, "Hey, guys, do anything you want out there." Making Billy pay for his excessive gravity, the outfielders act dumbfounded, walking in circles like movie zombies. Billy prevents this unknown quantity from reaching base, and the next O.B.P batters don't do much better.

I'm feeling more comfortable with my position and enjoying Mike's loose and needling approach, which is in great contrast to the annoying Dick's and, at least for now, Billy's. In the last inning, one of the Percentages hits a dribbler that eludes Billy. Mike has to swoop in from shortstop to recover. As Mike is making the play, I tell Billy that his effort was "pathetic," cracking up Mike to the point that he sails the throw. Keith bails him out with a leap, catch, and sweep tag, shaking his head at both of us for our lack of seriousness. We win the game and sweep our second doubleheader of the season, finally emerging over .500. On the bench after the game, the team is in a happy mood, and overtense Billy is taking the brunt of it. Mike asks Billy about his fielding performance on the last play.

"I don't have as much time to react when I throw the fastball," he explains.

"Who are you, Randy Johnson?" Mike asks.

Mike is not done with Billy. Responsible for paying Manny forty-five dollars, Billy is collecting three dollars per player per game. Mike notes that this tariff should generate about twenty dollars more than the umpire's fee. "Where does the rest of the money go?" Mike wonders aloud. Although it's certain that not everyone is paying Billy, he can't publicly identify the culprits. Mike continues, quizzing Billy about the cost of our screen-printed T-shirts, then reports, "Machinegate seems to have more layers than an onion." My two hits and good fielding haven't won me anything yet here, and beating O.B.P is not a big deal, but it's nice finally to be part of a winning effort and to feel a little like part of this team. And I'm glad that Mike is focusing his attention on Billy and not me.

## *Out in Left Field*

Today is like the opening day of midseason for Pamela's Foxes, who face the Friars Club and our former teammate Zeus. At home, I spend the morning doing laundry, the upcoming game precluding work that involves sustained thinking. We are desperately short in the outfield. The flexible positioning precepts of Eddy Ball are now working against my personal fielding ambitions. Our best lineup has me playing the outfield.

When I get to Central Park, there are the usual last-minute personnel problems. Penny is late, and our team is on edge. Since we are up first, I have so much thinking to do before the game, and it's my turn to take one for the team, I have myself batting last. I adjust the lineup, placing Dog at second base, moving around Cookie and Artie, and advance everyone but me in the order. That raises the wiry Q to number four, and he seems flustered by the imagined responsibility. "Cleanup, wow," he says and whistles in disbelief at being placed where a team's most powerful hitter traditionally bats.

As I'm trying to get loose and escape my teammates' anxiety by running in the outfield, Klem the umpire calls me over. Sport, the Friars Club manager, is challenging the eligibility of two guys on the field, one of whom is taking batting practice. I have no idea who they are, but it wouldn't have surprised me if they were with Sport's team. The Friars Club, which got off to a slow start, has been loading up its roster. Sport remains nominally in charge, but Zeus has taken over, driven by his great desire to win into doing what he said during the off-season he wouldn't do. Today the team has at shortstop a Puerto Rican guy from the Lower East Side named Jorgy. One of Zeus's few under-thirty players, Jorgy was recruited from the East Village Softball Association. He wears a 3XL New York Giants football jersey and jeans so massive that he can wear his softball togs underneath. He plays with high emotion, making Rickey Henderson–like snatches on pop-ups. Jorgy gets visibly upset, a la Paul O'Neill, when outfielders run down his deep fly balls to left. Unlike O'Neill, though, Jorgy will stop in his tracks and fling his bat in disgust as soon as he realizes his ball is likely to be caught. Jorgy's friend, neighbor, and constant softball companion, the strapping, sloe-eyed Juan, sometimes called "Home Juan," is now at second base. Like Jorgy, if Juan wears a cap it is backward, but Juan can hit with power to all fields, notably to right center, and is as easygoing as Jorgy is high-strung. There is also a new left-handed slugger in the outfield. Zeus can add these guys with impunity because he knows I won't call him on

LEFT FIELD AT HECKSCHER #4—BALLS THAT CROSSED THE
FOOTPATH WERE WORTH TWO BASES

them. Jorgy and Juan play with me in other leagues, and I don't want trouble over Trey. For all I care, Zeus and Sport can have the guys taking BP.

Shooing the trespassers off the field, Klem goes over the ground rules with Sport and me. One of them is new. Klem's World now has a dress code. Players must wear shirts with sleeves, and he rules ineligible the wife-beaters modeled today by Q and Little Bobby. They put their jerseys on over them, and for the second time this season all the Foxes are in uniform. As we come to bat, Penny appears and I add him to the lineup at shortstop. We go down on three fly balls to left field, as everyone seems to be shooting for the stand of maples, where the sacred bumps up against the profane. The branches of the maples intrude on the field's air space and upgrade routine flies into ground-rule doubles; an asphalt footpath curving into fair territory does the same for balls hit on the ground. Spectators will sometimes stand on the path, as if backing up the outfielders. There's also a park bench that's only a few yards into foul territory and inevitably occupied on nice days, though not always by people watching the game.

I jog out to left field myself. Jorgy leads off for the Friars Club and has the same idea as our players. He pulls a curving shot deep and down the left-field line. I can almost hear Klem shouting *"Two bases!"* as I start after it, because it's to the left of the footpath and that's what Jorgy will get if the ball touches turf. I have a good jump, and clackety-clack clack clack go my plastic cleats on the asphalt. I'm afraid of skittering like a dog on a waxed floor, but I hold my balance and make the catch. My little fan club on the park bench applauds, and Jorgy kicks the dirt and throws down his hat.

The game settles down into an unlikely pitchers' duel. The unlikely part of the duel is their pitcher, Bro, who got the ball because Zeus's first-string pitcher, the fireballer Burnsides, is unavailable today. Bro is a Central Park fixture, a portly fiftysomething with an elfin face who calls everyone "Bro." He encourages abuse by changing his shirt on the bleachers, but counters that his voluptuous man breasts make women jealous. Bro employs control and change of speed, and has a couple of trick pitches he uses when he's ahead in the count. He walks few and strikes out fewer. Today he is relying on our getting ourselves out, and it's working. In the fourth we break through when Mule singles and Cookie, running for him, dashes to third on Roger's single to left center. Daunted by batting in the cleanup spot, Q pops to short, but Papi lifts a fly ball, and Cookie comes limping in, having pulled his hamstring on the previous play. We threaten again in the fifth and sixth but can't score.

We are granting Billy no margin for error. I watch Manny tap a roller. Cookie charges and barehands it, and it is going to be close, as Manny is fast and hustling all the way. He finishes with a dramatic headfirst slide. This last move flouts the Book of unwritten rules and prejudices governing baseball strategy. Sliding into first is considered a bad play because it risks injury and slows the runner down, the latter effect being partly why players slide into the other bases. That said, it is an aggressive play with some surface plausibility. Outfielders are expected to dive for difficult chances after making a long run in hope of making the catch, and the headfirst slide is more dive than slide. The play also has fierce proponents in the majors, notably Roberto Alomar. It's bang, bang at first, and Klem calls Manny out. Zeus is apoplectic—not at the call, but at Manny, for his defiance of the Book. It's Zeus's turn to bat, but he still has not completed his lecture to Manny, who takes it, eyes down, hands on hips, silently dissenting.

Zeus's approach to plate appearances could not be more different from mine. Billy leaves one up high and Zeus takes his left hand off the bat and traces the ball's errant path. At one and one, another pitch misses, and Zeus shakes his head, offended by Billy's supposed fear to give him something to hit. When he walks, Zeus is a documentary of disdain at the pitcher's cowardice, flipping the bat and sauntering to first. Klem calls Billy's next offering strike two. Zeus protests, and an argument ensues. Klem's response is not persuading Zeus, who is already angry and has been engaged in a running

MANNY TURNED THE TABLES ON ZEUS

war with Klem over his dislike of wearing the mask. Zeus thinks that Klem misses calls by ducking away at the last moment. Klem for his part is fed up with Zeus's penchant for arguing and is not above suggesting that Zeus seems afraid to swing. When Zeus is really arguing, he will waggle his forefinger like Dikembe Mutombo does after swatting away a lay-up attempt. I can't hear him, but Zeus's gesture can't be missed, even from left field.

Zeus has crossed an imaginary line with Klem, who has thrown him out of the game many times over the years, and he knows that on the next close pitch he had better be swinging. Unfortunately for Zeus, Billy knows this too, so here comes a head-high fastball, impossible to hit hard yet almost certain to be called strike three if Zeus were to take it. Zeus lifts it feebly, not leaving the box and instead offering some profane parting remarks to Klem. With a chance to turn the tables on his mentor, Manny yells at Zeus, "Hey Zeus, why you not run it out?"

We fail to score in our half of the seventh. Zeus calls one of his frequent team meetings to rally the troops and set strategy. I head back out to my position, where I've had no action since the first inning. Cookie's dive has aggravated his hamstring injury, so Dog replaces him at second. The new lefty power hitter lines a single. The next batter shoots one down the line foul, scattering the occupants of the park bench. I razz one of them, acting angry and admonishing him: "You've got to make that play—that's why we put you there!" The guy shrugs and says, "I was afraid of the ball in Little League—still am." We watch together as Billy allows his first walk. The tying run is on second, the winning run on first.

A can o' corn later up steps Rock, another left-handed pull hitter, and even from the distance I can see Sport and Zeus's strategy. They're going to test Dog. Rock shoots one hard and low to Dog's right. He dives and gloves it,

ZEUS LIKED TO CALL TEAM MEETINGS

and flips to Penny for the force, as the tying run heads to third. Sport steps to the plate. He was the goat in our last contest, having struck out with the game on the line, and wants to make amends. He also tries Dog, but the veteran comes up with the grounder and throws to Papi to end it! Klem tells me to retrieve the orange cones demarcating the foul line, the chore of the winning team. Zeus wants to have it out further with Klem, but the busy arbiter is hustling off to his next game.

My teammates are so excited that they don't want to go home. But I don't hang around. I feel more like a spectator than a player. On the way back to the subway, I'm wondering if it is worth winning if I always have to play myself in positions that I don't want to play. My own theories have left me out in left field.

WEDNESDAY, JUNE 4, 14 WASHINGTON PLACE

## *Waiting Game*

There is nothing Francesca hates more than waiting, but now that is all she does. Her tenure case, on which her academic future and our future in New York may rest, is still pending. Tenure is an academic institution that was devised to protect the free speech of professors. But nowadays it is the keystone to the academic status system. After five to ten years, an academic in a tenure-track position is deemed worthy of a job for life or is let go. It's up or out, promoted or fired—like being forced to play in the minor leagues for a specified period, then deemed ready for the majors or released and consequently stigmatized, making it difficult to catch on elsewhere.

To make matters worse, there are no agreed-upon ways to judge scholarship—no scholarly equivalent to on-base and slugging figures to compare across different stages of a career. Decisions on worthiness frequently have nothing to do with the quality and quantity of a scholar's work. A candidate's tenured departmental colleagues, who typically are not experts in his or her particular area, vote after reviewing the work and letters from scholars who are in the candidate's field. The vote has to be unanimous or very close to it, meaning that tenure can be denied on the whims of a few senior colleagues. Others higher in the university hierarchy must also sign off before tenure is granted. If there had been tenure in baseball, Jackie Robinson would never have made it with the Dodgers.

We are cautiously optimistic. Francesca sailed through the departmental vote, and she's heard through the grapevine that her letters were uniformly strong. That would clinch it at most universities, including my own. But Columbia adds a bizarre layer of bureaucracy and arbitrariness. The provost chooses a secret ad hoc committee that sends out for its own letters, many more than most places ask for, and himself sits on the committee, giving him extraordinary power to decide who will advance. Information about the meeting of the committee is jealously protected, as if it were the release date of a summer blockbuster. Francesca knows that it has to meet some time before the end of the month, but meanwhile she has to play a waiting game.

On top of that, the fertility drugs have enlarged Francesca's ovaries from the size of walnuts to the size of grapefruits. Her inadvertent juicing is nature's way of taunting us. Francesca has the look of a woman four months' pregnant and is under doctor's orders to avoid exercise and sex until the swelling recedes. And for all the advances of assisted reproductive technology, there's still no way for a woman to tell whether she is pregnant until a day or two before her period is due. All the same, Francesca can't bear to wait and has been taking home-pregnancy tests. The first few showed nothing, which she found upsetting, despite the fact that she knew that it was far too early for them to be accurate. And although yesterday's test stick showed a very faint pink line an hour after Francesca peed on it, this morning's stick has come up negative, with no trace of a line even hours later.

It's pouring, but she has to trudge uptown to the fertility doctor's office for a pregnancy test and a checkup. The doctor tells her that her swollen ovaries will force us to skip this next cycle and probably the one after that. Myself, I need to take yet another specimen to the lab. Some bacteria were detected in a previous test. It was likely only a surface contaminant, but I worry that I may have spoiled our last chance to get pregnant this summer—or maybe altogether. Forced indoors, we are isolated with our thoughts. Francesca starts talking about our leaving town and heading somewhere warm like Miami Beach. Softball season or not, I'm ready to agree. Then the doctor calls. Francesca is pregnant! I would like to say that once we heard the news the clouds lifted and the skies brightened. Instead it rained so much that the next day's games were called off before the evening was out. And having been pregnant before, our joy is mixed with caution. But we stop talking about Miami.

## Letting Go

I'm fiddling with lineups before the Pamela's Foxes game against the Gotham Comedy Club when I get a call from Francesca. The secret ad hoc committee has completed its review, and the provost has ruled. Despite overwhelming support from the department and uniformly strong letters, she has been denied tenure at Columbia—fired. I've never heard her so hurt. It's as if the good news of her pregnancy were years ago. We stay on the phone until a quarter to two when she reminds me about my game.

When I reach Central Park, the rest of the guys are already at #6, warming up. Q says he was wondering if I was going to show. We take the field, and I head out to left. If I sometimes feel like a spectator when I'm playing the outfield, today I'm in such a daze that I'm like a spectator reading the newspaper. In the first we get out of a jam when Big Artie, whom I have at shortstop today, catches their runner leaning off third base after a single to left. I had been unsure where to throw and sent it his way when he called for it, and he took if from there. The Gotham hard thrower got a job and left town, and they now have a soft tosser on the hill. We reply with two runs.

Close as the game is, I can't focus on it, feeling sad and angry and then angrier still at something that has happened uptown, and trying to figure out what, if anything, I can do about it. Francesca has published plenty in prestigious outlets. Her work has been very well received and given the stamp of approval by experts in her field. She is strongly backed by her chair and passed her department's deliberations with flying colors. She is an award-winning teacher. She has more ivy on her CV—Brown, Yale, Columbia, Harvard—than there is on the walls of Wrigley Field.

In the fourth I'm up with two on and a chance to break a tie game open. I swing for the nonexistent fences and foul a long drive toward the Ballpark Café, then on the next pitch overswing and pop one up. I head back to the field and wonder whether the provost's decision will stand. Francesca's department will certainly contest it. I am trying to think through what I would do as chair, but the Columbia administration is byzantine. If the decision stands, it doesn't mean the end of Francesca's career. Smarter places will be certain to snap her up and give her tenure. But there aren't a lot of options in New York, so this could mean the end of our run here. Worst of all, this is going to be devastating for her. I start to think all sorts of crazy things. Will she miscarry because of this? Are we going to split up? Miscarry, then break up?

All this is running through my mind when Cookie approaches me concerned. He tells me that Artie "doesn't look comfortable at shortstop." I don't see the problem. Possibly I've missed some plays. But to appease Cookie I move myself there, telling Artie that I want to see some infield action. It's true too, as moving to the infield will help me focus on the game and take my mind off these other things.

Shortstop remains Grand Central Station, and I throw out three guys. I'm swinging at anything, but otherwise our bats are hot. We keep building the lead. In the sixth, I reach first on a fielder's choice, fastening on my day's oh-for-four collar, and Mule grounds to second. I break up a potential double play by letting go with a hard slide, the shortstop jumping out of the way. The baggy, retro Mitchell & Ness pants, aside from looking cool, have a reinforced knee. When I get up, I notice that the slide hasn't left a mark on me and doesn't sting at all. Just the opposite—it feels great! I am transformed into something like the enthusiastic baseball neophytes in Philip Roth's *Great American Novel*. Once they learn to slide they enjoy it so much that they send the dirt flying at first base on walks and after outs on their way back into the dugout. Mule reaches first, and since he takes a courtesy runner and I was the last out, I dust myself off and run for him. Penny hits a grounder, the play is at second, and I go sliding in hard again. We finish them off in the seventh, but I will no longer wonder what my teammates might be thinking about when they don't know where to throw the ball.

## *Fringe Benefits*

The atmosphere in our apartment is like the moments just after a team has lost a big game. The only difference is that the moment has been extended since Monday afternoon. Francesca's chair called her yesterday and left her an inspirational phone message that says her work is excellent, the department is behind her, the decision is wrong, and he and key senior colleagues are devising a strategy to reverse it. He adds, unfortunately, that he has never been in this situation before. Instead of working, Francesca and I sit facing each other, with nothing to say.

At noon I pedal across Fourth Street toward the East River to play a game for d.b.a. in the archaically named East Village Softball Association. I've played rarely in this league and if things were different at home might not be playing today. But I feel trapped at home. I've been working there most of the time, when I'm not on the softball field or at the New York Public Library, because I don't want to go to the office and face my colleagues. This league includes twelve teams representing local bars and restaurants. It is more social than competitive and aims to promote community. League rules stipulate that each team must field at least three women at all times, a requirement that charges the games with a sexual undercurrent. Often couples will play together. A lot of the men are looking to meet women and vice versa, and almost everyone is pretty fit.

It is exciting to play with attractive women, sure, but the appeal for me is different from what it is for some of the other men. I'm not looking to meet anyone, and Francesca doesn't play. What I like about having women on the field goes back to the earliest days of baseball. Although women rarely played baseball at first, they were often spectators, and their presence placed the game a civilized cut above all-male sporting pursuits like boxing, horse racing, and ratting, a failed candidate for the national pastime that centered on the speed with which dogs could kill rodents. Women were a deterrent against boyishness in players and gambling, drinking, and rowdiness among fans. Having women as teammates works even better. Women don't argue calls nearly as much as men do, and men tend show off their better selves, and argue less, when among women. Women give praise for routine plays, and men often follow their lead. I also love to play with novices who are hungry to learn. Women are far more likely to make great strides during a season. We men tend to think we know everything about the game already.

EAST RIVER #7 WAS LIKE A MEMORIAL TO NEW YORK IN THE 1970S

In the East Village, there is also a two-tiered pitching policy—modified pitch to men and slow pitch to women. But the supposed emphasis on fun, the uneven talent pool, and the enforced pitching chivalry do not always make for a friendly game. Our sister team, Josie's, which has the same ownership as d.b.a., is led by Weasel, the little goateed actor who is gunning for us. And last year an opponent did a Pete Rose into our (former) catcher Rosie, tearing her ACL.

Like all the East River ball fields, the ramshackle #7, which hosts the league's games, suffers from poor acoustics, the whir of autos on the FDR deflecting conversation—which leads to botched relays and, sometimes, collisions. But East River #7 is in far worse shape than the refurbished, artificial-turf East River fields down by the Williamsburg Bridge. It doesn't have an infield so much as a minefield of pebbles, moguls, and foreign objects, and the outfield is a patchwork of weeds and cigarette butts. Now that our city has become such a Disneyfied, family-friendly tourist destination, a cunning entrepreneur would do well to buy this ballpark, disperse some vintage crack vials among the pebbles, spray graffiti on the concrete bleachers, and convert the field into a theme park, a kind of memorial to the New York City of the 1970s and 1980s. Call it the "Field of Broken Dreams."

Andrés, the umpire for the league, is a proud, elderly Puerto Rican man from the neighborhood with thick glasses and a walrus mustache. He has been an umpire for so many years that his accustomed way of wearing his cap, backward, has come back in style. Andrés, like Klem, relishes his status as a public character, but unlike Klem, Andrés has the air of not having anywhere else to go or anything else to do. This league has games almost every weekday, and Andrés is responsible for seeing that they are played. There is nothing like a Central Park Conservancy here, so he also serves as the league's groundskeeper. He is meticulous about measuring out and repositioning the bases, though they are inevitably short and usually uneven. Andrés also deems it necessary to carry all two dozen league-owned bats from one team's on-deck area to the other every half inning. All of this activity is partly to deflect attention from his decision making, which is handicapped by his extreme myopia. He always relies on a base umpire to help him out but never learns his name, always referring to him as "blue," which is what players call umpires whose names they don't know or don't want to acknowledge. Also, only partly to get a better look at pitches, he leans right over the catcher, almost always one of the aforementioned attractive young women.

Andrés's talent runs more toward broadcasting, a little like the soccer announcer Andrés Cantor, who makes the really long "goal" call. He has several lines that are so catchy players can't help imitating them, usually employing Andrés's thick, possibly intentionally exaggerated, accent. When at long last he is ready to commence play after his between-inning delays, he will shout with irritation, *"Gator ow!"*—get 'er out—shorthand for "please return the practice balls to the dugout as I would like to restart the game." The league's favorite catchphrase is bellowed whenever any batted ball strays outside the baselines. Invariably, and with far more drama than warranted, Andrés enunciates over the traffic noise, "Eet ees a *foul* ball!"

The league also has an air of arbitrariness about it. There is an expectation, though no strict rule, that players will live in or near the East Village, the gentrifying hipster district that is annexing much of the Lower East Side and Little Italy. The assumption that the games are about having fun is often understood to mean that the teams are not supposed to be very talented or serious about winning. For these reasons, the other teams are generally hostile to us. We have several players, like Zeus and Penny, who play in a lot of leagues and live in New Jersey. And although most teams recruit outside the sponsoring establishment's labor force, we take this to an extreme. No one who works for d.b.a. plays for d.b.a. In the wake of complaints by opponents, Andrés, who can't even see all the way to the rubber, ruled Billy's motion illegal—he sometimes raises his arm too high, which usually just tips off a changeup—and barred him from pitching last season. Not coincidentally Billy had just pitched d.b.a. to the championship over the pizza parlor Two Boots, which is led by Bart, an

GINA WAS A PROMISING NOVICE

impresario who also serves as the league's commissioner.

The league, however, has its advantages. Near the top of the list is its schedule. There is no set day when any team plays. Players on a lot of teams can miss a lot of games and remain in good standing. Better still, there is a vacation hiatus in August, when the other leagues have playoffs, and then play resumes in September, when the others are finished. The finals take place during the World Series. Last fall, I was pitching against Two Boots, defending our championship. Billy's disqualification and my bad hamstring had forced me onto the firing line. I was like the Kid from Tomkinsville or the Natural in reverse, with injury leading to my conversion from position player to pitcher. But Billy appealed to be reinstated, and the league managers agreed, so I'm back to being a position player here.

Just before we take the field against the Niagara Fish, representing another East Village bar, my teammate Parker becomes incensed at Billy. His plan is to have our four women rotate through the three designated spots for women. This means that a new teammate, Gina, will be cutting into the veteran Parker's playing time. Gina is a promising but novice player, tall and athletic, with short highlighted hair and a ready smile. At this stage in her career she looks a little like a young Geena Davis with shorter hair playing a ballplayer, and she has the same throaty voice. Parker is a good outfielder and is also irked that Billy has requested that she start at catcher. Parker has stylish little clear glasses, pigtails, and usually a cigarette between her lips. A park rat, Parker, who in real life is a theater production manager, plays in the Broadway Show League on a team sponsored by Playwrights Horizons. Although she has worked at *High Times* and plays for their team, Parker is far from mellow. Last season, I saw her get a big hit and from second base she started jumping like a displaced cheerleader, chanting: "You say hi. I say risin'. *Hiiiiii—risin'*" (apparently signifying "Horizons").

PARKER DID NOT WANT TO PLAY CATCHER

An unhappy side of Parker's exuberance is now focused on Billy. She is already packed up and on her way out when she runs into a knot of us. Parker calls Billy sexist, saying that he thinks women can play only undemanding fielding positions and that she's sick of it. "Bye-bye, I'm out of here, have a nice season," she tells him. Billy requests, more urgently than usual, that we place our hands in a circle.

As we take the lead, I am more and more unhappy that Parker isn't with us and can't help thinking about her charges—and not just about Billy's attitudes, but about the coed leagues generally. Women here almost are always consigned to catcher, right field, and second base, and are are almost never seen in left or left-center field or at third base, and never at shortstop. The three-woman minimum tends to be treated as a maximum. The standard excuse for the stereotyped gender positioning is that competitive softball, like baseball, is a ruthless meritocracy—a talent hierarchy built from social equality. It doesn't matter who you are, where you are from, or what you look like; if you can play, you should get to play, and the better you can play, the more challenging your position will be. Managers who do not rely on their best players will lose both games and the confidence of teammates who want to win. On good coed teams like ours, it's rare for a woman to be a better fielder than a man, and so, the logic goes, men should play the more demanding positions.

93

Working against the meritocracy explanation is the observation that soft-ball managers rarely deploy their talent efficiently. The sabermetricians and Michael Kelly's *Moneyball* argue that even major league baseball teams mostly fail to do so—despite their tremendous incentives to win, vast monetary re-sources, and extensive data. They are too invested in conventional wisdom and what their eyes tell them to pay attention to the statistical record. In soft-ball the situation is worse. Very little information is collected, and manag-ers rarely know what to do with it. Softball managers rely a lot on reputation and face cross-pressures of favoritism, seniority, fear, and prejudice. On coed teams the benefit of the doubt almost always goes to the man.

Had I been calling the shots, I would have been tempted to sit the limp-ing Miles, Billy's co-manager, and to start four women. But we recently suf-fered our second loss of the season—and Billy is focused on returning the defending-champion d.b.a. team to its winning ways. He doesn't want to take any chances—either with losing the game or with being criticized. Playing the man in coed softball is a little like playing by the Book in major league baseball. Making the expected managerial moves minimizes the chances of being blamed if something goes wrong. We win the game, which is closer than it needed to be because Zeus and Penny didn't show up until the game was halfway over.

But there is no danger of mass defections, in part because of the fringe benefits of being a d.b.a. team member. I almost never go back to the bar, as I'm always behind on work and never have been big on daytime drinking. But today I'm definitely going, because the alternative is going home. Although I have my bicycle, I walk it east with Zeus for the twenty minutes it takes to get to d.b.a. I rarely get much chance to talk with him about anything but softball. Now as we walk, he tells me about the various programs he works for in the East Orange school district. He mainly deals with African American youth of-fenders. Often they are being home-schooled, and he sometimes has to testify in court about what his charges are accomplishing in the way of education. He spends a lot of time checking in with them over his cell phone.

We reach d.b.a., which has the long bar and dark interior of a neighbor-hood hangout, with occasional wooden church pews standing in for booths and an offbeat, upscale, niche drink menu, featuring a wide selection of im-ported draft beers that change weekly. Because d.b.a. doesn't serve food, there are few patrons this early in the afternoon. Aside from paying our fees, our sponsor stakes us to one free beer and pizza. We order traditional thin-crust cheese-and-basil pies from Lombardi's—not the Louisiana-Italy hybrid fare from our rival Two Boots.

94

There's also a standing invitation to the opposing teams to join us, opening the possibility for postgame events in the spirit of the early days of baseball. The first between-club matches would often conclude in a banquet, with gracious toasts on each side extolling the day's heroic efforts and culminating in the ceremonial awarding of the game ball to the winners. Today almost the entire Niagara team is in attendance, but they form a circle with their tables, sullenly bemoaning their defeat, which they attribute largely to Andrés's myopia. Our gang, only half as numerous, jaded with victory and pizza, forms its own congregation. The game ball is in Miles's bag and will be used for batting practice. I take a sip of my free beer and turn the rest over to Big Artie. But I'm in no hurry to get home and hang around until all the pizza and teammates are gone.

THURSDAY, JUNE 12, HECKSCHER #2

## Story Problem

I have been playing on and off in another coed league, the Broadway Show League, and because our apartment is still the losers' locker room, I am definitely playing today. The Show League was founded fifty years ago by an employee of the group whose team I play for, Thespian Aid, a charitable organization whose initial purpose was to insure that impoverished actors were granted proper burials. The Show League is designed to promote camaraderie within what it likes to think of as "the theater community," which includes the often-wrangling unions and theater companies. Most of the scheduled games this season have been rained out.

On the bleachers, Matthew Broderick is joking with a few of our guys about our jerseys—white cotton/poly T-shirts with navy pinstripes and sleeves that attempt to affect a Yankees look on the cheap. About five teams have independently discovered this cheesy style. Though departed from *The Producers*, the smash hit, Tony-award-winning show, Broderick plays for the team, which has just finished its game here. Last year John Lithgow and Tim Robbins played in the Broadway Show League, and the Show Business League has a team run by the film critic Jeffrey Lyons, but most of the players in the performers' leagues are not nearly A-list. The weekday leagues have the bald guy from *The West Wing*, one of the brothers from *The Brothers McMullen*, and probably half a dozen guys who have had bit parts on *The Sopranos*.

Though coed, this league is intensely competitive and very talented, especially the division I play in. The eleven-thirty and one-thirty divisions are

CHAD WAS LOOKING TO MEET SOMEONE AT HECKSCHER

made up of patsy show teams, but the three-thirty division that comprises the unions and theater organizations is formidable. The greater organizational stability and larger pool of possible players makes for greater talent. And although anyone not serving the theater community is strictly prohibited and certifying paperwork must be filed every game, in the late afternoon ringers run wild. It is far easier to disguise a lack of connection with an organization than with a show. Ringers are also encouraged by the fact that all the teams are fully sponsored and the league itself is sponsored by Michelob, which springs for parties and refreshments. Also pumping up the talent level is the late-afternoon starting time, which allows players with regular jobs to cut out early from work to make the games. Our best players' closest connection to a Broadway show has been as members of an audience. Since the last time a show team won was in the 1980s (*The Goodbye Girl*, a Neil Simon play that has since had a revival), those teams now have a separate tournament.

Chad, my Machine teammate who is the manager of the Thespian Aid team, runs the Chad-TV production company, which specializes in PR videos, and directed a documentary about a Screen Actors Guild job action called *Lights,*

*Camera, Strike!* Chad has endearingly crooked incisors and a persona of friendly and glib goofiness. He is definitely looking to meet someone, and his bantering skills are so refined that they work well even on the foreign female tourists who happen upon our games. On the bench, chat-'em-up Chad is boasting to a tall German woman what close friends he and the now-departed Matthew Broderick are. She's never heard of him. Earlier this season I took his photo for an Internet dating service, in case nothing pans out at Heckscher.

But Chad is highly competitive too. He became a Mets fan mainly because his older brother was a Yankees fan. He has a game that is similar to mine. He can consistently line the ball to a spot between the first and second basemen. Chad told me that when his time comes "I've got an agreement with Parks and Recreation to have myself buried there." How he gained charge of the team is a complicated story, but suffice it to say it does not involve his having worked at Thespian Aid.

Today Chad has his A-team present and accounted for. The team, which came in third last season, is a mixture of regular players from several of the Central Park leagues and a few actual employees of Thespian Aid. We have the reliable Billy on the mound. For some reason, most likely my versatility and equanimity, plus the strong likelihood that Zeus, with his established record as a revolver and shooting star, has lobbied him and is a plausible threat to defect, Chad has been playing me in left field and Zeus at shortstop. Today we have with us from Billy's Sunday team, the Machine, the slugger Tommy, whom Chad is excited to have recruited. Even Zeus's mysterious protégé Manny materializes, rushing up on his sturdy city messenger's bike. Chad's view is that if we can get everyone to show up and avoid injuries, we can win it all this year. Today we are playing the undefeated Nederlander Organization.

League rules specify that each team must field at least two women at all times and penalize pitching around men. If a pitcher walks a man with a woman in the on-deck circle, both man and woman are entitled to a base—even if the walk is unintentional. It is a rule well suited to my talents and temperament. There are two sorts of hitters who walk a lot. There are sluggers whom pitchers fear but who won't bite on pitches out of the strike zone—Barry Bonds, Frank Thomas, Jason Giambi. Then there are spray hitters who run the count—Bobby Abreu, Nick Johnson, Jose Cruz Jr. I am the second type, the type that works the walk. In Chad's scheme, I'm our top novelty hitter—the man batting before the first woman, the veteran catcher Tiny, a petite brunette who works at World Gym and has a teenage daughter and single-digit body fat. Tiny prides herself on her deep knowledge of the league, so she is OK with the unearned walk. Also, she has to get it all to get the ball out of the infield.

By the time I come up, it's the second inning, and we're already down two-zip with two outs and none on. Plan A is to try for the double walk—which is our only real chance to score this inning. Tiny instructs me from the on-deck circle to "be smart up there"—giving me her green light to take. It reminds me a little of assisted reproduction. My approach is much different here than in the modified fast-pitch leagues. Here I will usually take two strikes. When the pitcher starts me off with two down Broadway, it's time for plan B—to hit the ball to the right side to test the opponents' less proficient fielders. Here comes another strike, slightly outer half. I lace it down the right-field line, where the Nederlander brains trust has stationed its noncatching woman. Having been squeezed close to the line by the men playing the other three outfield positions, she refuses to play it safe and goes for a shoestring catch. And makes it! Shaking his head for emphasis, Manny tells me what I already know: "Eddy, keed, she miss that ball and you have a home run."

There is another notable sighting: my ex-d.b.a. teammate Parker, whose Playwrights Horizons team has merged with the show *Lost Highway*, moved down to the one-thirty show division and has just finished up. She takes a perch on top of the third-base line bleachers, above our opponents. From the coaching box in the first, I heard her offer the opposing players a fifty-dollar bounty for hard hit balls up the middle, the target being a spot well below Billy's head. In the third, in the absence of base runners, I coax Parker. I tell her that I want her back on d.b.a. She's fun and a valuable player. Our success in the East Village is due mainly to the dominance of our women. "What if Billy apologizes?" I ask her. No luck. I try humor, asking, "How much would I get for nailing Billy on the bench?" Parker snorts and continues heckling Billy.

Only in New York is softball also about real estate. During the Show League games, all five Heckscher ball fields are in use. As I head out to left, the right-center fielder from field #6 stakes out a spot a little in front of me to the right, and the right fielder from field #4 is stationed a few yards behind me and to the left. The worst thing that can happen to an outfielder at Heckscher is to chase a fly ball and get blindsided by an outfielder on another diamond doing the same. In the middle of America's biggest metropolis, I find myself in a square dance with the right fielder from field #4, the left-center fielder from field #1, and the right-center fielder from field #6. To gain sight lines to our respective home plates, we do-si-do between pitches and mentally plot safe passages to potential balls hit to either side of us.

When I return to the plate in the fourth, we are down 3–1. Again there are two outs, but this time there are runners on first and second. I go deep into the count as usual and work it full. The pitcher lets the next one fly, a high

IN THE SHOW LEAGUE, SOFTBALL WAS ALSO ABOUT REAL ESTATE

arching ball that appears to be headed high and a little outside. If I take, and it's ball four, we will have a 3–2 game and the bases loaded. But what if Blue calls it a strike? If I were to go by the Book, I should offer at the pitch. It's embarrassing to strike out, and players look down even more on teammates striking out in a slow-pitch league. Here is where Eddy Ball has its greatest deviation from the Book and macho softball culture. I'm trying not to think about the humiliation. I've already got myself out swinging at pitches out of the zone in trying to avoid a strikeout. An out's an out. And I've played well enough on this team that I feel secure.

So I see my predicament as a story problem, which I seek to solve as the ball hangs in the air. They now know in baseball, for instance, that a player trying to steal second base is helping the team only if he makes it more than 70 percent of the time. The unknown here is the likelihood that the umpire will call this almost-strike the ball that it is. The question, then, is at what percentage is swinging at the pitch a bad play? Sabermetricians have studied each of the twenty-four combinations of outs and runners on base throughout baseball history and know how many runs, on average, each of them is worth. My team's present situation—runners at first and second and two out—is probably worth, on average, slightly less than half a run. If blue calls the pitch a ball, both Tiny and I will walk, a run will score, and the bases will be loaded with two outs, a situation which is worth a little more than another half a run. If the pitch is called a strike, of course, no runs will score. One and a half runs are three times better than half a run, and so the break-even point for taking is a little less than one out of three. If I think the umpire has a 30 percent chance or greater of calling this pitch a ball, I should take. Complicating issues also incline me toward taking. The next batter, Tiny, will have a significantly smaller chance of reaching base than the batter following her, Billy. And with the ball on its way I can stand pat only if I foul off the pitch. There is also some chance I could put the ball harmlessly in play or miss it entirely—small, but greater than the infinitesimal chance that I will reach base trying to foul it off. So, all things considered, it would probably be irresponsible to swing if I think there is only a one-in-four chance that blue will call this ball—it is staying wide—a ball. Two seconds have passed.

But that is not all. To press the analogy with the steal, and I like to think of this taking as an aggressive, potentially game-altering play, the outside ball is like getting a good pitch to run on. But the other factor is the umpire, who is analogous to the catcher. I don't know this umpire at all. Does he have a gun back there like Pudge Rodriguez, who shoots down almost half of attempted stealers? Or is he a more forgiving receiver, the Mike Piazza type, who grants clemency to all but the tardiest thieves? That is, is blue like Klem, who has a wide strike zone and relishes calling the third strike, or like most other umpires, who tend to have standard strike zones and to avoid confrontations with the batter? The Clincher makes a dimple in the sand a foot outside, and I get my answer: Pudge. As I head to the bench to retrieve my glove, Tommy exclaims, "Jesus!" and I can tell his displeasure isn't with the umpire. Even Tiny is frowning.

I jog back out to left field and witness our fielders collapsing all around me. Zeus is having a trying afternoon at shortstop. In left-center field, my Machine teammate Tommy is having a choppy Show League debut. Tommy grew up in Chelsea and lives in Battery Park City. Like me, he has a Sicilian last name, though his is the same as that of the Profaci family crew member gunned down at Umberto's Clam House. Tommy is often called "T," like the mobster on the *Sopranos*, but in fact he's a federal parole officer, a tough guy on the side of the good guys, with a focus on violator retrieval. He has helped to put away members of New York's Five Families, though nowadays he concentrates on terrorists. With his closely cropped hair, powerful build, and air of menace, Tommy never gets joshed about the nickname. And during games he gets so fired up that I find it unnerving. Also, he throws left and bats right, making me wonder if something is amiss with his wiring. Tommy is only sometimes available for softball during the week and is enthusiastic about the opportunity to play today. But in his excitement he's made two overthrows, and now a base hit shoots between his legs. We do nothing in our final at bats and lose 10–1. Parker is standing and whooping at the end. She won't be coming back to d.b.a.

Witnessing the crushing of a Thespian Aid team that he thought could win it all, Chad is distraught. Some explanation now has to be advanced for this reversal. In softball as in life—and Ken Burns and company notwithstanding, perhaps this is the main resemblance—we seek meaning mainly when things go wrong. Winning never requires explanation, but defeat is the mother of a million theories. After unexpected defeats softball managers are especially drawn to speculation in which problems are diagnosed and solutions, sometimes dramatic, are proposed—especially early in the season, when there is still time to do something about it. No matter which players are deemed culpable for a loss, in the end the blame for losing falls on the manager. Unlike in major league baseball, where the manager is often merely the scapegoat for poor personnel decisions, in softball, managers are also general managers. They have recruited the team, and they have the potential to right the situation by adding or subtracting players, or both. Chad has his own story problem.

The softball post mortem is far more personal than its counterpart in major league baseball. Constant public scrutiny makes pro players circumspect. They are held ruthlessly accountable for any unseemly utterances. A talented reporter can convert one ill-chosen throwaway comment into a season-long controversy. So to avoid antagonizing their teammates or opponents, the pros master their polite clichés—the sort that Crash Davis drills into Nuke LaLoosh in Bull Durham. They develop an anodyne discourse of success based on luck, thankfulness, and appreciation of their teammates. References to a higher power are accordingly not uncommon. The script for loss is similarly impersonal, though it usually refers to trying harder. But softball players face no such constraints and will discuss their teammates more in the uninhibited manner of sports talk radio. Underperforming teammates are rarely seen as just not playing well; rather, they are considered to be unable or unwilling to play well.

In trying to diagnose problems and propose solutions, the way is open for democratic decision making, and softball players, unlike baseball players, can have a big voice in personnel moves. But it is not as if the entire team gathers around and trades ideas until there is a consensus. The discussion group is limited, with the manager relying on the advice of a few players, usually the better ones. Their opinions are valued not because they are more insightful but because the manager is concerned that they might jump ship if they feel they've been ignored. As we head to Columbus Circle, Billy, Tommy, and Chad trade ideas about what's wrong and what to do. Chad has long relied on Billy for advice and wants to retain Tommy. I'm happy just to be in the conversation, preparing to defend myself for taking strike three if the issue comes up. It doesn't. Neither does another possibility—that we just grin and bear the fact that our current team has no chance to win. If Chad were to indicate that that was acceptable—and he doesn't—Billy and Tommy might defect. Although none of us played well today—Chad couldn't get on base, Billy was shelled, Tommy couldn't make a play, I struck out—no one, of course, says anything about any of *us* needing to be sat down.

So instead there is talk of overhauling the infield. They agree that the third baseman, though a good hitter, is in over his head in a position where batters are pulling the ball hard. They also want to move Zeus off shortstop, but they don't want him to jump teams and want to keep his bat in the lineup. Chad suggests that I take short and have Zeus move over to third. But Tommy counters that Chad should recruit Mike the shortstop from the Machine. He is recently unemployed and no less connected to Broadway than any of the rest of us. Once I get past being upset at my summary rejection, I can see the logic of the move. Mike would shore up the infield and give us another power hitter, and Zeus wouldn't object to it. If they moved me over, he would likely view it as an offense to his status. They also think we need to make changes with our women. Everyone agrees that all Thespian Aid employees need to see less action. I'm a little worried that Tommy, who has seen me play only for the Machine, might criticize me to Billy and Chad. I know he wasn't happy with the strikeout. But logistics are with me. Billy gets off first, at Forty-Second Street, and Chad at Twenty-Third Street. Tommy's heading to Battery Park City, so he can't say anything about me to either of them without my hearing it.

## Father's Day Presents

My father and I have had a testy relationship since I was a teenager, arguing bitterly over many things, large and small, and never really making up.

Though I think about him often, and imagine he does the same, we don't talk much. This morning I wish a happy Father's Day to his machine.

My father gave me an undying love of sports. Though sports-crazy, his generation of urban working-class and lower-middle-class men did not play team sports as adults. For them, it signaled a transition to adulthood to replace basketball and softball with smoking and drinking. If a man made it in the world, as my father did, in dentistry, he would refocus his sporting efforts on individualistic country-club pastimes like golf or tennis. My father became an avid golfer, lowering his handicap to six, but like most men of his background remained a fan of the big three U.S. sports. These days, the only other time we are certain to talk is in March to exchange NCAA basketball tournament brackets. He also encouraged my brothers and me to play sports. The only one he objected to was wrestling, because of its weight-loss requirements. I disagreed then, but now would have to concede the point, since my most lasting wrestling accomplishment was an eating disorder. I always thought I would take up golf and play with him once I was unable to play what I would tell him were "real sports," but that hasn't happened, and now he can no longer play golf. Although he has always been proud of my academic successes, I wonder sometimes if my pursuit of athletics so far into adulthood is about proving something to him.

Unlike Mother's Day, Father's Day has a full slate of games scheduled. The Machine's opponent is the new team in the league, the Skins. On the Great Lawn the sun is glowing dully through the clouds with rain still threatening. Still, much of Manhattan has come out to frolic. Many are sitting on blankets or towels in bathing suits, as if they would rather be at the beach but didn't want to risk the trip. We have only ten players. Before the game, guys discuss Father's Day presents. The outfielder Clooney was granted his wish to play today. The catcher Superman said that his wife Lois and their two daughters, all here today, got him a singing telegram. It was in Spanish, as Lois's background is Puerto Rican. We ask Superman how he could tell that he wasn't being ripped off. He shrugs and says, "I recognized *feliz* and *padre* in there, and the rest I'm taking on faith."

Dick is pitching the first game, but because we have only the minimum he has to bat and Billy has to play first base. In the first two innings, Dick gives up five runs, two on walks. Between innings, he sits off to the side in the shade with his niece or someone on beach chairs. The Skins' pitcher is easy to read, and my teammates are feasting. Even Dick scratches out a couple of hits, as we win going away. I smack the ball every time but have only one hit to show for it. In the second game Dick and Billy switch positions. In the warm-ups I learn something about our ace. Dick can throw the ball overhand only with great difficulty. He throws, as the saying goes, like a girl—and not nearly as well as Lois or the women on my coed teams.

We jump out in front. Billy works far more efficiently than Dick and sets the Skins down with ease through four. In the fifth, Mike breaks every baseball taboo. "Can you believe Billy has a no-hitter going? I'm so nervous—I hope they don't hit the ball to me," he says so loudly that Billy can't help overhearing. Billy tells him to shut up and retires the Skins in order. But the damage has been done. With no one to keep score on the opposition, we have to rely on memory and someone recalls that a Skin had an infield single in the first, retroactively ending Billy's bid.

Another thing I acquired from my father was his thick, curly hair. His hair remained dense and almost black, without a trace of gray, until he reached his sixties. Mine now is only somewhat less thick, but it's curlier and holding fast to its dirty brown hue. Perhaps I was shorted in the initial allocation of testosterone. When I was growing up, I absorbed nonstop hair-related abuse from kids who were, conveniently for them, much larger than me. Most of the taunts added prefixes to the word "head": Fuzz-Head, Frizz-Head, Kink-Head, Burr-Head, Pubic-Head, and once even Toaster-Head (my tormentor explained that I looked as though I had stuck my finger in the aforementioned electrical appliance). With my hair still very much present at this advanced age, I thought I had the last laugh. But now the veteran outfielder Tommy decides that my hair and my disturbingly high headband remind him of certain, nonmacho breed of dog. He is calling me Poodle-Head.

Big league fun quickly degenerates into Little League redux. Every time I touch the ball or pick up a bat, there is yipping and growling. Mike joins in because he seems to think I'm expressing too much anger. I may well be angry, as Francesca's situation is always on my mind. When I lined out in the first inning, I swore at my bad luck. Perhaps Mike is deploying some counterintuitive idea from the theory of communications that a stiff dose of yipping will embarrass me into a more placid state of mind. The preoccupied MikeHargrove, whose position on the team is as tenuous as mine, is uncertain how to respond. He is strongly built with short red hair and looks even cleaner-cut than the absent Keith. At thirteen MikeHargrove was an all–junior high everything in several sports, but injuries cut short a potential pro career. He joined the team last year on the recommendation of our star outfielder Matt, his high school teammate from the Cleveland suburbs. Like me, he's getting a chance today because of low numbers. On the bench MikeHargrove often seems to be lost in a daydream, as if replaying in his mind some youthful contest. The spell seems to be broken only when he is quizzing me about what the Olsen twins might or might not be doing at NYU. He tentatively joins in the barking. Superman and Lois's daughters, always looking for trouble, are woofing away.

I know that making fun of a teammate can promote solidarity. And I like hard ribbing, but I never imagined that I would be teased in such a juvenile way, as I was in Little League. They could easily do this with someone else. What about Woody, who threw a fit over his precious bat a few weeks ago and today is crowing about how he's making us all forget Zeus? Or Dick, who when he isn't cursing umpires or shot-putting the ball around the infield, is off on his makeshift throne making out with a young woman who apparently is not his niece. It would be OK if it were just rookie hazing, a ceremonial transition marking my move from neophyte to full teammate after a period of ambiguity. But this is my second year with the team, no one else seems to be going through it, and my trajectory might be simply to be cast out. In any case, my experience is that this line of harassment is usually unconnected to any particular rite of passage and can proceed endlessly without a better future in sight.

One potential way out is the method recommended by the old John R. Tunis line of sporting books. In classics like *The Kid from Tomkinsville* or *Keystone Kids*, a fresh young busher like me would go jaw to jaw with bench-jockey hotheads, challenging them to slug it out to show that he can take it, that he ain't yellow, that there ain't no quitters on this here ball club, no sirree. For good measure, he might go jaw to jaw with opponents and fans too. That approach doesn't seem compelling. Although I would have a decent chance to take the younger of Superman and Lois's daughters, I'm not about to challenge a SWAT team star with a Cosa Nostra name. Then there is the therapeutic response. I could express my feelings and say something like, "What you are doing is hurtful to me and I am asking you please to stop." This being New York and the Machine having a relatively upscale roster of players, probably a third of my teammates have had close encounters with therapy. But it would open me up to the certain derision of the majority of my teammates—those who had been in therapy might even be especially vocal to keep from blowing their cover.

More plausibly, I could fight verbal fire with verbal fire—better insults. That, along with the occasional tactical relinquishing of my lunch money, is how I usually handled bullying as a child. Being forced to outwit bullies may in fact have launched my academic career. Before I can stop it, my mind has devised a line of counterattack. For hair-related harassers, Mike and Tommy are on thin ice. Mike's hair is definitely thinning, and Tommy's close crop can't hide the march of his hairline toward his neck. I could say that I understand their jealousy and call them "Bald and Balding—the minoxidil poster boys." Even better would to be to isolate Tommy. "I've been called lots of hair-related names in my day," I could say, listing a few. "But never have I taken so much shit from someone with so little hair."

I think it through. Their return fire doesn't need to be verbal. Most likely, they would just bark in a higher register. More important, because I'm new and marginal, nothing I could say would stick given the disparity of status between us. I had the same problem with the guy who called me Toaster-Head; I was an incoming freshman and he was a big-time sophomore. I can't fight or talk my way out of this. I have to play my way out of it. I need to start plastering that old persimmon. As I stand in, Tommy says, "Show me something, Poolie"—he has already shortened the nickname. I line a hit, and we go on to win 6–0. Despite the abuse, I'm happy because I finally have three hits and a walk and solid play in the field.

I cross the park and head to the C train with the guys. Billy, Tommy, Walker, and I are making Manhattan stops, and Mike and Woody are heading to Brooklyn. As soon as Billy detrains at Forty-Second Street, they start talking about him. I get off at West Fourth, knowing that I may be the next topic of conversation. Under the circumstances I am happier to get off than to hear about someone else. What can they say about me? If I can keep this up, Tommy will have to pick on someone else. Or at least he will have to call me *Mister* Poolie. Happy Father's Day, Dad! All things considered, I'm grateful for the hair and everything else.

◀ MONDAY, JUNE 16, HECKSCHER #2 ▶

## *Big Enough*

School is out, but I have nothing but tests. This morning I have a dissertation defense, scheduled so that I can make my afternoon Foxes game. It's bizarre to be in the office. To avoid having to chitchat about the chair debacle, I've been working at home or at the New York Public Library. It is embarrassing for my colleagues when they see me. They don't know what to say and act a little weird, as if they had bumped into Al Gore. Possibly I am making too much of it. Only the committee and grad students are here today, my friend Jeff and most of my colleagues having scattered all up and down the East Coast until Labor Day. The dissertation is excellent, and after I toss the candidate the usual mixture of curveballs and softballs, the champagne corks fly.

As I head to Heckscher, Francesca reports to the doctor's office on the other side of Central Park. We learned to our dismay over New Year's that, contrary to the popular saying, it is possible to be a little bit pregnant. And it turned out that we were not pregnant enough. The amniotic sac grew too slowly, leaving us with the unhappy knowledge that Francesca was going to miscarry weeks before she did. The doctor is concerned that this time the sac is positioned so low in her uterus that it might again jeopardize the pregnancy. This appointment is to check out its progress.

Back on my side of the park, Pamela's plays Production, the only team that has beaten us this season. Papi is out with back trouble, but everyone else is here. The game is plenty big enough for Billy, who is spoiling to avenge his only loss. With Krishy back in the outfield I can return to shortstop. To ward off reinjury, I have Trey playing first base. This is almost the team that I imagined when I was drawing up the roster over the winter. Just as the game begins, Francesca appears, and we head behind the bleachers for an impromptu conference. A second test has been aced. She is a lot pregnant. The sac is in a better position and is plenty big. And there are two more! Before I can absorb this news I'm up to bat, and by the time I finish popping up, Francesca has exited.

The third test is touch and go. We are down 1–0 in the fourth when it happens. Roger and Big Artie single. When Penny singles too, Roger has the sense not to try scoring from second—and we're lined up for the big inning. Then, instead of trying to lift a sacrifice fly, Q hits one down and hard and brings in Roger, Krishy's single scores Big Artie, Billy singles in Q, and Little Bobby sends one between the right fielders, clearing the bases. The rout is on! By the seventh, all that Production can do is mock Swanny's chatter. When one of them walks with two out, they are falsely enthusiastic, whooping it up and calling after him, "Great at bat." But they haven't mastered Swanny's lines and don't have his flair. They should've been saying, "We need a setter" or "It hurts more with two," and telling the next "sticker" to send one "right back through the originator." Lacking proper encouragement, the next guy is quickly retired, and Production loses, 12–1. We are a new team, and this is a whole different league.

Even though all the tests have been passed, I am in something of a panic. I'm glad that the one sac was big enough, that we are not detouring toward miscarriage again. And I know that these tests were just preliminary. But I don't know what to think about the possibility of three babies. I worry about handling even one. I'm not sure that this is a league that I'm ready to play in.

## Rained Out

It has rained for the last three days and thirty of the last fifty-three, according to the *Times*. Spring, it seems, has decided to run up the score. This June is going to have at least three times as much rain as the average June in New York City. After several rainouts, the Central Park Conservancy today planted the red flags on the Heckscher fields, ruling out the Sunday-league doubleheader. The rainouts have given Francesca and me all week not only to think about the possibility of triplets but also to mull over her response to the tenure decision. On Wednesday, Francesca's chair, who has been working nonstop on the case, reported that he had convinced Columbia's vice president to re-review her for tenure. Because of how secretive the process is, we can only speculate what that means. On the one hand, it may be a tacit admission that the ad hoc committee and the provost made a mistake. Granting a second review is almost unprecedented. On the other hand, the process will be stressful, grinding on for another year or more. She decides to put herself through it. But we agree that we will have to look for new jobs outside New York, where I've lived for the last fifteen years and she has for twenty.

I am proud that she is fighting on, but also all bottled up about it, the emotional equivalent of being forced inside, off the field. Here are anonymous people who have made an unjust decision that is hurting someone I care about more than anyone, which may also force us out of our home, and there is nothing I can do about it. I cannot even express anger, because when I criticize the people involved it upsets Francesca all the more, reminding her of what happened, instead of pointing to brighter possibilities for the future. I wish it would stop raining.

## An Eddy Ball Lesson

The batting order is even more a part of the status system in softball than in the majors. And amateurs, even more than the pros, expect it to go by the Book. At the top should be fast guys who get on base, followed by power hit-

ters, and then everyone else according to their place in the manager's pecking order, with maybe another leadoff-type hitter at the very bottom. No
manager should mess with something that seems so obviously essential to
a team's success. But with a conventional lineup we Foxes have been scoring
runs only late in the game. Even though we won our last game by a blowout,
we've scored a grand total of three runs in the first three innings of our last
five games—three runs in over two games' worth of innings. And when we
do go on one of those quasi-magical rallies, they are as likely to start at the
bottom of the order as at the top.

Our lack of early production is most likely random. Chance plays a far
greater role in hitting than most fans find plausible. My teammates like to
think that someone who gets six hits in a row is hot. But if any of them were
to spend batting practice flipping a coin instead of pretending to stretch
while ducking their shagging duties, it would come up heads six times in
a row far more often than they would expect. The sabermetricians have figured out that the batting order doesn't matter much. In terms of managerial
decision making it's far more important to put the most productive players
somewhere in the lineup.

Partly because I've been forced indoors with a lot of time to think, I have
decided to provide a lesson in Eddy Ball. I am using the fact that we haven't
been scoring early to shake up the lineup. We are going to bat according to
our position numbers, starting at a number picked by someone on the team,
although I don't divulge why I'm asking for the number. I want to get across
the idea that I'm confident in everyone's ability to produce in any slot.

Mule calls out "seven," and right away I can see that the resulting order isn't
going to be optimal for me. This means that the left fielder, scored as number
seven, will lead off. As shortstop—number six—I will be batting last. That
doesn't matter to me. But Trey is at third base today, so he will be batting just
ahead of me. He has probably not batted this low in any order, ever. "So, I'm
ninth?" he asks me, smiling broadly and expectantly, as if there were some
joke that I'm about to let him in on. Because the guys we have today include
more mobile fielders, I have Papi at DH for Little Bobby, who is playing left
field, the position with the lucky number. That puts Papi at leadoff, no doubt
for the first time in his life. But since he's not playing the field he is sulking,
as if he were Frank Thomas.

Today Pamela's Foxes are on field #2, where umpire Teddy presides over a
dangerous infield. We have the mucky field to ourselves for warm-ups because
our opponents, the Cornelia Street New and Improved Guys, remain on field
#5, where they have been practicing since noon. We take infield practice for

the first time since Opening Day. The weather, as requested, has turned on a dime. It is already in the eighties, sunny, and very humid. A spring's worth of moisture on the Heckscher fields radiates up into our faces. It is as if summer were angry at spring for piling it on last season and as payback decided to transport us directly to August.

Cornelia Street has now morphed completely into a men's team. Billy is scattering their hits, and our defense is flawless, with Little Bobby gunning down a runner going first to third on a single in the second. But my shake-up produces nothing but goose eggs until the sixth, when their pitcher, a guy with "Mike the Strike" stenciled on the back of his T-shirt, walks me, Bobby, and Mule, and a throwing error puts us up two-zip. Billy holds them down for the shutout.

I promised that I would stake any of my teammates to a beer if we won and they would make a postgame pilgrimage to Pamela's Cantina to meet our sponsor Mickey. But this afternoon only Artie, Penny, and Swanny take me up on it. We head back to West Fourth by way of the A train. It feels odd to traipse through Washington Square Park in the middle of a Monday afternoon, past the dean's office across campus, in my softball uniform in the company of my teammates. My sporting and academic circles never overlap like this, and I worry about being seen.

Pamela's is deserted during the late afternoon happy hour. We get draft beers, and I learn that two of the others, like me, played pickup ball every day during the summer as kids, Artie in East Rockaway, Swanny on Staten Island. Swanny would play two games before lunch and three after. Sometimes kids from his neighborhood would form their own team and challenge kids from other neighborhoods. I wonder whether this is what we are trying to re-create by playing in so many different leagues, and whether we are part of a dying breed. Kids today are so tightly scheduled with organized activities that they never play pickup games.

Penny and Artie leave, and it's down to Swanny and me. He turns out to be a strict adherent to the Book of ball-playing wisdom. In our newfound beery camaraderie he reveals that when I shook up the lineup, it shook him up too. If I wanted to change the order, I should have done it conventionally, and if I don't do that, in his view, we are going to lose. By five, Mickey still hasn't shown, and Swanny and I step out of Pamela's and onto the NYU campus, blinking, our eyes adjusting to the brightness.

Swanny makes me realize that I have pushed an Eddy Ball notion too openly and too far, and that in doing so I have strayed from core Eddy Ball principles. It is as if I were so proud of my approach that I felt the need to draw attention to it—the way too-full-of-themselves players can't help pointing at their chests after a big hit. But Eddy Ball is all about making unorthodox moves in a subtle way without disturbing what everyone else deeply believes from his teaching and experience to be true. If the batting order doesn't much matter to me, or to scoring runs, there is no need to ruffle the feathers of teammates who do care about it.

## *Easy Rider*

At Francesca's doctor's appointment today she will learn whether any of our little sacs have heartbeats and, if so, how many. Thinking about this, along with everything else, has started to wear me down. I am hoping that we have just one beating heart, one rice-grain fetus. Multiple births usually translate into low birth weight and often into unhappy outcomes. I worry that one baby may gain advantages at the expense of the other, or others. On top of that I'm afraid that Francesca and I will be unable to cope. When we talked over having children in counseling, the discussion was always about one baby, not three. Francesca fears that there are going to be no heartbeats at all, which would send us back to the conception drawing board. (On which I see the equation "0 heartbeats = IVF.") By the time we get done talking this morning, she has converted me to her way of thinking.

It's another brutally hot day with another softball game, this time in the East Village—d.b.a. versus the Agitators. Today also marks the return of our superstar, Robin, the dream girl of every man in the league and some of the women. Robin gets a lot of modeling work in bridal magazines. With her shoulder-length blonde hair, mischievous sky blue eyes, and turned-up nose she looks like the prototypical girl next door, except way hotter. She grew up a tomboy on a farm outside Atlanta and loves nothing better than playing ball—unless it is riding her Ducati, on which she has been touring the South this spring. She can hit and field. She also has considerable distraction value. Opponents often fail to keep their eye on the ball. Back in New York like a migrating bird, Robin is flush with career plans for a life after modeling, and recounts them in her unreconstructed diphthongs. She wants to start a business designing motorcycle apparel for women. When she goes out on her bike for the evening there is nothing but men's clothes for her to wear. She doesn't have a place to live yet, but she isn't worried about it.

ROBIN ALSO HAD DISTRACTION VALUE

Robin is not really my type—motorcycles scare me, and I'm already spoken for. Actually, at some level she's every man's type but I'm not hers. I would be no more likely to willingly attend the Burning Man Festival, which she treks to religiously each summer, than I would my own cremation, and I don't go out unless it's to movies, while Robin goes out every night and often appears at the field complaining of a hangover. Being her teammate is probably similar to what it was like playing with Mickey Mantle. I fell in love with Robin for reasons other than the usual ones during last year's championship series. We were tied with Two Boots, in extra innings. They were the home team, I was pitching, and with no one out I walked a woman to load the bases. I struck out the next one, but found myself face to face with Two Boots' pesky leadoff man. He tried to shoot the first pitch to the right side but missed, lifting a harmless foul out of play into their first-base dugout. Robin, though, did not see it that way and took a dive onto the asphalt in front of the Two Boots bench. For her effort she earned two scraped forearms—and the putout. I got the next guy, and we went on to win the game and the championship.

It being a Wednesday, with no competing Central Park leagues, all our men are available, and the managers Billy and Miles have me batting second behind Billy and playing shortstop. Our opponents, despite their incendiary name, are surprisingly mellow. The only complaints are from our bench, charging the Agitators' pitcher with throwing excessively hard to our women. They immediately replace him, and we rock the reliever. Zeus, having arrived late, is ready to enter the contest, and Billy asks us to sort out where we will play. I have gloved several erratic grounders on this minefield and gunned across to Robin. Once Zeus is in earshot I say that I think that the game is still too close to risk putting him at short. Jogging out to the outfield, he waves to me cheerfully with his middle finger. With Robin's return, Gina had been consigned to catcher and is complaining about the toll it is taking on her knees,

I LEFT ROBIN TO BILLY

compounded by the weight of Andrés, who leans over her. I offer to spell her. The move is only partly altruistic, as catcher is the only position in the shade. Andrés elects not to lean on me. Zeus moves to short, and Gina heads to the outfield and promptly makes a nice play. I have another big day; all told I have reached base in thirteen of my sixteen plate appearances. If I keep this up I will get to stay at shortstop.

We trek back to d.b.a. on First Avenue, where there are more Agitators than us. It turns out they are political activists and are more about solidarity than competition. I sit with Robin and drink my pumpkin ale. She tells me about working as a research assistant for a professor in college. She is so engaged in telling me the story that I'm halfway wondering if she's coming on to me. I'm flattered and, with the beer in me, having a hard time focusing. Was she impressed by my throws to first base? Is it possible, to rephrase the classic Nike spot, that chicks dig the base on balls? When I took her photo it was as if she were looking right through me. I briefly imagine myself on a Harley, hair flying in the breeze, in Montana or wherever. Or just walking my bike over to her apartment. The logistics would be trivial. Like Robin, who sometimes discusses her breakups, Francesca worries much less about men sneaking around behind her back than about relationship exit strategies that minimize stalking. As I am remembering—right, Robin doesn't even have an apartment—the scene ends as abruptly as *Easy Rider*. The upshot of the story is that she quit because her prof was hitting on her.

I realize that I'm mesmerizing myself with free-as-a-bird Robin while blocking out the fact that Francesca's test results are back and may mean major misery. I leave Robin to Billy and head to the pay phone. This time they were able to locate a heartbeat—two of them. I am trying to talk myself into being relieved. Two is good. Two is very good. Two does not equal three, and two does not equal zero.

**THURSDAY, JUNE 26, HECKSCHER #5**

## Under New Management

Today Thespian Aid will learn if it's for real. To turn things around, manager Chad has recruited more players, and to effect the transition he has temporarily placed Billy in charge, a little like a military strongman during a social upheaval. Billy will put the best lineup out on the field against the undefeated Shubert Organization, one of three teams with perfect records in the Broadway Show League. Unlike Chad, Billy faces no personal cross-pressures to play Thespian Aid workers or other marginal players, most of whom Billy has little more than a nodding acquaintance with. To defuse complaints, Chad is being ceremoniously "benched" by Billy this afternoon. What can anyone else riding the pine say if Chad is sitting down?

The team has been revamped from top to bottom. Robin is now at first, with the reliable veteran Tiny catching. Chad has also recruited Penny, the sad-eyed, underemployed filmmaker infielder from Pamela's Foxes, d.b.a., and maybe ten other teams. He is at third. And shortstop Mike is starting at short, with Zeus agreeably sliding over to second base. Tommy, still in left center, replaces Chad as leadoff man. Billy stays at pitcher. Even Manny is here, replacing Chad in right. With our glut of infielders and lack of outfielders, Billy and Chad's thinking on my deployment has solidified. I am the left fielder and the seventh batter, before the first woman. We all put our hands together in a show of unity for the pregame shout, but many of these players are never going to see action.

Before the game, I have a chance to chat with Mike. He greets me with a growling bark, letting me know he hasn't forgotten my new Sunday-league nickname, then tells me he has found a summer teaching gig at Brooklyn College and is trying to make it permanent. I take a chance and break my vow of silence on Francesca's case, telling him what's happened and what it could mean for us. It is a relief to be able to tell someone who understands the situation but isn't interested in the story for its gossip value, as most so-

WE PUT OUR HANDS TOGETHER

ciologists I know would be. He is dumbfounded and sympathetic. For what it's worth, he says that Francesca's story seems to top his own nightmare at Nassau Community College. Also, he stops the barking.

It has reached the midnineties by the early afternoon and the discomfort index is well into the three digits. Panama, the ageless drink seller, has positioned his red coolers on the bleachers at each field in play. He has some subcontractors to help him, but he works largely on the honor system. He appears at the end of the games to collect on his top-selling Gatorades—at two dollars each they will probably set me back a hundred bucks this season—and to sell beers at three dollars a pop. His postgame pitch is "Win or lose, we booze!" It is now after three o'clock, and the trees in the left field of Heckscher #4 shade the first-base bleachers of #5, so both teams are set up there. I can't help noticing a pretty young blonde in a red bikini, apparently having lost her way to the Sheep Meadow, sunning herself on the park bench on the walking path behind first base and watching the game quizzically. Shubert's scores two runs in the first.

But the new lineup is working. The order comes around to me with one out, a runner on third, and four already across. It is starting to play with my mind to be always trying for a double walk. I've already proved that I'm not afraid to strike out and can bat and work out probability problems in my head

115

PANAMA'S PITCH WAS "WIN OR LOSE, WE BOOZE!"

at the same time. But it seems weird to try to take the bat out of the hands of Robin, who is batting behind me today and swings well. Maybe because the right fielder is playing a little shallow or maybe because I'm losing my grip, I decide to fly it over her head. I hit the ball hard but don't get enough lift on it, and when she nabs it, I have instead a sacrifice fly—the kind of out I am always imploring my teammates never to make.

We are up three, hold them in the second, and then tack on three more. Despite the lead, Billy is making only the most minor substitutions. When Billy calls Chad in to pinch-hit, he has to be summoned from the park bench, where he is chatting up bikini woman. As he goes to bat, Chad relates that she is from England, that she is in town for a week, and that he has been explaining the game to her. The rest of the Thespian Aid players, most of who actually work for the organization, sit the entire game. Billy refuses to acknowledge their presence, they say nothing to him, and we win a close one, 9–6.

Afterward, I go looking for Chad, who, despite seeing little action on the field, is at the top of his game today. He is back at the park bench, where the Englishwoman in the bikini has been superseded by an Australian woman in a sundress. I don't know what Chad's on-base percentage is, but no doubt he is leading the league in phone numbers. Since the leadership is making changes, I put in a bid. I'm tired of being a novelty hitter. The man-before-woman double walk is just a bad rule. It would be counterproductive in itself for a pitcher to give an intentional walk to a man batting ahead of a woman. The sabermetricians have revealed the intentional walk—especially routinely walking the catcher to get to the pitcher—to be a strategy that backfires. So I don't see why there should be legislation against it. Anyway, these double walks are usually inadvertent. Most of all, however, I no longer want to be a part of a scheme that takes the bat out the hands of the women players. For participation's sake they should always get a chance to swing the bat, or at least to earn their own walks. My dislike of the rule has been playing with my mind and making it difficult for me to play my game. I lobby Chad and Billy to move me up in the order. For all my bizarre at bats, I'm still doing well in this league, and they need me in the outfield. They agree to consider it.

**SATURDAY, JUNE 28, EAST RIVER #7**

## A Disgrace to the Game

Parks and Recreation has for some reason exiled today's pickup game to East River #7, the decrepit weekday stamping grounds of Andrés, the myopic Puerto Rican umpire/groundskeeper/announcer. I jog over there, exploiting any opportunity to work aerobic exercise into my extensively undemanding athletic schedule. We have only sixteen players by four-thirty, possibly because it's yet another oppressive day, in the upper eighties with residual stickiness from recent rains. The pickup game is becoming a chore to me now that I have so many league games to play in. If I could I would trade the remaining Saturdays on the permit for an equal number in the fall when there will be far fewer chances to play.

Every year there is a story in the newspaper pushing back the date of baseball's origin. A librarian finds a newspaper account of a game of "base ball," a booster locates a yellowed ordinance prohibiting the playing of "base" near the town hall, or a scholar uncovers letters of an American forefather referring to playing some version of the game as a child. No doubt someone will soon happen upon an artifact from Jamestown or Plymouth and end this childish and useless game of one-upsmanship. For baseball as we know it today separated itself from rounders and other children's games not in the earliest days of settlement and not even when Cartwright and his Knickerbockers introduced their many written rules. It happened as baseball was becoming a mass grown-up sport, in the wake of the Civil War, when the controversy over skill and "manliness" was in full swing. It happened by way of innovators who were

117

not petitioning a national association for rule changes to make putouts more difficult, but who were bending the rules in the heat of competition.

Baseball became baseball only when pitchers sought to retire batters by way of their pitching. The sport is often said to be the only one in which the ball starts in the hands of the defense. Yet what makes baseball unique is that it blurs the boundaries between offense and defense by placing so much control of the game in the hands of the pitcher. In Cartwright's day, the pitcher, or feeder, was a low-tech and dubiously reliable form of batting tee. Pitchers' attempts to retire batters were largely passive-aggressive. A pitcher's main tactic was to refuse to throw a hittable ball to the batter, who could demand that a pitch be high or low, in the hope that in frustration the batter would swing anyway. This tactic was also a means of stalling, as pitchers sought to hold a lead until the sun set. For the same reason batters would sometimes pass at hittable pitches. In response umpires started calling strikes, a rule that was formalized in 1858, and granting bases on balls. Pitchers could retire batters without their swinging, and batters could advance that way too.

Sometime between Cartwright's amateur Knickerbockers of the mid-1840s and the professional Cincinnati Red Stockings of 1869, the bulk of pitchers took the next step. They figured out how to whip the underhanded pitch in ways that defied the rules against wrist snapping but were not declared illegal. Thus exited baseball from the children's Garden of Eden, opening the way to the changeup, the curveball, and even trickier pitches. Ever since, baseball has sought to strike a balance between pitching and hitting, moving the mound back and forth and up and down and widening and tightening the strike zone by law or custom.

During the spring the pickup game has undergone a transformation, as if recapitulating the invention of baseball. In his search for an edge, Weasel has been throwing modified fast pitch to the better male players, and my team has responded in kind. This has produced a number of close and competitive contests and has shoved the game out of the sleepy 1840s into the raucous 1860s. Yet the pickup game has fallen into a rut. I have been choosing against Weasel, but he starts with his Josie's teammates and I with my d.b.a. teammates or some longtime Saturday regulars, then we select among the rest. This way of making teams has all the disadvantages of a pickup game without any of the advantages. First, there's the mortifying ritual that is choosing sides. I still remember having suffered as a kid the shame of being the last picked. We have toned down the potential public humiliation. Here captains write down their choices on the sign-in sheet during batting practice, so at least the remainders aren't forced to stand in isolation as the captains ponder who will hurt their teams least. Still, anyone can see where they stand in the picking order by checking the sheet. I'm a little tired too, after Francesca's job fiasco, of having to make judgments about the quality of players I don't know. Worst of all, Weasel's partial-pickup game reduces the redeeming elements of randomness and serendipity. In a standard pickup game, the likelihood that an opponent this week might be a teammate next week softens the edges of competition and makes everyone friendlier. Having the same opponents game after game can generate ill feeling, as it did between Whit and me. Tension does seem to be building between Weasel's teammates and mine.

I have a reform in mind—to use the sign-up sheet, which enumerates the players in order of arrival, to make the teams. So today it is the Evens against the Odds. There is no reason that the sides shouldn't turn out fair. Also, it should speed things up by eliminating the captains' deliberations. Cartwright's rules of baseball stipulated that the captains would choose fair sides but didn't say exactly how. For the first time I find myself on a team with Weasel. I ask him to take charge of the Evens. When he does I realize I would have assigned our teammates to the same positions he does. I find myself calling him by his name, Louie. He goes to the rubber to face an Odds team led by Carl, a social worker therapist and one of the best players.

I take up the umpiring duties and, inspired by the setting, do my best impression of Andrés. Instead of my catchphrase to get the game restarted, "Balls in, batter up," I give them Andrés's *"Gator ow!"* For every ball hit outside the lines, I declare, "Eet ees a *foul* ball." I am hoping to amuse Krishy, but if he or anyone is enjoying it they are doing a good job of feigning indifference. The teams seem fairly matched, but our Evens team jumps out to a big lead. In my second time up in the first I swing left-handed, hoping to retire myself, but single anyway. I wonder if this is how Shoeless Joe Jackson felt—trying to throw the 1919 World Series but unable to make an out. Carl wants to start over, choosing teams the old-fashioned way. I can understand. For most of the players this is the only game they play in, as it used to be for me. They want it to be good, and they want to win. My reform is a lost cause.

As Carl and Louie pick new teams, I take the time to hang out with my teammate Krishy. I am trying to convince him to play more with Pamela's Foxes. With our small roster and the impossibility of recruiting new players, we can't win it all without him. But I'm not sure how to approach him. I now address him as "Krish," which is how he refers to himself on his answering machine. In New York softball, there is a tendency to add a diminutive to everyone's name, and maybe he doesn't like it. He is hard to joke around with, and tropes are lost on him. If a teammate takes a pitch and another says,

"Good eye," Krishy will correct the speaker, instructing him that a batter has two eyes and thus he should say, "Good eyes." Either Krishy is clueless or, a more interesting possibility, he is making a postmodern statement about our postmodern condition by honing irony to the point that it has become posthumorous. Krishy looks tan and fit—he always does—but I learn that he has been suffering from a stomach virus since returning from Cancun and has been as sick as his dog was earlier in the season. His hamstring remains tender. He and Trey, both personal trainers, are vying for league leadership for time spent on the DL. Krishy also talks about vacation-related credit card debt and has only a dollar for the alternate's fee. I tell him not to worry about it. He offers me half of a chicken wrap, and I'm in a quandary. If turning it down would offend him, I should take it, but I don't want to deprive him of his lunch if he is hungry and is offering it in lieu of the fee. The tipping point is that the sandwich looks unappetizing.

A game that meant everything to me a few years ago now has no appeal. The organized games are just more exciting. As performances they seem more real, and the play seems more focused. I wouldn't have played at all today if I weren't feeling responsible. With my unserious attitude I've become a disgrace to the pickup game. It doesn't help that the first days of summer have been pitiless, and starting tomorrow I have a schedule so grueling that the Major League Baseball Players Association would balk at it. A few years ago I was ready to quit the pickup game and knew that would mean I was done with softball. Now I'm dropping pickup until I stop playing so much league ball.

## Dog Days

Francesca loves vacations. Having decided to go up for tenure again and anticipating a visit with friends upstate for Independence Day has improved her mood tremendously—we are getting along great and even going outside together again. I was wondering why we don't get away more often when I remembered that these occasional long weekends upstate with Robb and Joey was as much vacation as I have allowed us. Part of the deal of our getting pregnant was that I could play on all these teams this summer. I thought it was so important that I be available for all the Foxes' games that I wouldn't agree to a real vacation until after Labor Day. But sometime around the Fourth of July the dog days of the softball season set in. There are many meaningless games, as sportswriters would call them, with no implications for the postseason.

And they are held during the hottest time of the year—when tempers often flare and the city becomes an asphalt crucible. With the late June heat wave, the dog days have come early this year.

Even this little break I transform into a busman's holiday for Francesca. I prevailed upon her yesterday to read some of the entries from my softball journal since Memorial Day. It was my birthday, so she couldn't refuse. I gave her accounts of most the games, though leaving out the ones about her job and the babies. She finds discussing the job depressing, and discussing the babies makes her anxious. As she was reading I could tell that she liked it but also that she was grappling with how to tell me something without hurting my feelings.

"You've got an eye for detail, and it's good that you're putting so much down, Poopy," she said. "You never know what is going to be important in the end."

"But, what?" I replied, waiting for the other shoe to drop, while thinking briefly that Poopy, which is what she calls me, isn't so different from Poo-lie, which Tommy has taken to calling me. Maybe it's how they say it that matters?

"Well, there are a lot of games here, and I'm glad that they're going so well for you," Francesca continued. "But is anyone, aside maybe from Zeus and Billy—and me, of course—going to want to read about all of them? And what about you? Isn't this about you? What were you thinking the day you left me alone to clean the closets and lost the game for your team? I remember your coming home so upset. I think that's what other people will want to read about," she said.

She knows me well, and she decided to give me my medicine all at once before I could act all hurt and stop her.

"Do we really need to read about the league on Tuesday? It doesn't seem to be adding much to the story. It's a little harder than the league on Monday but not as hard as the Sunday league. And on Thursday there are all those characters, uh, players, that Chad just gets rid of, like the one who played in his yarmulke, Dockers, and crepe-soled shoes. It's too bad—I liked him—but who will want to read about him? Also, it might help your readers if you summed up a few things, like how well you and all your teams are doing. Isn't the season about halfway over?" she said.

Like most academics, I found these minor criticisms and suggestions upsetting, infuriating really. Some birthday present! And she delivered them with this superior, disinterested air, as if to say, she doesn't care what I do, but this is how real narratives work. The comments seemed unfair too. I hadn't shown her the entries where I wrote what I was feeling about the baby and the shit deal she was getting at Columbia because I thought they would upset her. And I didn't lose that game all by myself.

But today, calmed down, I can see her point. Since we academics can't publish anything unless we respond extensively to our expert critics, I decided grudgingly to take her advice. So I dropped the entries for the Tuesday Show Business League. I play second base for a team, Scentsational Shoppe, that is led by Zeus and consists of a motley assortment of Pamela's and Friars Club players, though without a pitching ace, plus new guys who Zeus keeps picking up but who rarely stick. On average the competition is only slightly better than on Mondays. The best team in the league is excellent, but the teams at the bottom are worse. Our team is headed for mediocrity. If ever anything interesting happens there, I'll let you know. I also telescoped the discussion of the coed leagues, eliminating several players, including Hush Puppy. And I wrote more about what I was feeling, if anything, as best I could remember, and added that part at the bar with Robin.

Last week's fifteen pages' worth of entries, which, I might add, were swathed in prose of heart-stopping beauty, I will merely summarize. On Monday, Zeus's Friars Club dumped my Krishy-less Pamela's Foxes. Maybe I should have eaten half of that nasty wrap. In any case, the Friars team is so loaded up that I'm almost glad we lost. Who knows whom Zeus would have picked up next if he hadn't won. Now I think he will finish the season with the team he has. Otherwise, Francesca is right—the results were happy. On Wednesday, team d.b.a. had its championship rematch against Two Boots and blew them away. Louie and Commissioner Bart won't have any chance against us unless they somehow induce umpire Andrés to rule Billy's pitching illegal on the grounds that he's too good. They might have to trump up charges against Robin too. Yesterday, the perfected Thespian Aid squad, having purged the final remaining Thespian Aid employees fifty years after one of them founded the league, raked Heckscher with two also-ran teams in a makeup doubleheader. Between games Chad offered screen tests to two blonde coeds from Nebraska sporting matching T-shirts with stick figures in bandanas captioned, "Born to be Wild, New York City." They were flattered to hear that he was certain he had seen them in *Vogue*.

Francesca was wrong about one thing, though. Independence Day may mark the middle of the season in baseball but not in softball. Around the Fourth, baseball GMs have to decide whether to go for it or give up, trade veterans, and play for the future. This season, for example, my White Sox, a team that hasn't won a World Series since 1917, traded a few minor league prospects to rent Roberto Alomar and Carl Everett in a bid to catch the Twins. In Central Park softball the Fourth of July is more like Labor Day in baseball. A few softball teams can still influence their futures, and some are still in contention for regular-season championships. But most teams' rosters are frozen, and most players know whether their teams are heading for the postseason. Most of them are. The playoff qualifications for softball here are forgiving—more like those for pro hockey or basketball than for baseball. Even the most selective leagues allow half of the teams to advance. Not only can adults now continue to play children's sports. We have also coopted their self-esteem movement.

For those of you who haven't been keeping score at home, here's the rundown of all five leagues, complete with my on-base percentages:

Monday, Performing Arts Softball League: Pamela's Cantina (Foxes) is 9–2, in first place out of six teams (four teams make the playoffs; and we've clinched a berth). OBP: .543 (19/35).

Tuesday, Show Business League: Scentsational Shoppe is 6–5, fifth place of eight (six teams make playoffs). OBP: .435 (10/23).

Thursday, Broadway Show League: Thespian Aid is 4–3, fifth place of eleven (eight teams make playoffs, clinched berth). OBP: .625 (10/16).

Monday-Friday, East Village Softball Association: d.b.a. is 7–2, second place of six (four teams make playoffs). OBP: .789 (15/19).

Sunday, Lower Manhattan Softball League: The Machine is 9–5, tied for second place of six (four teams make playoffs). OBP: .303 (10/33).

Pamela's Foxes are doing the best of all my teams. We have been in first place since Opening Day. If we win the regular-season title we will get a big trophy for our sponsor Mickey. It all depends on whether we can beat Zeus's revamped Friars Club. We will play them twice in the season's final four games and need to beat them once. Most of the main plotlines remain available, and

PERFORMING ARTS SOFTBALL LEAGUE, PM DIVISION, STANDINGS AS OF JULY 4

| Team | W | L | GB |
|---|---|---|---|
| Pamela's Cantina | 9 | 2 | — |
| Friars Club | 8 | 3 | 1 |
| Production | 6 | 5 | 3 |
| Gotham Comedy Club | 5 | 6 | 4 |
| Cornelia St. (New Guys) | 5 | 6 | 4 |
| Mickey Mantle's | 0 | 11 | 9 |

although Francesca has made me appreciate the narrative limitations of total domination—no reversal and so on—it would be OK with me.

As for my running the team, my teammates are not yet all adherents of Eddy Ball, especially recently when it was too crudely applied. But it is my team now—patient and flexible, no superstars, with little complaining or backbiting. I'm trying to get the players to believe that we are the best, but they still seem surprised that we are on top. When the Friars Club beat us, my guys acted as if some natural order had been restored. Also, I'm down to fourteen guys, and the availability of two of those remains uncertain—Trey with his hamstring and Krishy with his God knows what. It's not as if I can trade with eliminated teams for the equivalent of an Alomar or Everett to bulk up for the stretch run.

I do seem to have made a friend or two. Cookie and I talk a lot and commiserate about our teammates' complaints and their spotty attendance records. I ride home with Big Artie almost every Monday and Tuesday. He has been helpful during the various reproductive and academic crises. Shortstop Mike has been very understanding about the academic matters too. Billy and I talk a lot now, as he has numerous suggestions for the Monday team, and I'm even getting along better with Zeus, who is my manager on Tuesdays.

As for my personal struggles, the results are uneven. On Monday, my numbers have fallen earthward, but I'm still the most productive hitter on the Foxes and always play a difficult fielding position. On Thursday, in the slow-pitch, coed Broadway Show League, I am starting to heat up now that Billy and Chad are batting me second instead of seventh. I went four for four with a triple two days ago. And I am simply destroying the East Village Softball Association. But I still haven't made it on Sunday, with the Machine. My extensive playing time has been mainly due to poor attendance by starters. I'm hanging in mainly thanks to slick fielding and the fact that Billy has seen me tear up other leagues. I am going to have to heat up my tepid .300 OBP, though, if I expect to get the call come playoff time, when everyone will be available.

I will worry about that later. Today I am acting the way people my age normally do. Francesca and I combat the heat with dips in the swimming pool. Like the rest of the country we grill hot dogs and burgers. Distant, soundless fireworks from Hyde Park, Poughkeepsie, or Perkinsville sporadically breach the horizon. This is so relaxing. I can't believe that this long weekend is as much vacation as I would agree to. Aside from my needing to make it on the Machine and the upcoming showdown with Zeus and the Friars Club, we could have spent an entire month in Maine, Montauk, or Mendocino.

Francesca will be working like a dog on her book about narrative to give us a chance to stay in New York and has nothing to look forward to in the way of a break until after Labor Day.

## Up the Ladder

More games have gone by, but today's is marked with an asterisk because I'm playing to win a spot on the Machine. I've hit much better and continued to play well at second base, but I'm still trying to redeem my miserable start. Before the game, there is a sign that I am slowly climbing up the Machine ladder. With Trey still out, Billy asks me if I will play third base. Last week Woody had a brutal day at third against the Skins, and we dropped the second game of the doubleheader, Billy's game.

In softball, unlike baseball, second base is not considered a key defensive position. Most softball hitters are right-handed, and they usually try to pull the ball. So third base is more prestigious. Because of the greater number of balls hit there, the fact that more of them are hit hard, and the longer throw to first, it's considered a man's job. But I prefer playing second base. A good second baseman can turn a lot of double plays, and double plays are devastating to an opponent. Plenty of balls are hit to second in leagues where the pitchers throw harder, and the better leagues also have a lot of lefty batters. Because of the short throw to first a second baseman can play deep, increasing the chances to make plays; at third most plays are the do-or-die type, relying on reaction time.

My downward slide on this team began early last season when I made an error at third base and shortstop Mike told Billy that I didn't look comfortable there. That afternoon I wasn't. It was on the Great Lawn with the sun slanting in, bothering me even on bouncers. I was happy to move to right field, not dreaming that it would take a season and a half for me to be asked to return to third. If I'm going to make it here, I need to step up to challenges. I tell Billy that I'll play third.

It matters, too, because today the Machine plays Rif Raf, the team Zeus jumped to in protest over Dick's remaining on the team, and which is only a game behind us. I've realized that even though I am playing better it's not going to make much of an impression unless I do it against the better teams. Although it's Zeus's first year on Rif Raf, he seems to be running it. Juan and Jorgy have joined the team, and so has Mule, leaving behind the woeful On-

125

Base Percentage. We take the field, and I get tested immediately, making a backhand play on a scorcher down the line. Later in the game, with runners on first and second, another smash comes my way. I glove it, step to the base, and fire to Keith to end the inning. Twice I'm up with a runner in scoring position—and both times I single him in. We win, 6–4.

Manny is umpiring again today. Since he's at Heckscher all the time, he has decided to take advantage of the fields' two main moneymaking opportunities. He's worked his way into the rotation for the Lower Manhattan Softball League and boasts that by umpiring both league and pickup games he can clear three hundred dollars on a Sunday. League games pay forty-five dollars, and pickup players will kick in twenty-five dollars for the benefit of having an official. He has also become a drink seller, a subcontractor for Panama. His best day for that enterprise is Thursday. With all five fields in use all day long, and a relatively well-off clientele, the Broadway Show League is by far the best for selling—which accounts for his spotty attendance at Thespian Aid games. Manny has learned from umpire Teddy the technique of praising players, which promotes fellow feeling toward the umpire and can come in handy when things get hot. "You playing gooood!" he says to me between games, nodding his head for emphasis and knitting his brow in earnest to ward off my suspicion that he is teasing me. "You stopping balls that are doubles," he says, shaking his head as if in disbelief. Aw shucks, Manny.

We always have trouble winning the second game, even though the steady Billy is pitching and not the erratic Dick. I like our chances, though, because they have Mule on the mound. Game two starts like a replay of game one. I get a chance to drive in a run in the second, get a hit, and we jump out to another 3–0 lead. Manny stops the game. The maples in right are an inviting spot for fans or anyone else who wants to sit under a tree, and a mother and child are set up there on a blanket. But the maples are also in fair territory, so Manny is politely shooing them off. The woman refuses to move. She is holding a toddler by his feet, and we experience softball's first ever change-of-diaper delay. The child's father looks like a guy who used to play on Mondays but much more tired. He sees the issue and also tries to coax her off the field, but she is adamant, and the couple seems on the verge of a quarrel.

The weather is sticky, but the scene is bracing. I have gone from crisis to crisis this spring. I have had to deal with getting dropped as chair, while worrying about being dumped as Foxes manager and cut from this team. I have had to negotiate the mental maze of assisted reproduction, worrying about the size and number of the fetuses, not to mention Francesca's tenure case and its implications for her and us. I've been thinking that if I can just get through the latest drama, everything will be OK. Now it is starting to sink in that next year I won't be debating whether to play second base or third base or any base. I will be sitting on the bench playing diaper-bag holder. I wonder if I've been had on the deal with Francesca. I'd imagined that she would be so attached to the new baby that she wouldn't mind that I was sneaking off, possibly almost daily, to the park. But this guy seems overwhelmed with the one kid, and we almost certainly are going to have two.

When the game resumes I get a chance to end the third with another step-on-third–throw-to-first double play. But the videotape goes on the fritz. My throw one-hops Walker, who is subbing for Keith. Walker scoops it but, in trying to show Manny that he has the ball, raises his glove too quickly and sends the ball flying. Two hits later, Jorgy clears the bases. Down to our last licks, we're three runs behind, but Mule walks two guys and can't field a dribbler, loading the bases. Tommy then lines one past Mule, so hard that it makes him skip. But Jorgy is shading up the middle, converting Tommy's certain hit into the pitcher's best friend, as he steps on second and guns over to first. And now Walker turns the play into the pitcher's best friend dropping over with a pizza, a six-pack, and a DVD, as he tries to score from third and is thrown out from here to next week. Rif Raf runs off the field, jubilant, as we remain seated on the bleachers, stunned that the game is so suddenly over. A triple play? Afterward, I hear Manny praise Mule on his pitching. Mule is happy to explain exactly how he did it. Unlike with the pros, neither God nor luck nor any teammate appears in the account. Mule won't be kicking any more dirt on Manny.

I decide not to wait for the funeral procession to Columbus Circle. I'm not up for playing the blame-attribution game. Anyway, Billy, an equal-opportunity finger-pointer, has been going on and on about how he popped up with the bases loaded. He's not going to be blaming me. I finally had a four-hit day and fielded well overall. I may have well secured a spot in this lineup even after Trey returns. But something still seems to be holding me back here. When we needed a big play I didn't make it.

## Election Day

I boasted to Mickey that we would probably win him hardware for Pamela's Cantina, and I want to take care of it today. A win against the Friars Club would clinch the regular-season PM championship, but I'm desperate for players. Swanny, the underemployed stagehand, is somehow vacationing on Martha's Vineyard, and Trey and Dog are away too. Possibly I'm the only player in the league who isn't taking a summer vacation.

I can't help attributing this mess to Krishy. I have been trying to convince him to come back to Pamela's, but I'm starting to think of him as one of those clueless swing voters who know little about politics and care less but inevitably decide our presidential elections. They are herded into TV studios after debates and encouraged to free-associate about the candidates' posture, intonation, apparent sincerity, and other inane things. Campaign managers are forever trying to get through to them but at least know the date when they will be put out of their misery. This morning I get an e-mail from Krishy saying that it "looks like I'm not going to make it." It's not clear if he has a client, his dog is ill, he fears rain, or what. I call him and explain to his machine that I need him. For Krishy I am declaring it Election Day. If he doesn't show up, that's it. I hope he likes my intonation.

When I arrive at Heckscher, Zeus's team is already taking batting practice. Zeus is playing this contest without Sport, the Friars Club manager, whom he has deemed to be an offensive liability. Our only player already there is Mule, who badgers me about pitching. "I shut down the Machine," he says. Soon the Foxes file in, and when rock star Billy arrives at showtime, we have ten. It looks as though Mule is going have to play the outfield. Then who should come voting with his feet but Krishy.

Zeus's team takes the field. He is manning first, Juan is at second, Jorgy is at shortstop, and the fireballer Burnsides is on the rubber instead of stocky, control-pitcher Bro. The problem, I point out to Zeus, is that the Friars isn't the home team, and a standoff ensues. Gino, a smallish man with a droopy mustache and a retiring manner, is the third and newest umpire for Monday's Performing Arts League—serving on probationary status. Worried about losing control of this game before it starts, he is on his way to get Klem. But there are several guys from Irving Plaza, whose game just finished, here to scout the game. The longhair manager Mack has a schedule, and with this confirmation we take the field. I quickly wish that I had let the Friars stay there. Billy isn't sharp, falling behind to Jorgy, who rips a meatball for a single, and then losing Zeus to balls. Billy retires the next two, but another walk loads the bases. The next guy up is another of Zeus's new recruits, a lefty slugger. Billy falls behind, and Lefty rockets the cripple over the outfield. I know I said that I wanted to experience softball magic, but enough! In my last two half innings against Zeus's teams I have suffered a triple play and a grand slam.

It's 6–2 after two and a half. Billy is scheduled to lead off as our eleventh batter. He tries to beg off, saying his leg is sore. I ask Gino if Mule can serve as Billy's DH instead of an extra hitter. But the Friars bench, which consists of Bro, won't permit it. Billy pops up to Zeus at first, and Zeus holds the ball out to show it to him. On the bench in the fifth, Q and Little Bobby say we're missing the pepper that Swanny provides. I counter that what we need is to stop lifting the ball into the air, where they have proved they can catch it. We finally start to hit the ball down. With one out Cookie reaches on Jorgy's throwing error. Bobby hits one to Juan at second, he flips for the force, but Cookie's takeout slide upends Jorgy, whose relay thwacks off the bleachers. Zeus then displays the less endearing side of his managerial technique. If someone makes a bad play, he is apt to move the player to a different position—immediately after the error, showing up the offender. Zeus takes over short himself, exiling Jorgy to right field. We get one, but they get it back in the top of the seventh, and it's 7–3 when we come to bat for our last licks.

I bring the guys together and call a mock play, as if we were a basketball team down a point with possession and a few ticks remaining. My idea is to do the opposite of what usually happens—a manager providing tense advice to batters in a crucial situation who don't need it and are probably nervous enough already. Instead I say, "Here's the deal: Everyone hits, no fly balls. Billy gets the game winner, and then we carry him off the field on our shoulders in slow motion humming the theme from *The Natural*. Break!" I pick Billy because he didn't want to bat in the first place. This cracks up most of the guys.

And, better still, it starts to happen. Mule hits a grounder to Juan at second, who bobbles it, and, running as if in slow motion, still beats the throw. Penny singles, and Cookie grounds into a force-out, but Papi singles to load the bases. Little Bobby, the tying run, comes to the plate and hits the ball hard on the ground to Juan, who boots this one too, Cookie hustling home. Zeus benches Juan. Q singles to left, reloading the bases. Billy has his advertised chance for glory, though he would need to clear the bases to do it. Instead he loops a single into center, driving in another run, refilling the bases, bringing us within one, and sending me to the plate.

Zeus yanks Burnsides, waves in control pitcher Bro, and calls Jorgy back into the infield, stationing him on second in the hope of turning a double play. With right field wide open I can play the role that I'd assigned to Billy with a line drive over the infield. I duck under a pitch at two and one and get the call, which earns the ire of Bro, who seems equally angry with Gino and me. I'm still looking for a pitch to drive, but Bro sends one way wide. I take off before the pitch lands, and the tying run trots home. Up comes undecided voter Krishy, who lines Bro's first pitch decisively into the vacated part of right field, as if checking a box on a ballot. It's not at all like *The Natural*. All our guys are running helter-skelter, unsure whether to congratulate Krishy at first or Q at the plate.

I touch second base and just stand there and watch it unfold. I was acting as though we had them all the way, but I didn't really believe it myself. Now the chaotic scene seems to be a complete vindication of Eddy Ball, all the way from picking a team of fine but underappreciated team players to the displacement of anxiety-making chatter, with the midseason correction of downplaying minor, in-your-face Eddy Ball notions. A preseason bet on the "Sharkeys," who'd never before cracked .500, winning the divisional championship would have drawn steep odds, and now we've done it with two weeks still remaining in the season. I can't wait to tell Mickey about the trophy. More than that, I can't wait to see it up on the bar—and to explain to all my lunchtime academic colleagues this September how it got there.

## *Makeup Call*

Mule the salesman is as always making his pitch to pitch. "We've already won the division," he argues, poking me in the chest. "And I used to play for these guys. C'mon, I wanna beat them." I have a different agenda for the Foxes game against Gotham. There is an award for allowing the fewest runs in the division, and I want to win it as a tribute to the team's defense and Billy's pitching, and for Mickey's mantle. But we have only ten players. Krishy doesn't want to risk aggravating his hamstring injury, Roger is working on his new house in Jersey, Trey has a training client, and Penny has more editing work. With the playoffs around the corner, his work drought has come to an end at a most inopportune time. I know that the National Bureau of Economic Research examines more refined data, but if the incomprehensible Mule finds employment as a sales manager then the jobless part of the recovery must be over. I ask Mule to catch, and he reluctantly agrees, as the sun has beaten the temperature into the nineties, the humidity level having maxed out. "OK," he says, "but I'm not wearing the jersey." Its light cotton flannel is still a lot to take in this weather.

Umpire Teddy says, "Play ball!" and we do, going up 7–1. In the fifth, Billy runs into trouble. Six straight Gothams reach, waking up their fans—their girlfriends, some Irving Plaza guys, and the entire Friars Club team, whose

THE GOTHAM FANS WANTED MULE

opponent, Mickey Mantle's, had forfeited. Stoked with Coronas from Panama's cooler by way of Manny, Zeus is demanding a pitching change. "We want Myoo-oooole," he lows. Some of the other Friar's guys join in and are beside themselves with glee.

I found this amusing last week when I hung around after a game in the Tuesday Show Business League, where I often play, to watch a team run by the film critic Jeffrey Lyons, featuring Mule, battle P's & Q's, featuring Q. Zeus and Manny and some other park regulars were ragging them mercilessly, also using the Mule call. The cherubic Lyons, a diehard Red Sox rooter, doesn't play the field, affording him the opportunity to regale teammates and spectators alike with his deep knowledge of baseball trivia—Frank Thomas and Jeff Bagwell being born on the same day, the Griffeys hailing from the same small town in Pennsylvania as Stan Musial, and so on. Lyons treated us to his classic story about Mule. It's just before midnight, New Year's Eve, and Lyons and his wife are watching some 1940s American movie, which, sensitive to his audience, he dismisses as "some chick flick." They are clinking flutes when the phone rings. It's Mule. "I just wanted to tell you I'm playing with your team this year," he reports. I tried to one-up Lyons. Last winter, just before I stopped taking his calls, Mule leaves a message on my machine a little before ten-thirty. His tone is urgent. "Call me back tonight," he says, but leaves a different number than usual. A few minutes later, I do. A woman answers and asks me if I am aware of the time and that her mother is ill and

131

was asleep until the phone rang. I've rung up Mule's in-laws. He takes the phone and is breathless with excitement. He has a new idea for the batting order! But I'm not seeing the humor in this now.

Billy gets the second out, but they get another hit, sending in the tying run. Instead of firing home, Q aims at the Gotham manager, who is trying for third. The throw beats him, Cookie tags him, and Teddy, right on the play, calls the runner out. The manager is quickly on his feet and arguing, correctly, I believe, that the tag was too high. His anger is partly strategic. As in baseball, softball managers argue close calls to get the benefit of the doubt on future calls. In softball there is only one umpire, and he is going to miss calls. Good umpires "miss them both ways," with makeup calls—intentionally incorrect decisions—to compensate for the ones they blew.

But the Gotham manager's anger runs well beyond strategy. Softball games are rife with displays of righteous indignation over injustice. Your employer may be squeezing your pension or health benefits. Time Warner, Con Edison, or Verizon may add mysterious charges to your bill. The president may provide deceptive and shifting reasons for going to war. And these things matter far more than softball games. But here on the field players are eyewitnesses to obviously wrong and unfair decisions, and the legitimate authority is not tucked away in some corporate headquarters or the White House but is right in front of you. Wrong calls cry out for protest. Everyone knows Teddy is too professional to reverse a judgment call. Still, we've blown the fewest-runs award, the game is tied, and it's advantage Gotham. They have the fans, last ups, and Teddy looking to make it up to them.

We put up a goose egg in the top of the sixth, and Gotham leads off with a single. Dog and I turn a nifty double play, but Teddy rules the batter safe at first, an obvious makeup call. Billy gets out of it anyway. Papi leads off, hits one off the pitcher, and barely beats the throw, but Teddy calls him out. I can't get myself worked up enough about the injustice to argue. Billy walks, Bobby and Cookie single, and I line one down the right-field line. I am standing on second, and three runs are across. Gotham and their sultry-weather fans from the Friars Club have gone suddenly and satisfyingly silent.

Back on the field, I'm still irritated at them all. In the calm, I can't help thinking about Mule. Sure, he can be annoying, but now I'm embarrassed for having made fun of him. The guy shows up to every game and does everything asked of him. Billy likes throwing to Mule because he thinks like a pitcher. He's not our best pitcher, but he always gives his best. I have an anger-induced brainstorm. Why not give the fans what they want and bring in Mule to close Gotham out? That would be your managerial makeup call!

DOG TURNED A DOUBLE PLAY

Granting his wish would make up for the fun I've had at his expense. I huddle with Cookie. With the game still close and with Mule's penchant for walking batters, Cookie thinks my idea is a more like a brain cramp. I have to remember that the reason Mule isn't pitching for us isn't that I'm stopping him. Mule isn't pitching for us because my teammates don't want him to pitch. I'm just the person assigned to deliver the bad news, every game. I let it go, and Billy dispatches them.

Despite the victory and the heat, I head home with a cold feeling. I remember wanting at the beginning of the season to have what I thought of as big league fun, with hard teasing. But I wanted it to be good-natured and, well, clever, like when someone asked Jim Bouton, after he had spun a knuckleball, whether the homer that ensued was the longest he ever gave up. And I was hoping that at least occasionally someone would take aim at himself, the way Joe Morgan did after he struck out. Jeff Lyons's story was funny and sweet, and Mike's going off about Machine-gate was humorous, but for every moment like that I am taking very tired shit five times for having long hair, and players are lowing all afternoon at Mule, as if they scored extra for lack of originality. From this point on I rag Mule no more.

## Existential Question

The Machine has an eleven-thirty twin bill today against the defending-champion Hitmen, who swept us in May. If we can return the favor, we will tie them for first. I feel less than ready, having had no chance to warm up. I barely missed the A train, trapped in a MetroCard standoff with a detraining passenger at the West Fourth Street station turnstiles, and had to wait twenty minutes for the next one. Again I'm at third base, my position here at least until Trey returns. I wonder if when the playoffs begin I will be as in the way as my turnstile partner was this morning.

The Hitmen are up first, and I dive and nab a scorcher over the bag, gather, and gun, but Teddy misses the call, ruling that Keith came off the base at first. Thankfully no one is blaming me—even the tightly wound Dick says "nice play"—and nothing comes of it. In our end we have three in and Keith on second with two outs when the order comes around to me. Casey, their manager, pitcher, and all-star, tries to get ahead of me with a BP fastball, but I send it pinballing among the maples in right for a ground-rule double. Dick gives them three back, and in the third I come up with Keith on again. This time Casey starts me with risers. He loses me. We score another four runs. Casey replaces himself with his second-string hurler and substitutes out two of his better hitters, conceding game one and saving himself for game two. The noonday sun glares, threatening to become oppressive. Fortunately it's still early, and the oaks and maples around the diamond provide some shade for the infield and, more important, for the only bleacher—on the first-base side—where we are always set up. The Hitmen, as usual, are off with their chairs, coolers, and fan base back in the green space on the third-base side.

Dick has also set up there, at a little remove from the Hitmen, with his young wife in his and hers beach chairs with umbrellas for parasols. In the sixth, we are up 8–3, but Dick starts them off with a walk and then becomes irate at Teddy's pitch calls. In protest of one, Dick just glares menacingly at Teddy through his wraparounds and ignores Frank's return throw! I had never seen that one before. As infielders do when pitchers work slowly, I let my mind wander. Is there something more going on than petulance, an overwrought, child-pure sense of injustice? Is Dick's display strategic? If so, it isn't working. We on his team have all experienced his anger, and it seems indiscriminate. Maybe he thinks we will play better if we fear his wrath—but it seems just as likely to backfire, and we make so few errors anyway. When

Dick lets another one sail by, my confusion turns to anger. Does Dick even think about how his biggest supporter Frank feels as he watches his throws sail into the outfield? I reflect on the play in the first and how weird it is that I was so relieved Dick wasn't blaming me for something that was not at all my fault. Smelling blood, Casey substitutes his big guns back into the game. A couple of singles dart through the lethargic infield; more follow. Casey drives in the tying run, returns to the rubber, and sets us down.

Dick starts the seventh giving up a leadoff walk and a single, and Billy heads out with the hook. I talk with Mike, who wants to discuss professional matters. Having to teach so much and having taken time off to write his book on caregivers for cancer patients, Mike failed to get over some hurdle in the PhD program on schedule. A season that began with his losing a thankless teaching position is going to end with the director of graduate studies forcing him out on a technicality. Unbelievable. I don't know what to say, aside from that I'm sorry. He clinches the upset one-upsmanship championship.

Almost as difficult to believe, Dick is refusing to leave the game! He falls behind the next batter and ignores the return throw. Having retrieved the ball yet again, Mike instructs Dick, "Throw strikes or get off the field." Dick shouts back, "Just who the fuck do you think you are?" Mike leaves the existential question hanging, as Dick gives them the lead. On the way to his private dugout, Dick can't avoid Mike heading back to the bleacher. Dick offers a challenge: "Whaddaya gonna do now, get a hit?" If Krishy is an undecided voter, Dick, almost voted off the team last winter, is a politician who steals the election and reneges on campaign promises. Mike lifts the first pitch to third base—on distant field #2—and ties the game. That's all we get. From afar Billy waves off Dick, who is off the hook for the loss, and sets them down easily. We don't score either, and two flares put runners on. Rattled, Billy grooves the next Hitman, who skies one to the field #2 bleachers. We can't respond, and that's the ball game. Dick breaks camp without saying good-bye.

In the second game, the Hitmen can't touch Billy, but we aren't hitting either. More disturbingly, their outfielders now position themselves exactly where I like to hit the ball—shallow in right center and near the line in right. I line out on what would normally be a single to right center. Still, we scratch out a run here and there, play solid defense, and take a 3–1 lead into the seventh. In our end we get runners on, and I have a chance to do damage. This time I shoot one cleanly up the middle; we tack on more and win going away.

On the way back to the subway most guys are irked that we blew the sweep. Billy is particularly upset. Usually I'm concerned with what he might be thinking about me, but with my experience as a manager, I now see things more from his point of view. All season long he's been trying to hold together the Machine in the wake of the off-season flap over Dick, who today took on Mike, one of the team's best players, and refused Billy's request to give him the ball, his ego puffed up by his inflated won-and-loss record. The Machine rarely scores runs for Billy, so despite having given up fewer runs than Dick, Billy's record is under .500, while Dick's remains perfect. The league seems to be imploding too. The contentious Pitt Bulls have already run one good umpire out of the league, and now Dick has hassled Teddy, who after today may be done too. Worse still, on the A train I learn that the real world has been impinging on Billy. His mother has taken ill. His sister is staying with her in his mother's Arizona home, but they think she is going to need an operation. If that happens, he's going to be heading west, possibly for a long time.

( MONDAY, JULY 28, HECKSCHER #4 )

## *Regular-Season Wrap-up*

The magical regular season of Pamela's Foxes ends today with the anticlimactic "position" showdown against the second-place Friars Club. We are 12–2, and the Friars Club is 10–4. They can't catch us, and we can't drop them into third place. Cookie agrees that we need not pull out all the stops, so we are throwing at them a medley of second-string pitchers, including Mule, who is grateful for the opportunity. We don't want them to get another look at Billy until the playoffs. We've chosen to play in Klem's World, a brainstorm of the guys who showed to an impromptu regular-season championship party last week at Pamela's, in the hope that Zeus and Klem will mix it up. I make up a conventional batting order—as I now always do. But with Roger out again at his home in Jersey, I slot myself at cleanup. I'm not afraid of it. I'm still the division's RBI leader, a silly status falling my way only because our order is strong top to bottom and I also lead in plate appearances. But my teammates think that a lot of RBI means a player is clutch, so I am hoping to pad the stat.

The final league contest between the top two teams has all the urgency of a company picnic. Zeus, who has heard through the grapevine why we chose the field, is on his best behavior. He has also apparently patched things up with Manny, who is back on the team. I put myself in to pitch, facing my teammates from other leagues: Manny, Zeus, Juan, Jorgy. In the fifth, Gina, the d.b.a. novice whom I've asked to show up today and the Foxes' first woman batter of the season, shoots one the third baseman can't handle. The Friars Club takes a 4–3 lead into the seventh, and all we need is a bloop and blast.

WE TOOK A TEAM PHOTO ANYWAY

Big Artie gets the bloop and Little Bobby the blast, but it's hauled in. I'm in the on-deck circle when we make the final out—no win and no RBI for me today. But the regular season is over, and we're champs. So we take a team photo anyway.

One person is taking it all very seriously. After the game, Klem makes a pitch to officiate our first playoff contest, next Monday. As PM division champion, we have the choice of fields. "I love your team," Klem says. He doesn't add that he's concerned he might have to preside over the consolation contest between Mickey Mantle's and Cornelia Street. Working the losers' tournament game would be a big drop in status for the league's senior umpire and former commissioner. If we don't pick Klem, that would be his fate, because Zeus, as leader of the second-place team, has the second choice. Zeus, magnanimous in victory always, offers to buy me a beer; I take him up on it. He is already

PAMELA'S FOXES, END-OF-SEASON HITTING AND FIELDING ASSESSMENT

| | | Hit? | |
|---|---|---|---|
| | | Yes | No |
| Field? | Yes | Cookie, Eddy, Penny, Billy, Krishy, Artie, Q., Trey, Swanny, Bobby | Dog |
| | No | Roger, Mule | Papi |

137

discounting the regular season as being something like today—an extended warm-up—and is looking weeks ahead to the postseason.

I go home and enter the final regular-season stats on the league's Web site. The numbers seem to confirm that my makeover of the team was successful and to bear out some of my Eddy Ball theories. We outscored our opponents for the first time ever, and by a full fifty-seven runs. The only divisional opponent that did better was the Friars Club, though in the other division, disturbingly, Irving Plaza outscored its opponents by seventy-six. Our low runs-against total was a testament to Billy's pitching and our defensive flexibility and opportunism. We had seven players in the divisional top twenty in on-base percentage (OBP). Three are guys—Billy, Penny, Artie—I added to the team for this season. Eleven guys had on-base-plus-slugging (OPS) numbers over .800. More important, they also scored well on a more complex and predictive metric of my own making that counts on-base percentage twice as much as slugging average, adjusts upward for reached on errors and downward for base-running blunders, and involves multiplication and a cube root. We led the league in walks and as a team we got on base about 39 percent of the time, tops in the division. And we had only one home run. Looking back at my initial two-by-two table, I can see that almost everyone ended up in the hit/field box. I guessed right on Q, Swanny, and Little Bobby. Only Papi was a puzzle. I wasn't expecting him to help much in the field, and he didn't, but his batting fell right off the charts, with a sub-.700 OPS.

My own stats fell off after my fast start, but I ended up leading the team both by e-mail exhortation and example. Although my batting average dropped to .400, I finished at the top of the entire league in walks, with ten, and led the team in OBP at .520, which was also the eighth highest in the league, not that anyone pays attention to this stat. And I ended up tied for the divisional lead in RBI—a worthless situational stat, as I've said before, but my teammates found it impressive. In the field I could have been better, but I played well enough and wherever needed. This wasn't the MVP season I'd wanted, but I'll take it.

( SUNDAY, AUGUST 3, HECKSCHER #1 )

## Training for a Marathon

The dog days conclude in a blur of humidity. In the Sunday league, where I've been trying to solidify a spot on Billy's Machine team, we have a split double-header to make up for rainouts. We play the fifth-place Skins at two-thirty and then Rif Raf, led by our former teammate Zeus, which is vying with us for second place. When I get to the Heckscher fields, I learn that Mike the shortstop is going to be absent. I worry that he's quit over last week's tiff with Dick, but Billy reports that Mike is having a cortisone shot in his shoulder. With Trey still out, I am at the top of the infield depth chart—at shortstop. Woody has moved up to third, and Chad is at second. On top of that, Billy has me leading off for the first time since Opening Day last season.

Right before game time the placid sky is hijacked by an intense cloudburst that sends us scurrying for cover to the oak stand behind the backstop. Just as quickly the rain desists, leaving the afternoon brightly sunny and deeply clammy. Concerned about his win-loss record, Billy reverses the usual pitching order and starts himself in the Skins game, leaving the more difficult Rif Raf for Dick. Billy also may want to take advantage of our pattern of scoring a lot in the first game and not much in the second. As leadoff man I single. I don't score, but we gradually build a lead. The Skins have holes at the bottom of their order, and Billy is blowing them away with his serviceable heater. Our makeshift infield is making all the plays, with Keith hoovering the occasional low relay. We cruise to an 8–1 win.

A win against Rif Raf in the nightcap would clinch us second place, which is mainly an issue of bragging rights. No matter what, we will face each other in round one of the playoffs. Still, this is not an unimportant game, and I am playing shortstop in it. Billy has, however, moved me back down in the batting order, to seven, my stay at the top as evanescent as the afternoon's downpour. Clooney, the emergency MD and left fielder, has been hot and is now slotted at leadoff. Dog, the substitute hurler for my Pamela's team, is pitching for them against Dick. If Dick is sorry for his outburst last week, he isn't saying. When they come up in the first, Billy is shouting from the bench, "pull hitter," and waving the outfield around to the left. I shade toward Woody at third. The batter drills Dick's heater, and I dive to my left and snag it at dirt level. Dick pumps his fist and says, "Big play!" In May or June I would have been on cloud nine with such praise. Now I ignore him, as I throw the ball around my infield and think, "Just pitch the ball, son."

Our bleachers start to fill up. There are several attractive women, in obvious need of softball guidance, but Chad is unaccountably ignoring them. And for the first time this season I espy the Machine's number-one fans. Last season, a Hasidic family followed the team. I thought at first that they were Dick's family, as they were such vocal supporters of him, though it seemed odd as his personal manner is so profane. But it turns out the family just happened into the park one day and became attached to the team and its most annoying play-

I SHOWED THE KID HOW TO
THROW OVERHAND

er. Billy doesn't even know their names. Our fan club includes the mother; a girl, the eldest, dressed in a long drab jumper; and two boys, each with earlocks, button-down shirts, dark trousers, and yarmulkes. I find it surprising that we have such fans. In each of my New York marathons, the Williamsburg streets were lined with Hasidim, but they just stared uncomprehendingly, the route becoming eerily silent.

The boys have brought their gloves today and are throwing baseballs around behind the backstop with Frank's kid, who is in his Little League uniform, only intermittently paying attention to our game. I go over between innings, where the older boy, modeling himself after Dick, is throwing underhanded to his sister, who has appropriated the younger boy's glove. I show him how to throw the ball overhand. As I am tossing it around with them, I think about how different they are from my teammates. I am teaching them something, but they don't act insulted or as though I'm crazy. They seem pleased to be learning. I see Frank, who is demonstrating a pitching grip to his son, and he seems more engaged in that than in the game, which continues behind us as our teammates rally. Frank is still playing in the league, and Superman is often here with his kids, playing in our game and then playing with them between games and innings. Maybe having twins is not going to be the end of my playing career—maybe it will be just a sabbatical before adding new coaching duties. The kid was grateful that I had straightened him out, but I probably should have thanked him.

The kid's hero is as usual pitching in and out of trouble. Twice we convert Dick's walks into double plays. Then we turn the power on, and he has another win. Dick calls his wife on his cell phone and tells her he's gone ten and oh for the season. He doesn't mention that pitching wins and losses are highly situational stats, that he has benefited from a ton of run support, and that Billy has given up fewer runs. Still, it's an impressive record for a pitcher almost voted off the team who can't throw the ball overhand across the infield. He has won a kind of redemption.

It reminds me of my own. I began this season as the team's second-string right fielder, batting last. I started out two for thirteen at the plate and seemed on my way to being barked off the team, but I worked my way back with my glove and gradually picked it up at the plate. I am ending the season batting .333, with my OBP up to .400—not great, but not bad either. And Billy has gained enough confidence in me to play me at shortstop and even, once, to let me lead off. This isn't how it's going to be when the playoffs begin, when all the guys will be here and Billy will place his best team on the field. But I've played well enough to be in the lineup somewhere. Also, I am no longer being yipped at, and only Tommy still calls me Poolie, and then only rarely. More and more I'm hearing "Steady Eddy."

Somewhere in Ken Burns's *Baseball*, a talking head doubtless declares that the baseball season is like a marathon. This is one of those grand analogies that glom themselves onto no sports other than baseball—it is also alleged to be like life, to be emblematic of the struggles of youth, to recapitulate primordial desires to return home, and blah blah. Once pronounced, these supposed truisms are repeated endlessly, as if in an echo chamber. But they wither under the slightest scrutiny, suggesting only that the opportunity to pontificate on baseball is like a drug that inhibits the firing of neurons in a middle-aged man's critical synapses. Take the biggest cliché of them all. I have news for Mario Cuomo, and when the time comes, he can pass it on to Bart Giamatti. Baseball has nothing to do with wanting to go home. Arguing that it does is the analytical equivalent of trying to yank a curve in the dirt for a tape-measure home run. Baseball is about scoring runs and stopping opponents from scoring runs. Going home is what happens when the game is over. Even in terms of figures of speech, this formulation has it backward. Being sent home is what players are trying their utmost to avoid.

I have played ball and run marathons, to return to the point, and the shortest baseball or softball season lasts at least a few months, while none of marathons I ran took much longer than a few hours. This summer I've been on Heckscher #1 in the nightcap of a Sunday softball doubleheader when, with the same amount of time having ticked off on a marathon clock, I would already have my shiny Mylar wrap cinched around me, a one-size-fits-all also-rans medal dangling from my neck, and be padding my way gingerly to the Seventy-Second Street C station. What's more, the pokiest runner in a marathon will elicit the cheers of tens of thousands of strangers, whereas even

141

professional-quality softball players draw a sleepy audience numbering in the tens, consisting of teammates, opponents, an occasional friend or relative, and a smattering of curiosity seekers whose numbers depend chiefly on the strength of the almighty euro.

If the would-be baseball sages would play within themselves once the cameras are on, they might realize that they've stumbled close to a decent analogy. The baseball season—or the softball season, for someone playing in several leagues—is like *training* for a marathon. Preparing for the twenty-six-mile race means starting months in advance. Although there is no set schedule as there is in baseball or softball, marathoners have to run five or six days a week whether they feel like it or not, and longer on weekends. Late-season marathoners will do the bulk of their training in the summer, it will end in the fall, as does the softball or baseball season, and the weather will often dictate whether and when it is possible to get the activity in. During training, as in the dog days of the softball season, most outings will be hot, often they will be boring, and progress will be incremental. Injury is always a threat. It is possible to get over the psychological humps in both by thinking about a big day in the fall, one that will not go well if too many of the smaller days in the summer are missed. On race day and the last game of the season no one knows exactly what will happen. But almost everyone will lose, and then they will go home.

# *Postseason*

**THE WEATHER CHANGES** only marginally, but the appearance of the post-season marks a dramatic shift in mental atmosphere. Despite the continuing high heat and humidity, games take a sharp turn for the urgent. The playoffs are what matters, what the entire season points to. Winning, always important, is all in the postseason. Everyone wants it, especially the elite players, who dodge dog-day games but clear their schedules come playoff time. Managers impart a deep sense of gravity to their players, demanding sacrifices and reaffirmations of commitment. With the heightened desire to win and the increased attendance, both managers and players face dilemmas.

During the regular season managers will often bat beyond the standard ten in order to get more players into the game, and they may allow the pitcher to hit. During the playoffs such practices will be seen as unaffordable extravagances. To maximize their chances of winning in the postseason, managers tend to tighten their batting orders and play only their best players. Marginal players who saw considerable action during the season, especially in dog-day contests, may see less now. Choosing the team's best lineup is a process fraught with trouble, as managers will be second-guessed by their players, especially by those being sat down but also by starters, who may favor a different deployment or have friends on the bench.

In the playoffs everyone who can show up does show up, but not everyone who shows up can play. It can be a rude awakening for players who see themselves as starters and central to the team suddenly to be transmuted into fans. It is, of course, much less fun to watch than to play. But being benched is also threatening. Unlike in professional ball, softball players can play more than one position, and there are no platoons. Righties bat against righties, lefties against lefties. There is no need for a rotation of starting pitchers. There is no major role for relief pitchers or pinch hitters. Players who are sitting cannot tell themselves that they are being saved for some special situation. They are being judged as not good enough to be relied on when it counts.

Hurt feelings and hot tempers provoked by lack of playing time are greatly magnified during the postseason. By August most players have paid their
league fees, which is not the case in April. More important, players who have
played most of the regular season feel as though they've earned a right to
continue playing. Often they feel as though they have established squatters'
rights to a specific position and a spot in the batting order. Those exiled from
the playoff lineup feel as angry and humiliated as if they'd been evicted, their
belongings scattered on the street for all to see.

Managers have different ways of making playoff decisions. One solution is
to play everyone who played most of the time. But managers who don't play
their ten best risk alienating the better players, who want to win and usually
have distinct ideas of who belongs in the playoff lineup. A more plausible
tactic is to establish a set lineup by midseason and stick to it during the playoffs. Doing so will avoid the worst of the hard feelings and confrontations
at playoff time. This strategy is not foolproof, however; during the regular
season not everyone will show to every game. A related strategy is to cull the
players during the regular season, signaling to marginal players that they
are not in the manager's plans, in the hope that by the end of the season they
will have dropped away. In doing this, though, one runs the risk of ending up
short of players come playoff time. Yet another approach is to have a big roster and try to get everyone on it to show up to postseason games. This gives
the manager the greatest degree of freedom to play the best players, or the
hottest ones. But it maximizes hard feelings.

Players on the outside looking in come playoff time have the economist
Albert O. Hirschman's standard strategies of exit and voice. For a regular-
season starter benched at playoff time, voice, also known as protest or bitch-
ing, is almost a given. A player cannot jump to another team at this late date,
and a complaint directed at the manager often can produce additional playing time. A manager uncertain about who the better player is for a specific
position will tend to give the nod to the noisemaker. Sometimes that happens because the arguments are compelling—the manager might even con-
sult the scorebook—but more often just to shut off the sound. A player riding the bench may also speak out to his friends among his teammates, who
then join in lobbying the manager. A star can often successfully intervene
for a friend on the bubble. Even when it doesn't result in playing time, protest helps players affirm their sense of themselves as players, as a few teammates will see the justice of their case.

A failed protest will often be followed by the only sorts of exit possible.
The benched starter will storm off in a huff, or sulk and then stay home for

the next game. Most players consider it better to be absent than to be shelved. Sitting on the sidelines after having started is for them a little like having your soothing white-noise machine suddenly stop playing crickets chirping and start screaming, "You stink! You're a loser!" Even if you can't afford a new one, you are better off pitching the old one. The third way to deal with postseason bench time is simply to wait for a chance. Playoffs are often long enough that a starter will get hurt or mess up. This is the least likely response, however, because almost all players left out believe that there is someone in the lineup who is less deserving than them. And it is not just a matter of bolstering their individual identities. Players usually see the team's chances of winning as linked to their own fate, so to bench them is also to threaten the team. Unfortunately, there is no consensus on the meaning of "team."

Next week is the first week of the postseason. I am going to be facing the problem from both sides. As manager I plan to put the best team out there. We don't have as many players as some teams, so I don't have as many options, either to improve the team or to piss off teammates. But there are some of each. As a player, I will be starting for all of my teams. If I'm going to be doing any complaining, it will be about where I'm playing or batting. I feel as though I have the worst of all possible empathetic worlds. I will understand why players are complaining to me and will wonder if they are right. But I am not going to complain much myself, even if I deserve more or higher quality playing time, because I sympathize with the manager. I fear that I am going to be like the New Yorker who rents a car but identifies with the pedestrians so much that he never gets through the intersection.

The prospects of the teams vary greatly. On Mondays, the divisional playoffs are double elimination. We Pamela's Foxes won the PM division and have proved that we are significantly better than Gotham and Production, but not the second-place Friars Club. Most likely we will face the Friars Club in a best of three to see who represents the PM division for the Heckscher Cup. I think we have half a chance to beat them but not much more than that, and there is always some chance that we will get knocked off by one of the other teams. So call it a 40 percent chance for the Foxes to win the division playoffs. The PM divisional winner then squares off against the AM champs, most likely Irving Plaza, in a best of three. I think we would be an even bet to beat them, which makes it a 20 percent chance we'll win it all.

I like the odds better in the East Village. Billy and Miles's d.b.a. squad is two-time defending champion, and we are the favorite again. Also in our favor is that all the series are best of three. But this year there are a few greatly improved teams, including Josie's, Welcome to the Johnsons, and Cedar

Tavern, as well as East Division power Two Boots. And winning means a long struggle, three consecutive series. We are highly likely to survive in the less difficult West Division, though Cedar could possibly upend us. If we win our divisional playoffs, I think we would be slight favorites to beat Josie's, the Johnsons, or Two Boots. So call it about an 80 percent chance of winning the division and maybe 45 percent of winning it all.

The other coed league, the high-anxiety Broadway Show League, is a far more difficult bet. Because of all the rainouts, the playoffs had to be shoe-horned into fewer days, so this year's tournament is single elimination. This should be to our advantage, since we are underdogs and would have to win only four games. We have the Actors Federal Credit Union in the first round, a team we trounced just last week. After that, we will almost certainly bump up against the undefeated, many-time defending champions Madison Square Garden—a team of stagehands that constitute the Yankees of the Show League. Our chances of beating them are probably one out of three, maybe higher given Chad's roster upgrades and the possibility that they may underestimate us. They pounded us in the early season before Chad revamped the team. If we get past MSG, we probably would face Nederlander's in the three-thirty "organization" division finals, a game I would rate as a toss-up. Then whoever wins the division title will crush the winner of the patsy "show" division. So, it's about a 17 percent chance for Thespian Aid to bring home the gold, or whatever it is MSG has been getting.

As for Billy's Sunday Machine team, it has as good a chance as any of the four teams in the Lower Manhattan Softball League to win it all. I think we have a sixty-forty chance to get past Rif Raf in round one, and if we do, an even chance to knock off the defending champion Hitmen. That gives us about a 30 percent chance to win. Each of the series is best of five. In baseball they say that anything can happen in a series this short, given the large number of pitchers, but in softball five games is usually plenty for the better team to establish dominance. The Machine is my only team for which I have a chance of being benched for the playoffs.

My chance of winning at least one championship is about three out of four, but which one—or ones! Maybe we will defy the odds and lose them all.

## *Twin Killing*

It seems unfair. The only advantages that Pamela's PM regular-season championship gives us in the playoffs are that in game one we get to be the home team, choose the field, and face the fourth-place team, Production. My morning anxiety is heightened by the fact that Francesca and I have a pregame appointment with her obstetrician on East Sixtieth Street. It's Francesca's twelfth week, and we hope and expect that the sonogram results will confirm the two heartbeats found earlier. This will be my first look at the babies. It is also my first chance to meet the OB. She is Indian, tiny with dark long hair, big glasses, and an intense gaze, very impressive in a nerdy way. When discussing risks she gives odds, as for the risk of losing a fetus during amniocentesis (one in two hundred)—a process that is four weeks away for us. The obstetrician says that if all goes well, as she expects, Francesca will deliver her twins in mid-January. The OB should be a manager. Listening to her makes me confident that everything will work out fine. By one-thirty, however, Francesca is still at the back of the sonogram line. Since we are expecting good news, and since she freaks me out every time she comes to the park, we agree that she will go straight home.

I have to run from East Sixtieth Street to make it in time for the game. On the way over I am wondering why a slang term for my favorite play in softball—the double play—is "twin killing." It seems so morbid and offensive and also impossible that there would be any quirkily redeeming etymology. In my pregame e-mail message to the Foxes I had urged the team to be there at one-fifteen to practice for the playoff game, but when I get to Heckscher it's almost game time. "One-fifteen, huh?" Q says, looking at his wrist, as I scramble into uniform. I realize that I'm not going to get to stretch and that I have a sunburn on my stomach and lower back pain. Sometimes I warm up before games without my jersey, to keep it dry, and I'm wondering if I took in too many rays over the weekend. Our air conditioner broke down too, and I may have strained my back trying to install the new one.

We are with Klem on field #4. The call was Billy's. The infield on #4 is true, and since we are the better fielding team, we don't want bad hops to influence the game. More important, Billy can exploit Klem's expansive strike zone better than Production's pitcher, whose control and stuff aren't in the same league. It rained yesterday evening, and the field is mucky but playable.

Now there is a dishwater sky threatening to drain at any time. Klem wants to get things moving.

My late arrival seems to have placed the Foxes on edge, and various team-mates are asking me about the lineup. There is bad news. Our slugger Trey is out of commission. His season of injuries is culminating in abdominal surgery, and he won't be available unless we are still playing in September. The catcher Roger is out for a third straight week working on his new home. He asked if it was OK to skip the game, and I told him it was. And Penny has not yet arrived from an editing job he has scared up, leaving us with eleven. One of them is the veteran pitcher Dog, who I am planning to start on the bench. I have to throw away my morning's handiwork and improvise. I end up with this: Eddy ss; Cookie 2b; Krishy rcf; Artie 3b; Billy p; Bobby rf; Mule c; Swanny lcf; Papi 1b; Q lf.

We take the field and start playing, erratically and nervously, as if we were the fourth-place team. Their leadoff batter rolls one on the damp infield toward third. Big Artie barehands it, as if it were a bunt. But he rushes needlessly. The batter's box is so muddy that the runner's feet make a sucking sound on his way out of it. Artie's throw is off-line, and Papi can't save it. Billy pops up number two, but number three bingos and sends home the run. The cleanup batter bounds a ball to Artie's left. He is close enough to make the play, especially with the slow track, but doesn't try, thinking, apparently, that I am going to make it. But I am shaded up the middle for the double play, and it's a seeing-eye-dog base hit. Billy is looking at Artie, more confused than angry, but says nothing and then grooves number five, whose liner to left scores their second run. A wild throw by Q advances runners to second and third, and it's Katy bar the door. But Billy strikes out the next two, the last one on a pitch a foot outside. The batter protests vehemently, but Klem says it "caught the corner," and we have avoided being blown out before we can bat.

I lead off for us and run the count full. The payoff pitch misses low, and I toss away the bat and head to first. Klem, of course, rings me up. I suppose I should've been ready for it, given the threatening weather, Klem's reputation, and the likelihood of a makeup call. But Billy's scouting report was that Klem was widening the strike zone in and out, not up and down. I protest, and Klem makes a looping gesture with his hand. He is indicating that the ball was at the knees when it went over the plate and then dropped off the table like Joe Morgan's motherfucking curve ball. With two outs, Krishy is sitting on the cripple—what is it with these baseball terms?—and launches one that would have tied the game had I been on base.

In the second, I do my part to settle things down by throwing two guys out. As we come up to bat, Penny appears. About four teammates simultaneously insist that I insert him at third base. It's as if we were already panicking. With two outs Mule doubles, and Bobby runs and scores for him on Swanny's single, tying the game. A slow drizzle has begun when their leadoff man singles in the fourth. For the next guy I am shading up the middle, hoping to turn two. I get just what I want—a hard grounder to Billy's left heading between me and second base. I'm ready to step on the bag and fire to first when the ball scoots under my glove. Everyone is safe. The drizzle graduates to rain. Teddy has waved the Friars Club and Gotham off field #2, but we play on. I cannot keep my glasses clear, and I am not sure if the steam is from my breath or the top of my head for having blown such a big play. The next batter hits one toward Penny, now at third, who knocks down the ball and has the presence of mind to tag the runner. Now it's really coming down. But Klem is determined to finish the half inning. The batter drills one to my right that splashes down hard a few feet in front of me. I try to stay in front of it, and it catches my wrist but ricochets away, and before I can recover it the bases are loaded. It's now coming down too hard even for Klem, and he waves us off the field.

I am every sort of upset. I can't believe that I've blown the double play and placed the team in such a desperate situation. I can't believe that Klem let the last two batters hit in the downpour. I also can't believe that I blew my chance at fielding redemption. My wrist is stinging too, balancing my lower-body aches. As the team gathers under the trees behind the backstop to wait it out, there is nothing I can do but listen to my teammates tell me to shake it off. It's more difficult than usual. Normally, after a bad play, the relentless advance of the game preempts foul moods and forces the mind toward the future. Now I have time to dwell on the miscues, and heaven knows how many runs they are going to score.

Once the rain stalls, Billy saws off the next batter and gets out of the inning with only one run across. But down 3–2, we can't do much. It's difficult to hit the wet ball far, their outfield is playing very shallow, and Klem's strike zone is widening as the game progresses. As we prepare for our last licks, I can't believe that my error is about to cost us a playoff game and maybe force an early exit from the tournament. If we lose we will most likely meet the Friars Club next week, facing elimination. I'm not projecting my usual calm and irreverent presence. I don't call any facetious play or single out any potential hero. I go to coach first base.

As the rain returns, it starts to happen. Billy and Little Bobby reach on grounders in the muck. Up steps Mule, a right-handed hitter who likes to hit to the opposite side. I tell Bobby the usual things first-base coaches tell runners in these situations—get a good jump, run on a grounder, go halfway on a fly, and make sure to let the line drive go through. Bobby gets a good jump and Mule lines the first pitch—right at the first baseman. I yell, "Back!" almost as soon as he swings. If this were a bad movie, the play would happen in slow motion, Bobby and I with agonized looks on our faces, and me mouthing "Nooooooo" in a too-deep voice as he strains back to the bag as if underwater. But it all happens very quickly as—bang, bang—Mule then Bobby are put out. We are down to the last out.

Swanny steps to the plate and, with the rain splashing down like pellets in a puddle by the plate, lifts a can o' corn to right center. But with the drawn-in outfield and the rain pelting down, the ball gets past them. Billy slogs home, Swanny hydroplanes into third, and the game is tied! Water is billowing in sheets as Papi steps in. The waterlogged shoe is on the other foot, and Klem is going to make Production play it out. Swanny is screaming from third base that it only takes one and hurts more with two. The quacking Swanny is almost literally on a pond. Papi lashes the first pitch over the infield, the left fielder isn't close enough to warrant a dive, and we have survived game one. We slap hands in fast motion, gather our stuff, and run. Swanny is so happy—and already so wet—that he doesn't mind hauling the bases over to the bins. The rest of us seek refuge in the tunnel behind the field. It's almost as if we can't absorb what's happened. In the underpass, it couldn't be more miserable—dank and smelly, the rain puddling at our feet. That is, unless you happen to be one of the Production guys, who are all here too, huddled in shock.

Which gives me time to worry about Francesca and the ultrasound. I wonder if some karmic trick is being played on me. So many times I have run off a string of hits in softball only to check my office mailbox and find that an article submission or grant proposal had been rejected. This game has worked out too well. The ultrasound results were expected to be positive, but we also were expecting to win easily today. I've worked myself into such a lather that I slosh right into the apartment, where Francesca is on the telephone. She looks at me, upset and perplexed, and I fear the worst. But the only thing wrong is that the living room needs to be mopped.

## *Facing Elimination*

This morning I was having a happy dream. I was a boy riding my Schwinn Sting-Ray around the subdivision with some neighborhood kids, as if we were rounding up other kids for a game. I felt the sunshine, and there was a quality of light and a feeling of eager anticipation stretching out in front of me like a lifetime. But the warmth morphed into the throbbing pain of a heat rash on my thigh. Jolted awake, I started thinking about today's Pamela's playoff game. We know where we are playing, Klem's World, our new home field. We know when we are playing, two o'clock. We just don't know whom we are playing. The Friars Club is down 5–2 against Gotham in the fourth, with the bases loaded and no one out when their game resumes at one. We get the loser, a desperate opponent facing elimination.

I get the Foxes to agree to show up early again, and today I'm on time too. On #4, where we will be playing, there is a battle to the death between AFTRA and McAleer's. The Irving Plaza guys are hanging out, watching their potential opponents beat each other up. We head over to field #6 to get in batting and fielding practice, while monitoring the Friars/Gotham game. For all my bizarre ailments, I'm loosening up in the sticky atmosphere. AFTRA wins, and Klem waves us over. The Friars Club is down by one, but has the bases loaded and one out with the game on the line and steady slugger Juan at the plate. He drills one up the middle, but the shortstop snags it, steps on second, and fires across for the double play. The dejected Friars Club is coming our way. They are not the only ones unhappy. "Now I have to deal with Zeus," Klem says.

Late as it is, Penny is still not here. I make some last-minute adjustments. With one out and one on, Zeus starts a string of singles, and his team goes up by two before we get to bat. Zeus has picked Burnsides, with his erratic heat, as his starter. He is apparently afraid that our guys will launch balls into the maple trees in left on Bro, the elfin-elephant control pitcher who stymied us in the final regular season game. I single, but Krishy goes out. Mule singles, but Roger goes out. Then it happens. Papi bloops one to right, and I score. The next five Foxes lash out more emphatic hits. Penny shows up, and I add him as number eleven. Zeus pulls Burnsides in favor of Bro, who retires Penny, but six runs are across. The Friars Club is finished. The next six innings just make it official.

This quick turnabout in their fortunes—from playoff favorites to playoff fodder—is a lot to take in one afternoon. Zeus is sitting on the third-base bleachers by himself. The backbiting on their side is now out in the open. Most of their team lingers, and a knot of their long-standing players comes over to discuss the game with us. One player openly questions why Bro, who has had success against us, didn't start. Another is unhappy about Zeus's unusual substitution patterns. He motions to Zeus and says, "You can have him back—he's nothing but trouble." For a recreational league, the words are pretty brutal.

Manny is distraught. He pulls himself together to sell some drinks, transporting beers to the first-base side, where our guys are celebrating. Only Jorgy and Juan remain with Zeus on the other side, but they aren't talking to

MANNY STILL DID SOME SELLING

him either. I'd go over and offer to buy him a beer, but he seems in a foul mood and his body language seems to be saying "leave me alone." He likes to buy a beer for the losing manager sometimes, but I think it is less about softening the loss than rubbing it in. I'm mainly glad that Zeus's fate isn't mine. At least not yet.

## Strike Zone

Since the tumbling of the Berlin Wall, in sociology, as elsewhere, Marx has been on the outs. Now I'm starting to doubt his dictum that when history repeats itself, the first time is as tragedy, the second as farce. Yesterday my dreams were preempted again, an intense, stinging sensation having advanced from the bug bite just above my knee, past the heat rash on my thigh, and all the way up to my groin. Somehow the back strain and nonred sunburn on half of my stomach had also intensified. All week I have been slathering on antibiotic cream like cream cheese, and it hasn't helped at all. I have also been swallowing Advil like Pez, which has helped. To counteract the resulting stomach trouble, I've been chomping Tums like Necco Wafers, which, curiously, they resemble in their chalky texture and nebulous flavors. With the location of the latest lesions I feared that maybe I had contracted genital herpes back in the swinging eighties, and it chose playoff time to come out of dormancy.

The pain became so excruciating that I sought out my GP, which I do so seldom that I had to call the number on the US Healthcare card to find out her office's location. In the last five years the only doctors I've seen are therapists, fertility specialists, the OB, and my learned PhD colleagues. My GP quickly diagnosed my various pains and lesions not as separate problems but as parts of a syndrome. I didn't have sunburn, back strain, bug bites, heat rash, or genital herpes. But I did have herpes—herpes zoster, better known as shingles, a viral echo of chicken pox. No one knows for sure what sets it off, but the main suspect is stress. Ten days into the playoffs, and already one of my major organs has cracked.

The first time you experience chicken pox it is a farcical itching; the second time it is burning, with tragic overtones. Since I was so late in seeking help, I face the possibility of what the GP called "postherpetic neuralgia." Left untreated, shingles can leave intense pain in its wake long after the lesions are gone, potentially endlessly. Having inadvertently rolled the dice for a chance at a lifetime's worth of searing agony is scary enough, but for me it almost feels worse to have contracted something so closely associated with old age. George's father on *Seinfeld* gets shingles, not someone playing ball five times a week. As an ailment, too, it seems particularly taunting to a softball player. With its scorched-earth policy toward my stomach and painful lesion outposts occupying territory down to my knee, shingles have attacked me in my strike zone.

To make things worse I've become a potential disease-monger. I can't give anyone shingles, but I can transmit chicken pox, and if I infect Francesca that could damage the fetuses. We spent all afternoon yesterday trying to figure out whether she has already had chicken pox or an immunization against it. Her mother has passed away, and her father couldn't remember, so she ransacked the apartment in a fruitless search for her blue book of vaccinations. She's pretty sure that she's had chicken pox. In case she hadn't, doctor's orders were that I wear long pants, sleep separately, and otherwise avoid contact with her. She took a blood test, but the results won't be back until Saturday, at which point I will no longer be contagious. And since I've had shingles for more than a week, we've been wondering if any of these tardy precautionary measures could possibly help. We both remember last week when I had her touch what I had alertly diagnosed as a mosquito bite.

Supplemented by new antiviral drugs, good old calamine lotion, ibuprofen, a complete baseball outfit, unorthodox conceptual worries, and a disturbing image of myself as an old-timer, I head to today's big Broadway Show League playoff game. Our Thespian Aid squad, having crushed the Actors Federal Credit Union as expected in round one, takes on the undefeated defending champions, Madison Square Garden. I run into our manager, Chad, on the path to the field and he has problems of his own. Our diehard gals are on hand, but he's having boy trouble. Tommy cannot escape from his federal parole office in Brooklyn, and the suddenly in-demand Penny is videotaping an interview. He will get here as soon as he can, but he's going to be late. Manny appears, but that still leaves us one man short. The other Thespian Aid men got the message that they weren't likely to see playoff action.

Teddy the umpire calls us over to field #5, where MSG will be hosting us this afternoon, so we will be starting the biggest game of the year with seven men and three women. Needless to say, MSG has a full complement of men. Before the game we stall. The MSG shortstop is trying to get Robin's phone number, but Teddy waves them onto the field. We have a potent front end of the batting order that has been productive lately. Our game plan is to score early and make them panic, as they are almost never behind. Then it would be a matter of holding the fort until Penny arrives.

The MSG pitcher has good control, uses the full twelve feet of arc, and takes a disconcerting step away from the rubber after he releases the ball. The game starts out according to plan, as Chad breaks ground for his eternal resting place with a liner that kicks up the dirt between the first and second basemen and shoots into right. I come up looking to help him with the task. My plan is to take a strike and then go after the first one I can drive to right. The second pitch is a little inside and Teddy calls it a strike. I must be more nervous than I think, because instead of just sighing or shaking my head, I use my bat to indicate the indentation in the dirt where the ball landed, inside. Teddy is rightly annoyed by my display. "I don't want any complaints about balls and strikes today," he says. "Now get in there and hit," he adds, his tone suggesting that his strike zone has just expanded and I had better be swinging. The next one is low, but I step forward to greet it and lace it smartly toward Chadsville between the second and first basemen. We are in business. But we get only one as Zeus pops up to shortstop, and shortstop Mike hits a long one that's chased down. In their end, the big, lefty first baseman drives one into the third-base bleachers on field #4 and scores before Chad can find the ball.

In the second Manny leads off with a single, takes a big turn, and is gunned down by the right-center fielder before he can get back to the bag. With two outs Billy works a double walk. We are looking around hopefully for Penny to come trotting down the embankment, as he could pinch-hit here, but there's still no sign of him, and Tiny grounds out to end the inning. Fortunately, MSG is still swinging for the fences in the second, and fortunately, aside from the bleachers on distant field #4, there is nothing approaching a fence at Heckscher. One of their sluggers breaks through with a long triple and then scores on an inadvertent sacrifice fly that I chase down in deep left as another guy also tries to homer. In the third, Chad and I lead off with hits again. Chad scores, but Zeus and Mike strand me again.

In the third, the MSG players take a different approach. They are punching the ball, aiming at Tiny at second base, and taking advantage of the deep positioning of the outfielders. Two guys hit balls in front of Chad in right; on the second one he rolls his ankle. A double-play ball cuts right through Tiny. As the inning progresses, our game is generating an enormous fan base. Large numbers of people are crossing the footpath, and many stay to witness the onslaught. I know the euro is up, but this seems ridiculous. When the inning finally ends, MSG is up 9–2.

The bottom of our order is going down meekly in the fourth when Penny comes charging through the crowd, fresh from a taxi, in uniform and ready to go. He replaces Tiny, and our defense holds them. We have the top of the order up in the fifth, but they deploy an extra infielder against Chad and me, and we do nothing. In the sixth, Mike goes deep to left over their drawn-in outfield and chases Zeus around the bases. In the seventh, we are still down, 9–4. Tiny leads off and reaches base, bringing it to the top of the order. It's our last chance. Chad drives one up the right side, but with their new five-man infield, they knock it down and get the force-out. I am shooting to drill one over the first baseman and down the right-field line, where there's now plenty of open real estate and the foul territory is lined with spectators. I hit it hard, but right at the first baseman. A single later, Zeus pops up to short to end the game. But the ball tips off the shortstop's glove, another run is in, Zeus reaches second, and it's 9–6. Having been burned last time, MSG is now playing Mike very deep. He can't tie the game with a homer but tries for one anyway, and his long drive is chased down by the left-center fielder.

When a softball season ends in defeat what sweeps over you first is a feeling of confusion and disbelief. It's hard to absorb the fact that it's over, hard

PENNY ARRIVED READY TO GO

to let go. Most players have running in their heads a story of redemption, or possibly total domination, and when the game turns tragic they are at a loss. Our disorientation expands to bewilderment upon learning that some time during MSG's big third inning the power went out over much of the Midwest and the Eastern Seaboard—the biggest blackout in U.S. history! Our sense of loss is made more surreal by the hundred-odd spectators in nice clothing, dressed as if for a funeral, and the hundreds more teeming across the park in a commuter processional. Having been sheltered from reality by our little softball world, we quickly sort out how to respond. Zeus and Mike are staying to play another playoff game in a different league. But Mike is worried about his dog, which he had locked in his apartment with the windows closed and the air conditioning on. He gives Billy some numbers to call.

Billy, Chad, and I head to Columbus Circle, where we would normally be catching the subway but won't today because there's no juice to power the trains. Once there, Billy goes west, as Chad and I head down Seventh Avenue. There are thousands of people, mainly flowing north, like refugees but better dressed. They are marooning autos like a protest demonstration that has escaped police control. As Chad and I press against the human tide, we encounter one and then another guy reading ominously from the Book of Rev-

A GUY WAS READING FROM THE BOOK OF REVELATION

elation. We discuss what might have been. Chad is talking about mistakes we made in their big inning. We both wish we had come through with hits in the seventh.

We limp to Times Square. Overhead in the twilight there is nothing but the blank stares of giant video screens and tongue-tied news zippers. It is difficult for me not to think of September 11, when I swam against the stream of downtown workers trekking up Sixth Avenue through the Village away from the smoke and debris in a useless bid to help. Today everyone seems more purposeful, as if to say, this is a relatively minor annoyance. But I am angry with Chad about something we don't talk about. I've been playing on this team just for this game, and we had no chance to win it because Chad cut the margin too thin. He scared off too many players during the regular season, and there weren't enough available for the big game. I can't figure out why he's projecting such a well-what-can-you-do? attitude. Then he confides that he can't wait to get home to his girlfriend! Was he having an all-day, first-blush-of-love sex-fest when he should have been on the horn making sure he had a full team for the biggest game of the season? He certainly doesn't seem to mind much that we lost. Before I can ask, he peels off to the west.

With no cars on the street during rush hour, I head right down Broadway. Now that the adrenalin and ibuprofen have worn off, my strike zone is ablaze. I feel as though more than a season has passed, as I face a dark and uncom-

fortable evening. It is going to be too hot to sleep, and I will have to choose between pain and acid reflux. Francesca and I will soon return to our discussion of the possibility that she is going to get chicken pox and thus of whether my being so out of touch with my body and GP will mean that our babies may be deformed. We both think it's highly unlikely, but it's something to think about, and we have until Saturday. Meanwhile, her computer will be on the blink. And I will be wondering if this pain is here to stay.

[ SUNDAY, AUGUST 17, HECKSCHER #1 ]

## *Annual Meeting*

It was a relief to learn that Francesca doesn't have chicken pox, and with that news she flew to Atlanta for the annual meeting of the American Sociological Association. I'm scheduled to give a paper there myself today. Until I sat myself down voluntarily a couple of years ago I had compiled a Ripken-esque streak of thirteen consecutive years of giving papers at ASA meetings.

Academics can finish writing projects during the summer, as teaching and committee responsibilities recede, or go on extensive vacations. I haven't done either. I was hoping to complete my book on the Townsend Plan—an old-age pension organization of the Depression era—and Social Security. It's been a long time coming. I started studying the Townsendites as a young man and now find myself fifty months away from my induction into AARP. I have one chapter remaining, but I haven't figured out how I want to conclude it—as tragedy, comedy, or a lost cause? I also thought I would be pressing ahead with a larger project on the consequences of the U.S. old-age pension movement. But the National Science Foundation sociology panel decided against funding my proposal and awarded it the consolation prize of being one of the select few rejected proposals for which the panelists encouraged revisions. It's probably a kiss-off, but the project and a lot of money are at stake, so my collaborator Neal, a PhD candidate, and I revised the NSF proposal and wrote a draft of the paper unfunded. Otherwise, my summer's work has consisted of playing in softball games and taking notes about them.

I like going to the sociology meeting. It's like a free vacation. I get to have dinner with friends from graduate school. Famous scholars buttonhole me in the hallway seeking my opinions. My talks draw meager but engaged audiences. But the meeting, unfortunately, always takes place during the Central Park softball playoffs. While I was away in Chicago last year running the business meeting of the Political Sociology section, the Sunday Machine team—then called the Nuclear Pencils—was being dismissed by Rif Raf in two straight. With my bad hamstring and poor play I wasn't in Billy's plans. This year I don't really need to go the meeting. My paper is coauthored with Neal, and he is willing, even eager, to take one for the team.

As far as softball goes, I'm in a much different situation. I am starting at third base for the Machine, at least until Trey returns. Also, I'm not injured the way I was last year. My hamstring is much better, and the pain from the shingles may be here for good but can be controlled in the short run with Advil. And of course this time I've told no one. Today we Machinists again have two playoff games against Rif Raf, which is becoming something of an annual meeting in itself.

The view of most managers is that showing up to playoff games is a player's chief responsibility in life. The only acceptable reasons for absence are injuries, funerals, work that absolutely can't be got out of, or the manager's instructions not to bother to show up. Long-scheduled family vacations are in a gray area. Billy is trying to arrest the decline of a team that won the championship just three years ago. In the finals two years ago his team went the full five games against Rif Raf before succumbing. Last year, the team lost in round one to Rif Raf, which then lost to the Hitmen.

Billy's e-mails establish a hard line in dealing with the playoff problem. He's treating us as if we were a professional ball team, demanding that we all show up but telling us that for the good of the team some of us might not play all the time, or at all. He is going to devise a lineup that gives us the best chance to win, batting only the minimum ten. Billy is planning not to bat himself in the games he pitches. For some time, he has been flying back and forth across the country to visit his ailing mother, but he's still been making the games. So he doesn't think there is room for us to complain or offer excuses for missing a game. Billy is talking more and more about folding the league after the season. It has become too much trouble. He has had to deal with temper tantrums, sweet-talk some umpires out of bolting and replace those who have quit, and negotiate permit extensions from Parks and Recreation, which has raised fees and restricted access. So for these playoffs, there is more than the usual sense of do or die.

But unlike last year there is no way any team can be sent home for good today. Our doubleheader kicks off a best-of-five series. Commissioner Billy changed the format with the idea that the longer the series the more likely that the best team will win, and with the hope that he is managing the best team. The plan is to finish the series next Sunday, with three games if necessary. Despite Billy's hard line on attendance, a couple of guys are not here today, probably having been notified that they would not be starting. We have fourteen. For game one, Billy's playoff batting order is Clooney lcf; Krishy rcf; Mike ss; Walker dh; Keith 1b; Tommy rf; Matt lf; Eddy 3b: Superman c; Woody 2b. Since I'm not batting at the very bottom and am playing third base, which is considered more important than second base and catcher, Billy would have to add three good players to bump me from the starting lineup. The somehow undefeated Dick gets the honor of pitching the first game, while Billy has scheduled himself for the nightcap. This afternoon, MikeHargrove is the odd man out. He has been occupying Billy's doghouse for having had the temerity to skip games in favor of his honeymoon. For the other side, Zeus is rallying what definitely seem to be his troops.

In the playoffs, the Sunday games have an even more intense feel than the already intense regular season games. The games are much tighter, and every defensive advantage—now that the teams all know one another's tendencies—is being exploited. Probably the batters are tenser, and the umpires call more strikes and outs. We take the field and Dick sets them down, but it quickly becomes clear that he is not going to get his usual massive run support, as we also go down easily in the first. It remains scoreless until the bottom of the third, when the top of our order strings together four singles to give us a 2–0 lead. Now the sky goes from sunny to surreal. A wall of dark haze forms to the west behind the outfield—Nature's way, as in blacking out the center-field bleachers in Wrigley Field and Yankee Stadium, of providing a good hitting backdrop. We take advantage and a three-run lead into the seventh.

For Dick there's no gift horse too big to look in the mouth. I track down a pop-up in the extensive foul territory behind third, but Dick walks the next two guys to bring the tying run to the plate. Not getting all of the calls he believes he deserves, he is stamping circles around the rubber. I try to ignore him and stay focused in case he throws a strike. Something bigger is brewing above. The sky is now completely colored in and drizzling has commenced. Dick pulls himself together and induces a couple of fly balls, and we take game one. It is a good thing too, because now the heavens open, and we duck beneath the oaks behind the backstop. The rain pellets start penetrating the leaf cover, and several of us dash past the Carousel to an underpass. There we find ourselves stranded with teams of tourists, plus some Hare Krishnas who are beating a drum and chanting rhythmically to a droning theme that sounds a little like George Harrison singing "This Land Is Your Land."

I realize that right now is when I should have been presenting a paper to my sociology colleagues from around the country. As I drip, watching the tourists photograph the Krishnas—those shots'll wow 'em back in the Quad Cities—my thoughts turns to what I'll write in my electronic softball journal when I get home. I've gone completely native. I couldn't be in any greater captivity if I were in a cage in the nearby Central Park Zoo.

## MONDAY, AUGUST 18, HECKSCHER #4

### *All Over*

It is just as well that we played only the one game Sunday. Today is an even bigger day—a doubleheader for the PM division playoff championship in the Performing Arts League. With two wins my Pamela's Foxes can advance to play the AM winner for the whole ball of wax—the Heckscher Cup. It's like going to the World Series. Or, to look at it another way, today is the first day this summer when the dream season of the Foxes could come to an end. Two losses and it's all over. This morning it dawns on me that despite the fact that we have won fourteen games and lost only three—and despite the fact that as the Sharkeys the team never even played .500 ball—if we don't win this series, we may be perceived as having gone backward. After all, last year, on the strength of Amanda's arm, a late-season acquisition by Zeus, we advanced to the playoff finals. Worse, if we lose, I will probably be held responsible for having lost the ground.

I waste the morning mulling over lineup decisions, although there aren't many to make. Billy is not going to bat. We will lose a little bit offensively, but I want him to concentrate on his pitching, and he may tire pitching two games in the humidity. Everyone except the injured Trey is going to be here, and I don't want to have anyone but Dog, our ace in the hole, in reserve. I am starting Artie at first, as he has proved more reliable there than Papi, who is going to be the extra player. He can sub for the novice Roger at catcher late in the game if the situation calls for it. Billy now prefers Mule to catch, but squatting wears Mule out, and he said yesterday that he would rather catch the second game if he were needed.

When I get to the park, a few of our guys are there, watching Irving Plaza and AFTRA playing extra innings on Heckscher #4. The game is tied in the bottom of the eighth, when Irving Plaza loads the bases with two outs. A hard grounder to first is played Bill Buckner–style, and just like that Irving Plaza is the AM champ and will get a chance to defend the Heckscher Cup. Some of the AFTRA players console their first baseman. Most seem inconsolable themselves.

Cookie and I huddle with Klem and the Gotham managers before the game. We want to stay on #4, Klem's World, despite the left-field obstacles, mainly because we don't want to play on field #2, with its dangerous infield. I'm also wary of moving from the field that we won on. The umpires aren't an issue. Since only two teams remain, Klem will be sharing his World with Teddy, each taking a game behind the plate. Umpires are friendlier to managers of winning teams. Lately Klem has been deferring to me, partly because we are the favorites and partly because I have been choosing his field for our top-seeded games. He lobbies me for an early starting time for next week's championship games. "Can you start at noon next week? You guys are probably gonna sweep today," he says. I put him off; his talk about the next round seems way premature and bad karma, especially as Billy and Krishy are running late. In other circumstances Klem might be tempted to start the game, but today he waits for Billy.

As I ponder last-minute changes to the lineup in case Krishy doesn't show, I am thinking that not only is managing not that much fun, it's also not so different from being the chair of an academic department. Both jobs provide an undercurrent of excitement, with little crises to attend to and minor decisions to make all the time. The officials in the institution are respectful, especially if things are going well for the team or department. And sometimes there are important general managerial decisions to make—like deciding which players or faculty to recruit.

But the general managerial decisions are a tiny part of each job, and the rest of the work is as extensive as it is thankless. Each involves a lot of demanding people insecure about their talents. It takes a lot of work to get teammates and colleagues to do things they should be volunteering for, like showing up to a game early for practice or serving on committees. The best thing for team and department alike is flexibility, but just as teammates want always to play their favorite positions, colleagues like to teach their favorite classes every semester. I hear out all my colleague-teammates, play everyone, worry about their reactions to my minor moves, kowtow to their schedules, and fear that I won't be able to retain their services.

To improve the team or curriculum requires making a few people very angry, while the majority who benefit will barely notice. Winning or success in hiring new faculty is simply expected. Losing or failing in hiring draws attention, and blame. Meanwhile, the manager or chair's own work suffers. As acting chair I spent lots of time tapping out upbeat e-mails to the faculty or deceptive annual planning reports to the dean when I could have been writing books or articles. In this league I'm often unable to get in batting practice or stretch before the game, as I'm busy consulting umpires and teammates or fiddling with the lineup. Sometimes I can't even give my plate appearances the concentration they deserve.

Despite the fact that we have dumped Gotham three times in a row, the Foxes seem tight. I ask them to play our usual smart game and make a statement—to blow them out. It has no effect. Swanny seems extra concerned with our putting our hands together and shouting "win." I have not been able to stop this ceremony and now join in with everyone else. Just as Klem orders us to take the field, Krishy appears, offering no explanation, and I add him to the lineup. I don't mind. I have to admit I had pegged Krishy wrong. He's late again and still too wild on the base paths. But he's become the epitome of the playoff player. He's committed to the team, so much so that he often e-mails me with suggestions that are surprisingly useful—thoughtful ideas well informed by the statistics on the Web site. It's like having another manager, in both good and bad ways. He's often adamant about his suggestions, and I have to explain in detail why I am doing something different when we disagree. Most of all, I envy his skin. Not the fact that it seems so tan, shiny, and healthy looking in contrast to my cracked and pocked hide—though of course that too. It's that Krishy's skin is so thick. He has an aura of certainty, and complaints and criticisms roll off him as if he were waterproofed.

Billy sets them down. I lead off, take a strike, and then line one. The right-center fielder dives but catches only divot, and I cruise into second. Mule lines one sharply to right too, but this time the outfielder one-hops it, and Penny holds me up at third. Artie pops up to the left fielder, too shallow for me to risk scoring, and then Roger grounds sharply to the third baseman, who tries and fails to tag me as I head back to the base but recovers to get Roger at first. Krishy hits one hard to the right side, but the second baseman makes the play, and our leadoff hits go to waste. The first inning sets the tone. We threaten but can't score. They break through with one in the fourth, on a swinging bunt that Billy throws away. In the fifth, they get another when Billy loses their cleanup man to balls with the bases juiced and only one out. I bring in Papi to replace Roger as catcher, in case of a force play. The grounder comes to me, but slowly. Unsure whether I can get the out at home, I go to first, and we go down 3–0. Gotham has a lot of vocal women fans on their third-base bleachers, and they are going wild at this upset in the making. We get out of it without further damage, but I see worry on the faces on my teammates.

Some of them ask our cheering section for a little countervailing noise, but our fan base today consists solely of Penny's and Swanny's girlfriends, and they are rooters of the more thoughtful variety. Mainly our section is filled with Irving Plaza guys who are here for the shade and are quietly rooting for us to lose, as they would rather face Gotham. Swanny picks up the rooting slack, calling out, "We need a setter here!" Penny obliges with a single and moves to second when Little Bobby just misses beating out a grounder to the right side. Q flies out, and I come up looking for something to shoot up the middle—"right back through the originator," as Swanny puts it. On the first pitch I get it, and finally we have a run, but that's all we get.

We hold them in the sixth, and I head over to the Gotham side of the field to coach third base. Roger flies to left, just missing the trees, but Krishy walks. Then it happens again. Swanny, Papi, and Cookie all bang out hits, and I wave Krishy and Swanny around. The game is tied, and the go-ahead run—Roger, running for Papi—is on third. On purpose Penny lifts a fly to right—a play he knows I don't like in general, but which seems OK under the circumstances—and Roger scampers home, giving us our first lead, 4–3. All we have to do is hold them in seventh. Billy gets the leadoff man but walks the second guy. Two hits and much cheering from the third-base side later, they have tied it. Now we need to score to win.

We've been here before. I goad my team with a tension-defusing rallying cry: "Does anyone has anything better to do than to win this game?" I don't have time to call a facetious play, because I am leading off, looking to get on base. I take a ball and then another low ball that Teddy calls a strike. I gasp as if sucker punched. Unlike Klem, Teddy will make it up you if he believes he has missed a call and isn't shown up. Also, I have two hits in this game, I am the leadoff batter and manager of the PM division's best team, which should work to my advantage. I run the count full, spoil the next two, and the Gotham pitcher leaves the next one low and outside, sending the winning run to first! It should not be possible for someone who has struck out looking as many times as I have this season to be surprised, but I truly am when Teddy rips the lawn-mower cord. "Same place as the first one," he explains, not looking up. I restrain myself. I don't want to be thrown out, but it's humiliating to strike out in such a key situation, especially after having won the battle. When in Klem's World, I suppose. No one on the bench says shit.

Mule is put out on a comebacker, but Big Artie smokes one through the right side and up steps our cleanup hitter Roger. He has enough dead-pull power to trim the maples in left and zips a shot down the line that skips past the outfielder. Artie comes around third with the winning run, but Roger's ball has crossed the footpath that trails into fair territory. From behind second base Klem is crying, *"Two bases!"* Had we been playing on field #2, as Gotham had wanted, the game would have been over, but here Artie has to go back to third. Krishy steps to the plate. Like the others he also has a chance to redeem the first inning, when Mule and I got on and no one could get us in. Again Krishy shoots the first pitch hard to the right side, but this time it goes past the second baseman, and game one is ours! Most of the Foxes are jubilant, but I feel only relief. Our season isn't going to end today.

By winning the first game we retain the choice of field and last ups, though in terms of fan support we still seem to be the visitors. In the pregame huddle I ask again for a blowout. Billy sets them down in order, exploiting Klem's wider strike zone. I come up swinging, but the pitcher snags my comebacker and we go down in order too, still tight. They score in the second when I muff the leadoff man's grounder. Their fans are whooping but shut up when Billy cuts off a peg to the plate and nails a runner trying for third, ending the inning. Dog announces that he's changed the scorebook to make each inning the seventh, trying to humor us into scoring sooner rather than later. It seems to work, as we accept a couple of walks and Swanny singles in the tying run, but only up to a point, as we leave the bases loaded. In the third, Gotham's first three batters single, making it 2–1. Billy holds them from there, and the game settles into a pitchers' duel.

With one out in the sixth, Q finally gets us off the schneid with a single. I shoot one up the middle, but the second baseman knocks it down and forces

Q. Mule singles me to third and is replaced by Q. Krishy grounds to the short-stop in the hole. He fumbles it and in his bid for instant redemption throws the ball away. I trot in with the tying run, and Q heads to third and Krishy to second. Roger smashes one in the hole; this time the shortstop snags it and tries to nail Krishy at third, but no luck. Q is across with the go-ahead run. Their third-base stands go silent. Billy goes back to the rubber, gets a quick out, and I'm praying for the ball. But Billy has a different idea. He intercepts a smash before it can make it to me and gets so far into the kitchen of the next batter that he can loop the ball only as far as the mound.

It's all over—the ballgame, the PM division race. The Foxes are acting like we won the pennant. We dash through the congratulations line and form our own little party on our baseline. There are hugs all around, and Panama materializes with his cooler and cry: "Win or lose, we booze!" The Gotham guys linger in little clumps on the other bleachers, not believing their season is over. On our side the Irving Plaza guys seem a little disappointed too. I go over to Cookie to congratulate him. "Hey Eddy—we did it, man!" he says. And we did it without Zeus, without Amanda, and without any major controversy. It's been many hours since my last Advil, but I can't help noticing that my leg, my groin, my stomach, and my back are no longer oppressing me. I'm over the shingles too.

## TUESDAY, AUGUST 19, HECKSCHER #5

### Forever Young

Yesterday's sense of excitement and possibility is missing here today. I have been playing on Tuesdays in the Show Business League for a team led by Zeus called Scentsational Shoppe. In this league show business is interpreted to embrace anyone who can afford to take off a couple of hours in the middle of a weekday, and most of the sponsors are bars, restaurants, and stores. The best teams, based in Fire Department of New York ladder and engine companies, are better than those that play on Monday, but the worst teams are worse than the New Guys. Our team is almost as good as the Foxes, except in the pitching department. Billy doesn't want to have anything to do with the Shoppekeepers. We are deficient in both talent and semiotics. Our official "uniform" is as cheap as can be: royal blue sleeveless cotton-poly T-shirts with the double-yuck name screened in white block letters. When firefighters sponsored by a macho beer-and-steak joint face off against our group of musicians, artists, and assorted misfits representing a perfume outlet it's as if we'd spotted them five runs. We ended up in fifth place in the AM division and play fourth-place Turtle Rock in the playoff opener. The tournament is single-elimination, and although we could win today, if we did we would be prohibitive underdogs against the first-place firemen, who have kicked our asses twice this season and await this game's winner.

As Zeus fills out the scorecard on the first-base bleachers, he seems to be preoccupied or lost, like a student taking a test that he hasn't studied for. I'm not sure if Zeus knows who has been helping the team and who hasn't. He doesn't like to collect statistics. Zeus usually has me batting somewhere around seven and playing second base. Earlier in the season I was at short-stop but took a bad-hop grounder off my neck and was demoted. In the final season game last week he rotated in three pitchers as if they were audition-ing. Today Zeus gives the start to Bro, the soft-tossing control pitcher from the Friars Club. Zeus picks up a new player almost every week, but few of them stick with the squad. Manny has been on and off the team. Zeus had to ask Manny to return for today, because Zeus had run our starting left fielder, the sponsor, off the team—which also means that this will be our first and last season.

The great baseball writer Roger Angell famously said that in baseball if you keep hitting, extend the inning, you can defeat time and remain forever young. This team doesn't have the talent to start anything resembling that sort of epic rally, but Zeus is keeping us young all the same—by running the team like a reform school and treating us like juvenile delinquents. He rides herd on his unruly charges, whose imperfect play he sees as directed at him personally, like so many spitballs. The pioneer sociologist Emile Durkheim argued that crime is a normal aspect of any society and that societies of saints would treat gossip as harshly as we treat assault. Zeus's idiosyncratic code of softball morality, with its strictures against both mental and physical errors, is designed more for saints than citizens. Throw to the wrong base, fail to tag up, or miss a game—or give up runs, ground out, or play one off your Adam's apple—and you've committed a crime against softball that demands swift and sure punishment. Zeus makes an example of the offender by replacing him with another, who inevitably messes up, and so on. He says he wants to win, but his softball code alienates players, who are interested in recreation, not rehabilitation.

With the Scentsationals, Zeus has re-created the unhappy, infantilizing atmosphere that I recognize from the Sharkeys. For so long the Sharkeys were my only team, and I used to get embroiled in the various controversies. Now I'm on so many other teams and they are so good that I have developed a dis-

HECKSCHER #5 WAS THE FAVORITE OF LOCATION SCOUTS

tance from this one, like a professional on a team that's out of the running. I'm playing my game, enjoying the occasional moments of glory, and going home, not taking it with me.

Zeus has one last move up his sleeve. Joining us today is Kevin, a short, powerfully built guy in his forties with a deep tan, a confident attitude, and a lower lip full of smokeless. Manny thinks Kevin's a minor-league instructor for the Yankees. Kevin says he runs baseball camps for the Yankee hero Bucky Dent and has coached in places from Austria to Utica. That would explain the tan and maybe the Skoal. His arrival inspires awe among the team—a player with any connection to organized baseball is viewed as magical. Zeus installs Kevin at shortstop and third in the batting order. Kevin's magic seems powerful as we score on an error by Turtle Rock's slick-fielding second baseman and Kevin's RBI. Maybe it's not hopeless.

Klem has relocated from his World and is working the bases here on #5, whose skyline sight lines make it the favorite Heckscher field for location scouts. An older gentleman I haven't seen before rings up the Turtle Rock leadoff man on an eye-high pitch, and he complains vociferously. The next batter looks at strike three down Broadway, but old blue calls it a ball. Bro, suddenly a strikeout pitcher, is livid.

I make a diving play to end the first, and Kevin says, "Atta boy, Eddy," a little like Kevin Costner's baseball lifer in the tedious *For the Love of the Game*.

In the second, Turtle Rock bloops two singles that couldn't have been better placed if the batters had lobbed them. With their catcher coming up, my new keystone partner Kevin says what sounds like, "Let's twist this one up." This is an expression I hadn't heard before, and it is definitely not in my *Dickson Baseball Dictionary*. The phrase means, I take it, to turn a double play. Is this how the pros say it? I find myself enchanted by my new vocabulary word, the way I was with the linguistic innovations of the cooler kids in high school, who were forever devising compelling synonyms for everyday affirmations like "yes" and "certainly." I'm grateful for Kevin's willingness to relay this one to me. Though I'm too old for peer group osmosis and mildly anxious about whether the verb is transitive, and if so whether the object is the batter or the grounder, and also whether the "up" is idiomatic, I find myself responding, almost involuntarily, "Yeah, let's twist him up."

I get a grounder but in my anxiety misfeed Kevin on the exchange and un-ravel the twist. Bro walks the next batter on another questionable call. Zeus tells Klem that a playoff game is no place for on-the-job training and that he should switch places with the rookie. Klem seems to be enjoying Zeus's pub-lic endorsement of his skills, but isn't inclined to help. By the time Bro works out of it, we're down 4–1. It's another humid day, and when I get back to the bench I reach for a Gatorade from Panama's red cooler. Manny stops me. He is now his own man in the drinks game too, having broken with Panama in a dispute over subcontracting fees. Manny collects from each of us and dis-patches an underling to a wholesaler.

In the fourth, Zeus lifts Bro. He has done nothing particularly wrong, but they are ahead, and Zeus has extra pitchers. Turtle Rock's lead mounts any-way. By the time I get to bat again in the fifth, we are down by six, with two outs and nobody on. We have no chance, but I exploit another loophole in baseball time. In New York softball, there is no limit on foul balls. I run the count full and then foul off pitch after pitch—the only way left to extend the season. After the seventh foul, the pitcher misses three feet outside. Even the elderly rookie can't call it strike. I trot down to first, but time catches up with the Scentsationals.

When Manny's drinks finally arrive, they are mostly Coronas. I realize that this was the plan all along. The drinks are for a postgame, postseason party, for commiseration and reminiscence. Team Scentsational Shoppe has made its final out. Zeus looks relieved. We are all being released, as if to our parole officers. I head back to the A train with Big Artie. I will miss some of these guys, but I won't miss this team. If I've made it here, I'm no longer sure that it's because I got on base regularly and turned a lot of double plays, even if I didn't know what to call them. More likely, I earned my place by reliably appearing at games and rarely being involved in high-profile bad plays. I always heard Zeus out and never showed disrespect. I was less a model teammate than a model inmate.

## The Ricochet Rule

Today I'm back to being Zeus's opponent, and, as the traveling secretary of Rif Raf, he has outperformed Billy of the Machine so far today. All the Rif Raf guys are present and accounted for, including one I haven't seen before. But at game time we Machinists have only ten. Neither Keith, the highly responsible and sure-handed first baseman, nor Dick, the pitcher and self-styled franchise player, is here. Superman is on vacation, and parole officer Tommy is on assignment. Frank will catch, and the patient MikeHargrove will take over for Tommy in right. I'll be at third. Had Zeus remained with our team, he would probably be the Machine's third baseman, and I would be at second.

Game one pits my two Pamela's pitchers against each other. Billy is going for us, and Zeus has tapped Dog for Rif Raf. This is a big assignment for Dog, a must game, because if we win this one, Rif Raf will have to beat us three in a row to advance. We are up 1–0, in a best-of-five series that has to end today because Billy is already behind schedule, and Parks and Recreation permits don't come with rain checks. We won't need one this afternoon. It is in the seventies, with the sun so bright that I need to borrow a hat—something I still can't easily wear—to shade my eyes.

Billy has induced Teddy the umpire to return. He is announcing a simple new ground rule—possibly a condition of his returning. All trees are in play. This rule eliminates a nagging source of controversy. Before, the umpire would have to make rulings about whether any tree branch had significantly influenced the trajectory of a ball. If the umpire ruled that it hadn't, the ball would remain in play. Many a pop-up was converted into a do-over, or a ground-rule single, by grazing a few leaves before settling into a fielder's glove. Having just lost a certain out, the team on the field finds itself compelled to debate the meaning of "significant influence," sometimes at length. Now if the ball is fair and tumbles through the tree branches, it's as much as the batter can get, but if the ball is caught before it hits the ground, the batter's retired. The out-on-a-ricochet rule, outlawed since the first Grant administration until its reinstatement in the ridiculous Metrodome, is back in effect at Central Park.

I am slotted at six because of the missing Keith. Dog walks Clooney, gets Krishy looking, then walks Mike the shortstop, and Walker's infield single loads the bases. The lefty Matt is up, as I wait on deck. Matt whistles one right past Dog's head, and it looks like two runs for sure. But Jorgy, at shortstop, had been shading Matt up the middle and snags the liner, swooping in stride to double Mike off second. Billy shuts them down, but Dog's back in trouble in the third. We load the bases again for Matt, again I wait on deck, and again he lines one right at an infielder. This time it's the second baseman, but no one gets doubled off, and I get the opportunity I almost had in the first inning. In the second, I looked at a lot of pitches, got ahead in the count, found a pitch to hit, and singled. I am thinking that now Dog is expecting me to look at a lot of pitches and may try to come right in with one. But then maybe he isn't thinking anything at all and is just going to throw his best pitch. Whatever—I am looking for something I can line to right. I get it first pitch and send one toward the trees. Two runs come in, and we go up 3–0.

In its attempt to mount a comeback, Rif Raf is fortified by the backdrop behind home plate. The area from the infield to the Carousel forms a deep-shadow sandwich. The fielders are in the sun, and the batter is in the shade, but then there is a sunny patch behind the batter that makes it difficult to gauge the ball off the bat. Standing in Rif Raf's way is Keith, who appeared in the second inning. He had already reached Columbus Circle by way of the F train when he realized he had left his cleats in his car, which was parked downtown. He briefly thought about heading to the field, but after weighing what was best for the team he went back for the cleats. After all, it could be a long day and in the long run it would be better for the team for him to be at his best. Since his arrival, he has indeed steadied the defense. What is worse for Rif Raf is that each time they start to rally they do something Zeus hates. Three times with runners on first and second a Rif Raf batter has hit a ball sharply to me at third. Billy has me playing near the bag and is throwing low and inside changeups. The first two times we get double plays, as I fight off the glare, step on third, and fire to first. On the last one, I handcuff Keith with an in-between hop, but he retrieves the ball and shoots it back to me as the runner on second foolishly tries for third. After that double display of bad softball, Zeus can barely contain himself.

It is 5–2 in the bottom of the seventh with two outs, but a double by Jorgy reduces our lead to two, and the tying run comes to the plate in the form of Rif Raf's ex-manager, a lefty power hitter and outfielder who would be pitching against us if I were running their team. Shifting around, shortstop Mike is playing almost on second base. Jorgy is getting a big jump, releasing on the pitch. Ahead in the count the ex-manager checks his swing, and Frank fires to Mike, who catches Jorgy off second. Billy and the Machine have a 5–3 victory, and we are one game away from eliminating Rif Raf.

For the next game's pitching assignment Zeus switches not to the lefty outfielder but to a guy named Sonny, who throws across his body, slowly but with good control and some changes of speed. His unusual motion and minimal repertoire proves disorienting. Inning after inning, we pop up, lunging after these slow pitches as if Sonny had set us up with fastballs. Dick now feels the brunt of the Machine's typical inability to hit in game two after having won game one. He is baffling them and walking them in about equal measure, and Rif Raf builds a 3–1 lead. In the fifth, a batter hits a ball down the left-field line; it's headed foul but is swatted by a branch overhanging the backstop and plops down onto the infield dirt by the third-base line—in fair territory. I field it like a bunt and get the batter only because, thinking he has hit a foul ball, he lingers in the box. In the sixth inning, they rally with one out and runners on second and third. Billy hops off the bench to confer with Dick about whether to walk their cleanup hitter. The decision is to pitch to him, and he plasters Dick's riser over the #2 infield on the fly and could have rounded the bases twice by the time Clooney locates the ball under the bleachers.

In the bottom half, Krishy pokes one off a tree trunk in right field and tries to stretch it into a double. He makes it, barely. Billy is quick to denounce the play. No one should ever risk making an out when the team is down by five runs late in the game. When certainties in softball are violated, Billy finds it incumbent upon him to express his outrage and gain the assent of others. Zeus probably would've brought in a pinch runner. Still, it is disconcerting because it is the way losers talk. Dick is not taking his first loss of the season well. He shouts that Sonny is "throwing nothing but meatballs," a taunt aimed in part at us for failing to hit them. When Sonny gets the last out, he crows to Dick, "That's right, all meatballs, but you can't do nothing with 'em!" Dick's reply is the kind that makes us want to run through walls for him. He says, "I wasn't batting."

For game three, it's Billy versus Sonny. Zeus is thinking that he might as well keep throwing Sonny at us until we hit him. He's not going to get tired. They build a 6–3 lead after five—even more disconcerting because we will have to rely on the volatile Dick's arm if there has to be a deciding game.

As we come to bat in the sixth, our Hasidic fans come parading to the bleachers like the cavalry from behind the Carousel. The mother and three children are fresh from synagogue and are toting several used plastic jugs filled with homemade lemonade. The recipe is minimalist, apparently water, ReaLemon, and melted ice. But we are thirsty and accept the lukewarm brew—and immediately start hitting, as if our bats had been suffering from scurvy. With one out Keith singles, then Matt drives him to second. Walker bloops a double to right, sending Keith home and Matt to third. I come to the plate. I skip one through the right side, sending Walker across with the tying run. Billy retires them in the bottom of the sixth, and in the seventh we pick up where we left off. The younger boy in his white shirt, dress slacks, and yarmulke has set up the plastic cups on our bleachers and is filling them as if on an assembly line, and we drink the tepid liquid as if it were a magic potion or the perfect complement to meatballs. We can't stop hitting Sonny. Near the end of the rally I single again, and two hits later Billy waves me around third. I should be out from here to Labor Day, but the throw sails over the catcher's head and before he can retrieve the ball I beat him to plate for the fifth run of the inning.

Billy has pitched two almost complete games and last inning stopped a line drive that ripped off his glove and aggravated an injury to his thumb, which he broke in similar circumstances last year. Billy sends Dick in to mop up, and he promptly walks the leadoff man. Two hits and a walk later, it's a verging on being game again, and Dick's game to lose, as Billy's cleats are off. Dick gets two outs, but gives up another walk and a hit and then walks the bases loaded, moving the winning run to second. Up comes Jorgy, who is seeking redemption for his blunder in the first game. Dick falls behind, and Jorgy rips a liner, but it's right at Krishy in center. Rif Raf is done, and the Machine is going to the finals.

I am happy with the victory and my role in it. For me that's four hits today, six for the series, and nimble work at third. Zeus hit well, but I don't think he outplayed me today. Somehow, though, I thought the triumph would be sweeter. After it's over, and I find myself feeling a little sorry for Zeus, as he sits apart from the other Rif Raf guys on the far end of the bleachers. He would have been playing with us if Billy had dropped Dick. During last winter's referendum, Zeus said he wouldn't play if Dick remained on the team, and he stuck to his guns. And now the team Zeus took over has ended its season in a worse position than it did last year.

**〖 MONDAY, AUGUST 25, HECKSCHER #2 〗**

## *Winning in the Purest Way*

Zeus is the least of my worries today. The Foxes face Irving Plaza, the four-time defending Performing Arts League champs, for the whole ball of wax.

I'm up early, with an almost welcome anxiety rather than pain. As I head to the park, there is a misty chill in the morning air. More bracing still is when I pass the NYU Bookstore. Delivery trucks are triple-parked out front, unloading texts for the new school year, which starts in just over a week. Possibly my book order for "Baseball and Society" is on one of the many pallets that crowd the sidewalk. I learned last night that Billy's left thumb had ballooned. He won't be able to bat. But it's his glove hand, and if he can pitch, I have to decide only whether Artie or Papi will play first base, whether Roger or Mule will catch, and whether to bat ten or eleven. I wonder who I'll pitch if Billy can't go. Dog or me? I arrive at Heckscher about an hour before the games. Dog, Mule, and Little Bobby are here on #2, the crappy field on which the championship series is always played.

Mack, the Irving Plaza manager, seems so settled in that I wonder if he camped out overnight. He wants to win in the purest way and is unique among the managers in the league. Mack recruited a team so talented that not only would it be wrong for him to play his preferred position, but in good conscience he should not play at all. What is surprising is that he acts on this, inserting himself in the game only during garbage time. Mack's stringy hair is even longer than mine, and last week it inspired a few of our guys to suggest a bet: the losing manager gets a crew cut. I told Mack I was willing to take the wager, despite its lack of potential costs to those proposing it—but only if the manager of each team were to lead off and play shortstop. He declined. Now he shoos us off field #2 and over to #4. Mack tells us that the umpires are "going to work on" #2 and heads over to #4 with the Heckscher Cup, the bronze traveling trophy for the league's champion.

The Irving Plaza guys could not be friendlier during batting practice. More than one of them says, "Let's have fun today." Their pitcher, a lefthander who relies on good control and good hands, is also displaying good sportsmanship. He is throwing BP—which Billy would never do, even if he were ever on time. But soon Billy is sighted heading down the hill from the West Drive with a metal splint on his left thumb and says he's good to go. For the first time this year, all the Foxes are here a full fifteen minutes before the game. The only player eligible for the playoffs who is missing is Trey, the slugging personal trainer who is recovering from abdominal surgery. And if we split today's games, he will be available for the rubber match in two weeks, the Monday after Labor Day.

I run the lineup past Cookie. I have opted for Roger at catcher, Artie at first, and eleven batters, with Papi the extra hitter/player and Mule the DH. I need Mule's bat and don't want him to tire out. Roger, it turns out, was irked that he wasn't behind the plate in game two last week. I know that Cookie would prefer Papi to play first, if only because they go way back and Papi has been chewing his ear off all season about it. But I think Artie is better, and that's how Billy sees it too, and as pitcher and team MVP he has the most important vote on the matter. Papi can come in to catch if the situation warrants or at first in case of an injury.

Because of the games' importance and because there are no other games, all three of the league's umpires, Klem, Teddy, and Gino, are here to officiate. They are even decked out in matching scarlet shirts, from some David Cone–sponsored event from years past. The morning fog has burned off and is replaced with a creeping humidity. Both teams set up on the shady first-base bleachers. Dozens of fans have already congregated. Just behind the teams are players from both divisions, including Juan and Jorgy from the Friars Club, the manager and several players from the Gotham Comedy Club, and other faces I recognize from the AM division. Klem's personal heckler, a player from Local 802, is there, emitting the occasional reedy cry of *"Two bases!"* like a birdcall. The usual European curiosity seekers are forced into the far reaches of the bleachers. There are perks to being in the finals. A heavyset kid of about ten, with curly brown hair and wide dark eyes, asks me very seriously if he can be our batboy.

There is no top seed, so Mack and I head to home plate for a coin toss. I win, and so we are the home team. In the pregame huddle, I ask the team to make a statement but most of the guys seem preoccupied as we end with the usual on-three chant. We are treated to Mack reading out his lineup like a public address announcer, with clapping and hooting for each name. He stops short of having the players jump off the bench, through a burning hoop, and into a high-five line to blaring music and strobe lights, but it's a little intimidating all the same.

We take the field, and Swanny betrays some tightness in his patter. After Billy's borderline, two-strike "honey shot," Swanny crosses a line by offering that umpire Teddy shouldn't "be afraid to ring up" a batter on strikes. Teddy seems nervous too, in his overreaction, as he tells Swanny to stop chattering altogether. Billy dispatches them easily. I step in. Since the umpires have been extending my strike zone for the playoffs and since Teddy, prompted by Swanny, may now be looking for an opportunity to show his lack of fear to call a third strike, I decide I'd better be hacking. I inside out one to right, and we are in business. But Mule and Krishy both line to right center for outs, and Roger's deep fly to left is hauled in.

Their second begins with an error by Cookie, and then their left-handed first baseman skies one to the backstop on field #1. We are down again. This shouldn't be a problem as we've been here before and our defense has settled down. But we aren't hitting, not nervous so much as lulled. Irving Plaza guys touch gloves with our guys as we come off the field between innings. In the fifth, their first baseman launches another long fly ball to right. Little Bobby goes back for it but is in trouble. It dawns on me that he hasn't had to go back hard on a ball all year. This one too goes for a homer, and we are down 4–0. We don't respond. Billy and I both make errors in the sixth. A few well-placed singles, and they go up 6–0. In our end of the sixth, with two outs, Q and Little Bobby single. I lace one up the middle scoring Q, and a wild throw sends Bobby scampering across behind him. But in the seventh, more errors by us open the floodgates. For the first time this season the Foxes are being blown out! Now Mack comes in as a pinch-hitter—and singles, clapping his hands as he rounds first. The final is 9–2.

There is not much time between games, and I have to decide quickly if I want to make any moves to keep the good ship Pamela's from going down. But I don't see any good ones. Instead, I'm ready to pull out all the stops in my pregame pep talk. Little Bobby is sitting by himself on the bleachers, possibly mulling over his misplay, and I think momentarily of lying to the team and telling them that Little Bobby is dying of Hodgkin's. This time, though, I'm afraid they'll recognize the dated film reference, and anyway Bobby will probably hear me. Instead, I go in the other direction. In ironical professorial mode I tell them I've detected a pattern with our season. We win four games, then lose a game, win four more games, then lose one, and so on, to the point where we are now 16–4. Thus, according to my careful scientific analysis, we are due to begin another four-game winning streak!

We come to bat, and our batboy now knows my stick, a twenty-six-ounce Louisville TPS Slugger I call White Betsy in honor of its ivory paint job, and hands it to me. I slap one past the second baseman, who knocks it down and throws needlessly to first, where the first baseman drops it for good measure and sends me to second. Mule slugs a home run over the right fielder's head. I am waiting at the plate, but Mule being Mule, he stretches it into a triple, panting noticeably when replaced by his courtesy runner, but not so much that he can stop himself from telling us, "I got all of that one." The Klem-imitator from Local 802 asks Mule if he needs a defibrillator. Krishy bingos to right for the second run. Although Roger flies to left and Krishy is thrown out at second, Billy shuts them down through two, and we seem to have regained our poise. I find myself slapping gloves with the Irving Plaza guys between innings. I notice that my sociologist friends Jim and Sarah are here, tucked away near the top of the third-base bleachers in the crowd. I have been talking up my team all year, and they decided to check it out. It's very touching, as aside from Francesca cutting across the park with the occasional frightening test result, they are my first fans this season. Under the circumstances, though, I can't acknowledge them.

In the third, Irving Plaza gets two on with two outs. The next batter is the prototypical softball shortstop: the team's best athlete, with great range, a gun for an arm, and power to burn. Billy gets ahead of him and he lunges at a change and lifts a high fly to medium left—can o' corn. Except no one is calling for it. Swanny and Q are racing in, as they were way deep out of respect for his power, and I am running out, back to the infield like a wide receiver, but the ball drops in for a double to tie the game. The next batter singles, and we are down 3–2.

In the fourth, Krishy gets an infield single with one out, and Penny chases him to second on a trough-aided hit to shortstop. But we can't get them in. Dog now changes the scorebook. The rest of the innings are headed "7" to see if this will spark an early last-inning rally, but nothing doing. It's as if we are waiting for our last ups to work our magic. Billy is holding them, but they have the top of the order coming up in the bottom of the sixth. Again they get two on with two outs, bringing up the first baseman. Since his two home runs Billy has been pitching him carefully, and semi-intentionally walks him to load the bases. But the strategy is foiled by a liner up the middle, and two insurance runs come across. We now need three to tie. In our last licks, Roger cracks a one-out single, but a fly ball to left and a grounder to short end the season.

The Irving Plaza guys are jubilant but gracious, saying in the slap line that the game could've gone either way and that they know we will be back. Mack embraces the Heckscher Cup as if it were some long lost friend and hadn't been resting all afternoon in his gear bag. The Irving Plaza team goes to set up a photo on the rubber. They are as much as saying that they own this field, this league. All the umpires join the shot. Even the little chubster who was handling our bats wants in. Mack sets him up front and center with the loving cup. Many of the players seem to wave, raising an open hand that signifies their five straight championships.

I have my camera with me, but I know that for any halfway serious team it's worthless to try to take a team photo right after elimination. No one smiles. And there is no trophy or award for second place. Panama has suddenly materialized with his standard postgame pitch, "Win or lose, we booze!" Settling in, Mack is buying beer after beer, treating the umpires, who break down

OUR BATBOY SAT FRONT AND CENTER WITH THE LOVING CUP

just this once and fraternize with the players after the game. Even Klem has nowhere to go.

Meantime Jim and Sarah drop by to offer their condolences. Then, like the rest of the fans, they quickly disperse. Only the umpires and players remain. It is like one of those postgame banquets after the first baseball games, but without toasts or food. I sit by myself on the bleachers. It's all happened so quickly that I can't take it all in. I go back and forth between disbelief and wondering how it all went wrong. A few of the Foxes come over. Q asks me, "Are you OK, man? Hey, we had a great season." Big Artie offers to buy me a beer. Even Panama feels the need to cheer me up. "What's wrong? You act like I just lost my business," he says, failing to stifle a laugh. He is making a killing today. I perk up if only to make everyone else feel better and take Artie up on his offer. I look around, and most of our guys seem not at all distressed. It's as if the rest of the team had been expecting us to lose and was happy to have been a part of it. Just by being here, the focus of attention, they are now all winners. Only Papi seems upset, sitting off by himself. It's not because we lost, however, but because he didn't get to play in the field.

I head back to the subway with Big Artie, who is trying to buck me up about our quick exit. "What can you do—they were just better today," he shrugs. He is right. We did not play well. We made six errors in game one and didn't hit much in either game. On another day, it might have been dif-

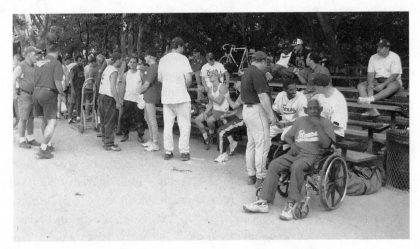

THE TEAM WAS HAPPY TO HAVE BEEN A PART OF IT

ferent. Any team can lose two games, and no team is going to win many championship games scoring only two runs. It wasn't as if their defense or pitching was so dominant that we couldn't have put up our usual numbers. Maybe we came too far too fast, and no one really believed that we could be champions. I feel as though there wasn't much I could do. There were so few managerial buttons to push. Artie and I part ways at West Fourth Street, and I feel a little better.

It was nice of Artie to cheer me up, but on the way back through Washington Square Park, I wonder if there wasn't something more fundamentally wrong. It's very difficult to beat a good team twice in a row, and they made it seem easy. Probably we would lose to this team seven times out of every ten. I may have set my sights too low, recruiting a team good enough to win the PM division but not good enough to win it all. Possibly I created a team too much in my own image—a team of Seabiscuits, guys with heart, making the most of their skills but lacking sufficient raw power. As we saw today, it helps to have some guys who can powder the occasional shot to the other fields. Maybe I should have picked up shortstop Mike from the Sunday team, plus another power merchant. But is it possible or even worthwhile to compete against someone like Mack who wants to win so badly that he doesn't play himself in the game? If we were doomed to lose, I should've played Papi in the field so that he would have shared more in the rest of the team's sense of being winners. I realize that it's like the chair debacle from the winter. I had a lost cause and played it for a tragedy.

179

On Washington Place, I have to walk into the street as the sidewalk is too clotted with deliverymen, hand trucks, and books for me to pass. I head to Pamela's, where we might have gone to celebrate had we won today. Mickey, the restaurant owner and team sponsor, has just had his establishment remodeled. Freeing himself at long last from the previous ownership, he has built a place according to his own vision. He is going for broke. Gone are the siennas and the faux-southwestern ambience of the cantina. In their place is a brighter Mediterranean look, with bleached imitation-stucco walls and painted cobalt lanterns. The menu cover now displays gauzy images of Near Eastern hotties. In addition to being an NYU luncheon spot by day Pamela's is now seeking to be a club by night. The bar area is shrouded in white boudoir curtains, and near the back of the room there is a chocolate leather daybed. There are notices announcing DJs and live music. Between them, the makeover and the menu give off the effect of a postmodern harem. The restaurant-bar's new name is Pamela's Global.

I want to ask Mickey about something he had mentioned a few weeks ago, when I told him that about winning the regular-season championship. Mickey said he might want to throw a party for the team. Today I compliment him on the new look and ask him about a celebration, but Mickey has bad news for me. As always he is up-front about his finances. He has invested a lot in the remodeling and doesn't think it would be feasible to throw a party any time soon. I remind him about the trophy that I will soon have for him, but it doesn't help to make the case. He raises his palms and says, "I have so many trophies—I don't know what to do with them." It seems clear that sporting this sort of hardware above the bar wouldn't fit the new ambience, and I realize that he was being happy for me when I told him about it. He is too polite to say so, but we have been globalized out of our sponsor. I will need to find a new one for next season. Pamela's Foxes is going to be a one-season team—like the Seattle Pilots or the Bingo Long Traveling All-Stars and Motor Kings.

<hr>

**( SUNDAY, SEPTEMBER 7, HECKSCHER #1 )**

## *Pitched Around*

Labor Day has come and gone, and on Wednesday I handed out the syllabus to my new "Baseball and Society" class, but I still have unfinished summer business. The Machine is trying to wrest the championship from the Hitmen in the difficult Lower Manhattan Softball League. Two games of this best-

of-five series are scheduled for today, with the rest—three games, if necessary—slated for next Sunday. At the beginning of the season I wanted to see
if I could make it on a contending team in a tough league, and now I will find
out. Billy will tap me to start the first game, but I wonder whether I will stay
in the lineup, given how many good players we have. Billy won't hesitate to
yank anyone who's messing up, especially a player as marginal as I am.

When I get to Heckscher, I can see that Billy is facing the playoff personnel problem in spades. Except for Chad, whose sprained ankle has ended
his season, every eligible player is here and available, including Trey, whose
third-base position I have been keeping warm. Billy is planning to bat only
ten, in order to maximize the plate appearances of his best hitters, but he has
fifteen here today. Even with a DH, four guys—an outfielder, an infielder, a
pitcher, and a catcher—are going to have to sit down each game. Billy calls
for infield practice. He wants to play Trey at third but first wants to see if he
looks sharp. Trey looks fine. Woody stations himself at second base, where
he has been playing, but Billy calls him in and sends me to second, bumping
Woody off the bottom of the infield totem pole. Billy sits himself too, granting Dick the start in game one. Also benched are the catcher Superman, in
favor of Frank, and MikeHargrove, the newlywed outfielder.

Dick is matched against Casey, the Hitmen manager, ace pitcher, and all-
around superstar. Casey has closely cropped hair, a powerfully thick body,
narrow suspicious eyes, and an expressive face. He gives off an appearance
of being wrongly tormented, beset by invisible burdens, and if he weren't our
opponent I would have to be rooting for him. There is some bad blood between the teams because they have a few hotheads, and we have Dick. They
are a largely Hispanic team, while we are mainly Anglos. Also, none of us
plays with or even against any of these guys in other leagues. And they often
act as though we have some advantage because our manager Billy is also the
league's commissioner, as if the umpires were in Billy's pocket. It is difficult,
though, to imagine the always professional Teddy showing favoritism. Not
to mention Jack, the formidable umpire working the bases today, who is as
unfriendly as possible to all the players, to ward off taking shit for having a
glass eye. The bad feeling between the teams is aggravated by our ecologi-
cal battle lines. We are as usual in the sun, on the sole bleacher by the first-
base line, while they are set up on folding chairs in the shade well beyond
the third-base line. For once this does not seem like much an advantage. It
is a beautiful, glorious day—sunny, with a brilliant sky, temperatures in the
seventies, and little humidity in the Central Park air—the kind of late summer day New Yorkers will always associate with September 11.

Casey sets us down easily in the first. As usual, Dick is pitching in and out of trouble, walking the leadoff man in the first and the first two guys in the second. But he is getting it over when he has to, and despite the fact that his fielders' attention often wanders, our defense is solid. So is theirs, and we are tied 1–1 after three. On the bench Dick is riding us for not walking. "This guy's got a lot of balls in him," he says, referring to Casey, trying to lighten his annoying patter with a modicum of almost humor. It is as if Dick believes that the Hitmen are gaining so many bases on balls because of their greater patience, not the errancy of his offerings. With nothing else to do, Billy is urging us along similar lines, reminding us to hit it down and hard instead of popping up or flying out as we are doing all too frequently. I take the advice to look at some pitches, and Casey loses me, but nothing comes of it. In their half, a walk and a swinging bunt put a runner in scoring position with two outs. The next guy lines one over my outstretched glove at second. From left center the tart-tongued Clooney yells—ironically, I think—"Where are your hops?" I jump pretty well, but given my lower starting point I still don't command much air space. They lead 2–1. The score stays that way until the sixth, when Dick's high-wire act gets shaky. He walks two, and then one of the beefier Hitmen—the right-center fielder and one of the few non-Hispanic guys on the team—blasts a pitch so deep to left that even the speedy Matt has no play except to look under the bleachers on field #2. This large gentleman is surprisingly agile, like a lineman in football. His three-run homer gives them the game.

I am stretching my hamstring on the bleachers between games, when a voice behind me says, faux-excitedly, "Omigod—there's Kenny G.!" I recognize the Chicago accent of my sister Marybeth, who is visiting for her birthday. She is trying to induce me to respond to a hair-related nickname so insulting that it makes "Poolie" seem dignified. It's OK for her to say it—she has the same hair. I ignore her until she and Francesca roll up in front of me on bicycles. Marybeth hasn't seen me play since the early 1980s. Back then I chastised her for calling me "Eddy," at a time when that wasn't yet established as my softball tag and I was for some reason resisting it. She has pointedly called me "Ed" ever since, repeating the story often, though I've said I was sorry and have come to embrace the inevitable diminutive. The older I get, the better "Eddy" sounds. They plan to spin around the six-mile Central Park Drive, this being the only form of exercise Francesca's OB now allows her.

I tell them the unhappy story of game one and that we are in a do-or-die situation, as it would be almost impossible to beat this team three straight. They haven't lost a doubleheader all season. But I can't linger as it's time for the next pregame huddle. Billy has moved Trey, who hit well, up in the order, and I am now batting ninth, just ahead of Woody, whom Billy has tapped to start at catcher in game two. The good-natured Superman is again the odd man out. He has hit well all year and often sits out one game of the double-header, but never both. Possibly Superman is being benched because he was on vacation for the deciding games against Rif Raf, but he's irked and has a different idea. Superman nods toward Woody and says, "I guess I should've bitched." MikeHargrove is again sitting and not saying much.

We run out onto the field, and Billy walks to the rubber. Solid in game one, our defense falters at the outset of game two. Mike misses a grounder at short and Billy allows an uncharacteristic walk. It looks as though he is going to get out of the jam when one of their lefties lifts a fly to right field and Tommy camps under it. But instead of settling into his glove, the ball gets lost in one of the trees—which again are being treated as if they were part of the sky. Keith dashes out from first base to await the ball's reentry, but it emerges far closer to the line and bounds past them both and two runs are in. We cut the gap in half on Clooney's Little League homer, and in the second I am up with a runner on and one out. Chino, their second-string pitcher, is trying to throw just strikes to me, having seen Casey lose me to walks twice. I know his name because the pitcher is the only player whose name is incessantly repeated: "C'mon, Chino." "Way to fire, Chino." "Whaddaya say, Chino." He is short and wiry, with a little mustache, multiple tattoos, and almond eyes so squinty that they look as if they had been salted. I send a rope to right, but the second baseman climbs the ladder to snag it.

Krishy, one of the few Pamela's Foxes unfazed by the gravity of the Monday-league championship series, seems to be feeling the pressure this Sunday. He struck out looking in the first game, and in his first at bat in this game he popped up; it was all he could do to keep himself from throwing the bat and earning an automatic ejection. In the third Krishy is way out in front and pops up again. He asks Billy to replace him, complaining that he isn't "seeing the ball well." The patient MikeHargrove gets the opportunity to see his first action of the day. He heads out to right-center field, where his former high school teammate Matt greets him with the cry "Ranger pride!"—their team's nickname. Instead of barking in my direction as he once did, MikeHargrove has created a ritual with me that makes fun of the overseriousness of our teammates. At the beginning of each inning I call out his name, give him a grave look, and wave my fist, and he responds in kind. This signifies that our heads are in the game and that we both are aware that there is as yet nobody out.

In the game, there is almost nothing but outs. Each team knows the other's tendencies and is setting the defense batter by batter. Billy is especially efficient in moving us around. There is one thing, though, that Billy can't counter. They have more left-handed power than we do, and they have been aiming for the trees in right. With a runner on and one out, another lefty Hitman sails one up into the branches. This time I join Keith and Tommy out there. We fan out grimly and methodically, like volunteers searching for a corpse in a thicket (though with our heads craned upward), and have a disturbingly long wait. I think I have a read on the reentry, but the ball comes tumbling suddenly out of the overbrush, landing just out of reach to my right and then trickling onto the footpath. It's a dead ball worth two bases—the footpath double being the only ground rule remaining. Billy is upset that another pop fly has gone for extra bases. We are trying to calm him down when Teddy emerges, also agitated, from behind the plate. Teddy thinks mistakenly that we are complaining about his interpretation. "Hey, it's a double! Play ball, fellas!" he instructs us. Everyone is on edge. A sac fly gives them a 3–2 lead. In the bottom of the fourth, I have a chance to tie the game with a runner on third and two outs. I'm aiming for back up the middle, having had no luck on the right side. Chino gets behind and gives me a pitch to hit, and I drill it back at him. But he picks the comebacker, and we are out and still down.

Between innings, I chat with my teammate Chad, who dropped by between games to check out the action. He is in street clothes, still hobbled by a sprained ankle contracted in the season-ending Thespian Aid game. Beside him on the bleachers is a petite and pretty brown-haired woman who has an active little gingerbread, mixed-breed dog on a leash. Chad has his arm around the woman, Lisa. She is very nice, and my anger at Chad for fucking up the Broadway Show League playoffs subsides. I find myself wondering if he met her online by way of my heavily Photoshopped image of him.

We are still down by one when we come up to bat in the sixth. The suspense is great enough that Marybeth and Francesca have postponed their bike ride. Francesca has retreated to a grassy knoll well behind the field so that she can lie down and take pressure off her back, which has been bothering her in this fourth month of pregnancy. She has a boy and a girl in there with her. I could see them on the ultrasound monitor when we did the amniocentesis on Wednesday. The OB made me sit down while she was doing it in case I fainted. This is another of those tests whose results take way too long to find out. So until the Wednesday after next, all I can report is that the OB did a nice job with the big needle, hitting all fluid and no baby.

With two outs, Walker on first and Tommy on second, and time running out, I get a chance at redemption. Like last time, this at bat I am looking for the first good one to hit. I offer at a fastball, inner half, catch it squarely, but toward the handle. Thank heavens for aluminum, as the ball lines into left for a single. Tommy is waved home, and the game is tied! As the throw to the plate gets away I cruise into second and Walker into third. Woody has a chance to give us the lead, but he flies out. No one scores in the seventh, and it's on to extra innings.

We hold them in the top of the eighth, and I try my Foxes trick. I draw up a mock play calling for me to be the hero, as I am the fifth person scheduled to bat. The Machine is mainly a new audience for this bit, and it draws a few giggles. We get something going. I find myself on deck with one out and runners on first and second, but Walker the DH has a different ending in mind. He drills a single to left center. The outfielder gathers it on one hop and comes up throwing, as Frank sends Tommy home, hoping apparently that the throw will again be off-line. It's not, and he's out from here to Columbus Day. I am now up with two outs, runners on first and third, and a chance to win the biggest game of the season. My triumphant *The Natural* scenario—the one from the movie, I'm hoping—is coming around to me.

Casey trots in from right-center field and holds a conference near second base. The urgency of the game and the glorious afternoon are filling the bleachers with many curiosity seekers. On the left side, the Hitmen's women fans have become increasingly vocal. Marybeth and Francesca, now back on the bleachers, seem worried for me. I am being psychologically frozen the way opposing teams call a timeout to harass a field goal kicker or a free-throw shooter when the game is in the balance. Billy walks over to the plate, and I worry that he is going to pull me. Instead he confirms my strategy. We agree that I am to hack at the first pitch that looks good. I have all kinds of time to think. The championship is at stake, I'm up to bat, and despite the fact that we have options on the bench, no one would think of calling in a pinch hitter. I've hit the ball hard every time, and when I haven't I've walked. The whole season is on the line, and I need to focus on the matter at hand, but I can't help thinking one thing: I've finally made it as a softball player!

Teddy breaks up the powwow, and, his decision made, Casey strides in from the outfield and warms up quickly, as if we had been causing the delay. He starts me with two risers that miss high and wide. Normally this would force him to lay one in, but his next pitch is yet another riser, which also misses. Their strategy is now obvious. He was hoping to blow me away or for me to bite on an unhittable pitch. Otherwise he is going to take his chances with the next guy. Being semi-intentionally walked never happens in *The Natural*, either the book or the sell-out movie. But how great is this? I am thinking. Not only am I in the game at a key moment. I'm being pitched around.

TEDDY BROKE UP THE POWWOW

Still, at three and oh I'm sitting on the nothing ball, inner half, as there is more room for me in left field, in case Casey elects to throw one. Maybe having grown frustrated with his own strategy, he does! It's low and a little inside, but also close to my miniature wheelhouse and what I'm looking for. I start to offer at it, but just as quickly think the better of it and check my swing. After all, Casey has just started pitching, and if he wants to walk the bases loaded, who am I to stop him? I shouldn't risk getting myself out on ball four. He might lose the next guy too, or be forced to give in. I head to first base trying unsuccessfully to project Zeus-like disdain at Casey's unwillingness to throw me a strike. But I'm far too happy for that.

The next guy is Woody. Casey grooves one that Woody sends back at him. Casey deflects the ball with his glove, and it dribbles to shortstop. I shout, "*Segunda!*"—one of the few Spanish nonswearwords I know—in the hope that shortstop will relay it to second base, where I'm already sliding in safely. But my bilingual ploy fails, and he guns to first, where he still somehow has time to nail Woody.

With the two Clinchers turned to mush, neither team threatens to score. Each team's fans, theirs especially, let out a cheer when a side gets set down. Francesca and Marybeth cancel their ride, and Francesca heads back to the mound to rest her back. In the top of the eleventh, their leadoff man hits a roller toward third. Trey charges in and makes a nice scoop but an errant

I HEADED TO FIRST BASE, TRYING
TO PROJECT DISDAIN

throw. Keith can't save it, and umpire Jack waves the runner to second base. A grounder to the right side and a fly ball, and we're down 4–3. Walker is leading off for us in the bottom half. I watch from on deck as he hits a bounder between first and second. The second baseman is so close to first that he could field the ball and step on the bag himself to record the out. He drops the ball, picks it up, still with plenty of time to complete the play. Then he drops it again, and before he can retrieve it this time, Walker has sailed across the base.

As I step to the plate, the outfield shifts way in. The right-center fielder is playing deep second base. The right fielder is patrolling the line like an umpire in the World Series. It is intimidating. Most teams have novices or unaccomplished fielders in right. The Hitmen have a former Philadelphia Phillies farmhand. I think briefly about trying to send one over an outfielder's head but decide to shoot as usual for just a base hit, hitting the ball where it's pitched, or a walk, if Casey wants to issue me a fourth one. Casey grooves one across the outer half and I line it over the first baseman's head, but the Phillie fanatic charges in, short-hops the ball, and comes up throwing like an infielder. I'm flying up the line, head down, but unlike trying to beat out an infield hit, I can't help seeing the play develop. It is bang, bang, but Jack punches his fist down, "Out at first!" Walker advances to second, but then Woody flies to left, Clooney grounds to first, and it's over.

The team gathers around the bleachers, not saying much and trying to absorb the loss, which has all but eliminated our chances to win the championship. Panama swoops in, crying as always, "Win or lose, we booze!" He is working our bench, as the Hitmen always have their own coolers and are breaking out the Bud. Like my teammates, I'm acting down, the way players are supposed to do after a tough loss. But unlike Monday, I'm can't say I'm

187

unhappy. I played well at bat and in the field. At the end I hit it well, and the guy made a great play. It's too bad that we are down two games and probably out, but I've made it here. And not a moment too soon. Francesca and I are finally going on a vacation and will be out of town next Sunday.

## No Day at the Beach

My relentless softball schedule had prevented Francesca and me from going on vacation until now. We've spent the last three days with Robb and Joey in Montauk, sitting on the beach, reading novels, eating lobster, and riding bicycles. We plan to enjoy one last day at the beach and return in the evening. But I have a different plan. I want to leave early. The Machine needs to dump the Hitmen three in a row today to wrest the crown from them in the Lower Manhattan Softball League, and I need to be there.

All weekend, I've been tormented by thoughts that have cut through the sun, sand, and seafood to roil my relaxation. All season long I've wanted just to make good on a good team in a hard league to put to rest my Little League trauma. I did well in the playoffs. I made plays, put up numbers, and restored my good name. When Billy kept me in the game, the Hitmen huddled about how to handle me, and Casey pitched around me, I felt that I had made it at last. I've seen my role as keeping innings alive, and the walk did that. If the rest of my teammates had been at the top of their games, we would've won.

Since I had this vacation scheduled for months, there was no refund on the deposit, and Billy's league went beyond schedule, I was satisfied to go out on a personal high note. Yet why should I settle for that? It's as if I had the attitude my Pamela's teammates had shown after the Monday-league loss—they were happily surprised with our better-than-expected results and content simply to be standing on the field in the finals. One thing had been bothering me in particular: Why didn't I swing at the 3–0 pitch that I might have drilled for the game winner?

As I watched the surf roll in, I figured out what was holding me back on Sundays: me. I wanted to be a star on Mondays and in the coed leagues, but wanted just to make it on Sundays, which I for some reason equated with my Little League experience. But there's only one game. It's the same. The Hitmen aren't so different from anyone else. I can't break up games with homers, but I'm always a threat to get a hit, regardless of the opponent and especially if the pitcher gets behind. So when I had the chance to help my team win its biggest game of the year, what did I do? I passed on a borderline pitch, one I could've hit, and left it up to Woody, whose peak softball years came and went during the Ford administration! I had a chance to be the man, and, without hesitation, I chose to be a cog.

No one is blaming me. No one even saw it—including, at the time, me. But there it was: the most dramatic moment of my entire softball season, hours upon hours of play, and when it happened I couldn't identify it. Had I got a hit, it would've been anybody's series. I realized that I let down Billy, who is heading to Arizona for his mother's operation as soon as this ends and is about to fold the league, my teammates—and myself. To redeem myself I needed to get back to Central Park.

My desire for redemption cost me not only the last day of the vacation but the last night as well. After dinner, I tried to convince Francesca that I needed to return. It was a difficult task, since I had already explained that it would be almost impossible to beat the Hitmen three times in a row. It's a lost cause. Also, I've agreed to so little vacation, and we are staying at a beautiful resort that will bar us once our babies are born. We argued fiercely but softly—probably not so quietly as to prevent Robb and Joey from overhearing us, but enough so that they could plausibly pretend that they hadn't when we broke the news.

So I'm up at dawn to catch the six-fifty-five to the city. I can already see it's going to be another beautiful day on the tip of Long Island. When I emerge from the subway at West Fourth Street, the sky is gray and the pavement soaking, apparently from a heavy rain that drenched the city this morning, and I wonder if I've made a major error. But an e-mail message from Billy indicates that the games are on. I take a cab uptown; despite my early start, I'm running late, and the C train isn't making local uptown stops. Today we play on the Great Lawn, where both teams are wandering from field to field, searching for the one with the least standing water. We have our pick because the Big Apple League's playoffs are finished. Also, on weekends New York, New York, is the city that always sleeps in. We settle on #2, on the northeast side of the Lawn. The red flags are up, but the Central Park Conservancy groundskeepers, zipping around in a green golf cart, give us the OK.

The umpires are already here. Jack is back, with his glass eye and forbidding attitude. I walk past him and nod. He spits. But the personable Teddy is not with him. Probably he reckoned it wasn't worth getting out of bed and making the trip, as we could lose the first game and minimize his payday. No doubt Teddy also factored in how disputatious these games can be. In his place is a base umpire I've never seen before, a skinny, pale guy with long hair and a mustache. It seems odd to have a new umpire for the last series in the finals, especially an umpire who seems to project so little authority. Although he and Jack mark out the bases with a tape measure, they appear a foot or two closer than usual. Chino, the backup pitcher of the Hitmen, is doing the best he can to disperse the puddles by third base and in the batter's box with a kitchen broom, the only implement available, the groundskeepers apparently having better things to do than to help us.

Casey, the Hitmen superstar, is matched against Billy in today's first game. In the playoffs, the steady Billy has reemerged as our ace, having outpitched the mercurial Dick, whose season-long string of luck seems to have run out. And if the series goes to five games, meaning we play three today, only Billy, with his arm-friendly assortment of junk and his noncombustible head, can hope to pitch two games well. The lineup is the same as for the last game, but Billy has taken a hard look at the scorebook and tweaked the batting order. Matt, who has got hot at the right time, is at leadoff, and Clooney is dropped to ten. I am now batting eighth. The catcher Superman has quit, upset that he was benched the previous week.

In the pregame huddle, I'm expecting Billy to pull some *Kid from Tomkinsville* shit, like reminding us that the season isn't over until the last out of the last game of the season. But Billy is asking us only to have a good time and to play our game. On the count of three, instead of shouting, "Win!" as we normally do, he instructs us to say, "Fun!" I am with him. I had been wearing my charcoal grey Machine T-shirt religiously throughout these serious playoffs. But today I have decked myself out in the most ludicrous major league baseball outfit of the last half century—the sunrise rainbow tiers of the early-1980s Houston Astros. Sartorially speaking, I'm going for broke. As the game begins, the Hitmen have their little knot of vocal and loyal female fans. Chino, their second-string pitcher, who doesn't play unless he is pitching, is whipping up excitement among them. It becomes clear why he had with him a tool to clean off the field. Chino is waving the broom—the traditional way bad-sport sports fans symbolize a series sweep. On the Great Lawn, the benches are on either side of the backstop, reducing the usual great distance between where we set up. So his little demonstration is taking place only about fifteen feet away from our bench, making it seem personal. Tommy points at him: "Look at the guy with the broom. Who does he think he is?"

We are the visitors and jump right on Casey, aided by their defense. Matt lines a single, and the shortstop drops Krishy's grounder. Mike singles in Matt, and the second baseman drops Keith's grounder, bringing in Krishy. Walker singles to load the bases, and Tommy sends in Mike with sac fly. Trey is up

TOMMY SAID, "WHO DOES HE THINK HE IS?"

and Casey points to first in the speeded-up softball version of the intentional walk. He wants to pitch to me—my big chance to make up for last week. Today I'm determined to be no day at the beach. I'm ready to hack and when Casey brings one in, I shoot it up the middle. The second baseman dives and knocks it down, but has no play, and another run is across. Casey loses his composure and walks in two more runs. Before we are done twelve guys have batted, and the score is 6–0. As Tommy heads out to the field, he asks Chino, "Where's your broom, champ?"

With the game seemingly in hand, Dick starts jawing with one of the Hitmen, who says he wishes Dick were pitching. Dick replies that the Hitmen are being beaten so badly that the wish will soon be granted—in game two. The Hitman has to be restrained from going after Dick with something heftier than a broom. The rhubarb consumes a good ten minutes, just as the sun has finally returned from the Hamptons for its afternoon's work in the city. Eventually Jack ejects the offending Hitman, the game continues, and we get the win.

Between games I get a Gatorade from an official green-and-white vendor cart, as Panama never ventures north of the Sheep Meadow. As I'm waiting for the skinny umpire to get himself a hot dog, I'm thinking that maybe this isn't impossible. If we can win this next game, they might fold. Already they are starting to turn on themselves, despite Casey's best efforts at diplomacy. Billy calls us in, and to stay with the theme declares that our on-three cry will be "More fun!" He has moved Trey up in the order with Krishy protecting him—so much for my making them pay for intentional walks. Dick is taking the ball, and Frank is serving as his personal catcher, a la Tim McCarver to Steve Carlton, as Woody sits. As we take the field, Frank isn't ready, so I warm Dick up. He has good stuff. He releases the ball almost backhand, snapping his wrist forward in a way considered legal that adds speed and a rise to his pitches. He is getting it over pretty well too.

But when the game starts, Dick loses his grip on the strike zone. With one out, he walks the bases loaded. The Hitmen fans are now noisily suggesting that his aversion to strikes is fear-related. I wonder if he is nervous. Frank asks Dick to throw to the glove, but Dick ignores him, circling the rubber in anger over a call, muttering curses, and glaring at Jack, but losing the stare-down. I'm trying to focus, after a sacrifice fly, another free pass, and then a 3–1 count. I'm only half ready when the batter slashes a hard grounder to the right side, but fortunately it's to the deadly serious Keith, who bails out Dick with just the one run across.

In the second inning, it's the same story. Dick gets an out and walks the bases loaded, with lots of stomping around and glaring. Billy comes onto the field. I'm trying to form a posse to ensure that Billy can force Dick out of the game, rounding up Mike at shortstop. He wonders out loud whether I'm afraid of Dick going off on me, and maybe I am, but Dick has got to go if we are going to have any chance. This time Billy is all business, and Dick surrenders the ball and walks to bench, to catcalls from the Hitmen fans, at last speechless. Billy induces a grounder to third, a potential double-play ball. But it skims through the muck. Before we can get out of the inning all three of the walks have come across, and we are down 4–0.

When we come to bat, a hit, an error, and a walk, again fill the bases for me, the tying run at the plate. I am facing Chino, who has, like Dick, a difficult riser and control issues. I'm still trying to rehabilitate myself to myself, but also want to build a big inning and not to try to drive in just one run by flying out. Because Keith has just walked, I also want to see if Chino has lost the strike zone. I take a ball and a strike and then what I think is ball two, but Jack calls it a strike. I protest, and Jack responds menacingly, "Do you want some cheese with that whine?" At one and two, I am at Chino's mercy with the riser, which he gets up and over. I go after it, but lift it meekly to the right side. My fly is too shallow to risk sending the runner home. I have managed to make an out without bringing in a run. On the bench, Billy pointedly advises me I should swing before two strikes against Chino, so as not to be vulnerable to the riser. Tell me about it. The Hitmen get out of the inning without any runs scoring.

We chip away, but after four and a half we're still down 5–2. On the bench Billy is muttering about the inning we loaded the bases and came up empty. "You've *got* to score in that situation," he is telling everybody and nobody, as if delivering the definitive postmortem on the game and season. For some reason, Billy is not complaining about Dick having walked us into a huge hole or about anyone else. I can't help thinking: I gave up another beautiful beach day in Montauk for this? Not to mention the all-expenses-paid, all-inclusive trip to Francesca's doghouse? It seemed preordained that we were going to lose at some point today. The odds couldn't have been better than one in ten that we would win three straight. I could be lying on the beach having gone out on a high note, having played well in last week's losing effort. Now I'm being held responsible for the missed opportunity that is already being chalked up as the cause of our demise. Has my reputation developed a death wish?

By the sixth, we have drawn within two, and with one out and one on I'm up—my last chance to make amends. Chino gives me a ball to hit, and I lace it sharply up the middle. As a fielder the second baseman is like my opposite. He makes some brilliant, athletic plays but sometimes muffs routine balls. This time he dives and backhands my shot, shoveling the ball in the same motion with his glove to the shortstop to nip Keith. I'm trying to hold my head up. I came back and did my best, but it didn't happen for me, or the team, which has played its last game. And all off-season Billy will be blaming me.

We are down to our last licks, trailing 5–3. Clooney, whose two fine over-the-shoulder catches in left center have kept us in the game, is first-pitch swinging and lifts a popup to second. It's the sort of easy out that has been killing us, and the frustration is so great on our bench that several Machinists are audibly groaning—until the second baseman drops it. Matt lines one to left, bringing our bench to its feet, but his ball is right at the left fielder, who was cheating way in. Two outs left. Tommy, whose slump has ended with his three hits this game, draws a walk, and it's up to Mike the shortstop. The outfield is playing a kind of prevent defense, but Mike goes right at them. He sends one deep, deep to left, and the outfielder goes racing back, with time and room to haul it in. The runners tag and the tying run jogs into scoring position, but Billy and some other Machinists are irked that with all the green space granted him Mike didn't try to poke a single instead of going for it all. We are down to our last out. A base hit will tie the game, and Walker is looking for the first good ball to hit. He gets one and drills it—but on a short hop right to the shortstop. He fields it cleanly and gathers himself, with all afternoon to throw to first and end our hopes. But he thinks too long, his peg handcuffs the first baseman with a nasty in-between hop, and the game is tied!

They intentionally walk Trey and pop up Krishy, but we're alive, and they're shaken. Billy retires them easily in their part of the eighth, and the only sounds heard from the Hitmen side are bickering. Tommy, who is fired up, which he gets when he is playing well, is encouraging the bench: "We have the hammer now," meaning last ups. "Let's use it!" Keith flies out, bringing me up. I have learned my lesson against Chino and am looking for the first good one to hit. He gets one over, and I shoot it between third base and short. One out later Clooney pops one weakly, not even all the way to the pitcher, and it looks as though we are headed to the ninth. With two outs I'm dashing on automatic pilot. When I look up the ball is near the backstop, and the Hitmen are in a tizzy. The ball had landed in front of Chino, but with the backspin English on it, it boomeranged off the leg of the catcher, who had ventured into fair territory. I'm on third, courtesy of Clooney's minus-ten-foot double. Chino walks Matt semi-intentionally, and up steps Tommy. His bat still has nothing but ropes in it, and he shoots one cleanly into center. I'm clapping my hands and stamping on the plate with both feet the way players do on TV. Our victory huddle migrates to first base, where Tommy's high-fives are dangerously hard.

After the game, I go back to the cart for another Gatorade, less out of necessity than superstition. The skinny umpire is there again for another hot dog. He seems famished. He wolfs it down, his Adam's apple bobbing. For the rubber match Jack is going to be behind the plate yet again. He can't risk having the new guy call the balls and strikes, and fortunately there have been no close calls at the bases. But Jack is worried about something else. He wants Billy to collect the umpires' fees from the Hitmen, who are beside themselves on their bench, the beleaguered Casey trying, over raised voices and gestures, to get his flaking charges to focus on the task at hand. Jack fears that if the Hitmen lose again they might be so hostile that they would welsh on the umpires' fees. "Me and my partner need to get paid," he tells Billy. "No matter what happens, Casey's good for it," Billy replies, not wanting to disturb the internecine squabbling. Let fighting dogs fight.

Switching from commissioner to manager, Billy calls us together for "Even more fun!"—although with his intense intonation and military cadence he might as well be shouting, "Win!" Despite having pitched almost two complete games this afternoon, Billy is starting again in the finale with no argument from Dick. The undefeated regular-season ace/playoff cousin is done.

**BILLY STARTED AGAIN IN THE FINALE**

Billy urges us to jump out to the lead. He sees the Hitmen as being on the verge of implosion and wants us to shove them over the edge. They were expecting to sweep and thought they had the last game in the bag. Now Casey has his hands full trying to hold them together. Their better record gives them home-team honors for the final game, so we come right back up to bat. Casey, who has called his own number, gets Matt to ground out, but Tommy, Mike, and Walker all line hits for one run, and a fly by Trey brings in another. For the first time we have a lead in the series! But the Hitmen don't fold. In their half, their leadoff man doubles and moves up on Casey's long fly. The next batter hits a comebacker to Billy. He looks the runner back and throws to first, but the runner heads home, Keith's relay is a little wide, and Woody can't bail him out. In the second, they lead off with two singles, and two fly balls later the game is tied.

The sun beats down, evaporating the pool on the diamond, drying the grass, and summoning drowsy New Yorkers from their beds to the park, but hits are becoming scarce, as Billy and Casey duel it out. In the bottom of the fifth, there is an auspicious sign. Our Hasidic fans, having wandered Central Park all afternoon in search of their team, have finally found us. But the Hitmen's leadoff batter, the last in the order, singles. I'm thinking it would be huge to twist this one up. Casey is up next, and he would be far less dangerous with two out and the bases empty than with one out and a runner on first—or two runners on base. As if following my thinking, the next batter hits one down and hard to Mike at shortstop. I have a chance to make the big play! Mike shovels the ball in one motion, and I pivot, not wasting time by stepping out of the baseline. With the shortened bases and a great jump

195

the runner is on top of me, and his hard slide cleanly knocks both legs from under me as I unload. I fall horizontally, my head going Wump! on the dirt like Charlie Brown's after Lucy pulls the football away. I get to lie out on the sand after all.

The next thing I know all the guys are around me. Clooney the sharp-tongued outfielder is for once deadly serious. He wants to know if I lost consciousness. I say I'm pretty sure that I didn't, though I'm not sure where my glasses are. With a concussion ruled out, other teammates lighten the mood. Up off the bench, MikeHargrove shows me his fist, our little joking sign, and asks, "How many fingers?" His ex–high school teammate Matt wants to get in on the hijinks. "What night is Quizo?" he asks urgently. When I answer, "Monday," Matt pronounces me good to go. I stand up, still a little woozy, and Tommy says, "Steady, Eddy." But Billy isn't replacing me, and there's no way I'm coming out. I realize that I don't know what happened. I fear I sailed my throw past Keith and sent the go-ahead and probably winning run to second base, but I'm holding out some small hope that I somehow completed the double play and shut down the inning. Maybe I'm the hero. So I ask. "Throw?" Matt replies, raising his eyebrows quizzically, as if I've stumped him or my condition might be more serious than initially diagnosed, "The ball rolled most of the way to Keith." Game resumed, Casey ropes one to the left side, but Mike snags it, and his peg to Keith easily doubles off the runner.

Between the arrival of our fans and my loopy performance I'm hoping the team becomes inspired. Matt drills one up the middle, but Casey snags it just before receiving a complimentary eyebrow piercing. Tommy hits one as sharply, just out of Casey's reach, and is on first with the go-ahead run. Mike has Casey in his crosshairs too, with the hardest of them all. But Casey somehow averts another optional cosmetic surgery, throwing his glove up, snaring the ball in the webbing, and then having the presence of mind to double Tommy off first. Three rockets, nothing to show for them, and nine outs later, it's extra innings, again.

I lead off the eighth, and Casey for some reason is starting me with risers, as if I too am a threat to detach his retinas, but he can't get them over. He goes down three and one. Billy and possibly our entire bench are advising me to take—as if I might be thinking of doing anything else. Casey can't get it over, and I am on first with the go-ahead run. Finally getting his chance, MikeHargrove comes to the plate, Billy being worried that banjo hitters like Woody will be thwarted by the Hitmen defense. MikeHargrove singles and sends me to second. Clooney flies out, and then Matt pounds one down and hard in the hole between short and third. My head is down as I slide into third. When I look up the ball is on the ground near second, and the skinny umpire has his palms down. The erratic second baseman has apparently dropped the flip. The bases are juiced with only one out and the white-hot Tommy coming up.

But as he steps in, the game is delayed. The second baseman is arguing with the skinny umpire, claiming that he had control of the ball and lost it while transferring it to his throwing hand for the relay. The umpire hears him out, looks a little lost, and then, as if acting out the fantasy of anyone who has ever contested a judgment call of an umpire anywhere, reverses his call. The runner is out! Now Billy is up and arguing. He seems certain the ball was dropped and is asking the base umpire to confer with Jack. He does, and they are quarreling intensely but quietly, in a way that reminds me of my trying last night to convince Francesca that I needed to be here today. The umpires separate, and the skinny one indicates that the corrected call stands. With two outs and an open base, Casey pitches around Tommy, and with the bases loaded Mike the shortstop still has a chance to break the game open. Their outfield, out of respect for his power, is positioned halfway to Delacourte Theater. Mike turns on one and plasters it high and deep to left. The outfielder turns his back to the plate, but he has great range and plenty of real estate to work with and makes the catch.

Now they have a chance to win. Their first batter, the last in their order, singles up the middle. This is bad. Odds are fifty-fifty that they win this inning, probably better. Billy gets ahead of their leadoff man, a dead pull hitter. I am shading up the middle, hoping to get another chance at a double play. But Billy gets deep in the batter's kitchen with a fastball. He fists it to the right side. I have no play. Keith goes after it, but it lands softly between us, just onto the outfield grass. The winning run is at second, no outs, and Casey is coming up. This is very bad.

Billy is working Casey carefully but can't afford to lose him. Casey swings hard and fouls one off. His plan seems to be to use his power to hit the ball as high, hard, and as far as he can. If it doesn't clear the outfield, a long fly will at least advance the runner to third, who will able to score on a grounder or another fly ball. Casey's next vicious cut sends the ball deep to dead center. Krishy and Clooney drift back, Krishy calling it, as the runner on second tags up. But Krishy twists one way and then another, and the ball drops behind him. The runner rounds third and heads home. Krishy hustles it in, and Mike's relay home is swift and true. But too late.

Casey is at second, skipping around jubilantly in an approximation of slow motion. From up close he looks beatific, as if this were the Rapture and he had just been summoned to the Big Club in the Sky. You have to hand it to him. What didn't he do? He shut us down, made defensive gems, talked his team out of imploding, and ripped a sayonara, championship-winning double. Casey breaks his trance, trots to home plate, and launches himself onto a celebratory dog pile. We have to wait until they untangle themselves to perform the perfunctory hand-slapping, as their fans serenade us with the theme song of ungracious winners everywhere: "Na na na na, na na na na, hey hey hey, goodbye." We head to our first-base sideline, change out of our cleats, and watch the Hitmen's photo shoot. Like Irving Plaza, they pose on the pitching rubber, alternately drinking from and pouring on one another a magnum of champagne, happy to risk being ticketed for a quality-of-life offense.

Meanwhile, our team is trying to sort out what went wrong. Everyone agrees that a team needs to score more than two runs to win a championship. Someone remarks on the shots at Casey. What if they had gone one or two feet either way? More point to the bizarre call by the rookie umpire that squelched a big inning. Probably everyone is thinking about one play or at bat he might have done differently. As usual, no one discusses more basic things. What, for instance, might have happened if instead of having Dick, who walked and talked us out of game one and almost game three, we had Zeus, whose bat might have put us over the top? Billy collects fifteen dollars each from us, given the number of games and officials, and reports back, dumbfounded, that Jack and skinny blue now agree that our runner was safe, but neither would say why the call went the other way. I wonder if they were afraid to make the correct call because it might cost them half of their fees.

I still wish I had swung the bat at three and oh last week. But I'm glad that I didn't exit on my apparent high note. I put my reputation back on the line, gave it my best, and tried to turn it around. It didn't happen. But now I feel not only as though I were accepted by my teammates. I also feel that they were relying on me and expecting me to help the team win. I'm also having a hard time reconciling the apparent facts of the situation with how I feel about them. The Hitmen are the champions. Anyone can tell because they are whooping it up at the rubber and mishandling the magnum. But we played out the lost cause for fun and pride and to win, and we almost pulled it off. In a way it feels as though we had. We beat them twice, and maybe a third time too. I want to be happy with what we've done, but everyone seems down, as players tend to be after losing a big game.

I am sad too, but it's not about the loss of the championship. The defeat in the game is preempting some larger loss. This afternoon marks the end of the team. Billy is a little like J. Henry Waugh, Robert Coover's accountant and fantasy baseball czar. Billy can't rig the dice to harm Casey, but without Billy the league can't go on and he has been frank about his plans to fold it. It seems unfair—even more than the umpiring. Now that I've become part of something tangible, it disintegrates. I will miss these guys, and I'm sure they will miss one another. This team has played together for years, and it's going to dissolve without anyone saying so much as a word about it, and to the taunting strains of "Na Na Hey Hey." Losing teams never take a picture. Losing teams never throw a party. My teammates peel off in different directions, and New Yorkers encroach on the field, reclaiming their park. With no better place to go, I linger until the last of my teammates has gone home.

**❨ TUESDAY, OCTOBER 7, EAST RIVER #7 ❩**

## *Playing to Win*

School is back in full swing, Washington Square is teeming with students, and the softball summer seems far away and unreal. It is as if my colleagues had been living their grownup lives in their adult summer homes upstate, while I went to camp. When they ask what I did for my vacation, they are duly impressed to hear that I "stayed in the city and worked on my book." But I'm only now back to focusing on my old-age pension movement project. "Baseball and Society" is again a big draw. There is the usual plurality of Yankee fans with their profound sense of entitlement. This time I have a Boston fan willing to mix it up with them about whether their deep-pocketed owner is good for the game. I have Jim Bouton lined up to talk to them later in the semester. Maybe I'm more familiar with the material, maybe I've had too much ball-related anxiety for one year, but, for whatever reason, I'm no longer worked up before class.

I am out of things as far as running the sociology department goes. As director of graduate studies, acting chair, and then director of graduate studies again, I felt responsible for almost everything that happened. Now my administrative duties have devolved to taking photos of new students and faculty for the bulletin board. I've had a chance to get to know the new chair slightly better, and he seems like a nice and sincere person. When I think about it I'm still unhappy about the way the decision went down, but who knows what the dean told him, and I'm thankful that he is chair and I am not. I wouldn't want his problems. There is a pattern in the department of colleagues getting all worked up over minor issues and taking them in a huff to the chair—and then maybe to the dean. When I was acting chair I used to think of those sessions as having to change my colleagues' diapers. I'm beyond it. Come February I'll be changing real diapers for twins.

With Jeff back from the Berkshires, it's as though I were exchanging my camp friends for my school friends. At Pamela's yesterday, he filled me in on some developments that would be keeping me up at night if I were chair. Although no one has voluntarily left the department in the time I've been a member, Jeff tells me that one of our junior colleagues is all but out the door to California–Berkeley. What's worse is that Jeff may follow. He's been a loyal soldier for many years—working diligently with students and doing all requested administrative work, while watching less accomplished colleagues blackmail the university into pay raises and other perks by seeking offers elsewhere. He is seriously considering a job at California–Davis. Francesca and I are also looking and may be California-bound as well—there may be jobs at California–Irvine, California–San Diego, and California–Santa Barbara. Maybe we will all move out west like the Giants and Dodgers half a century ago. In the meantime she is working day and night to finish her book on narrative and social movements in preparation for her second Columbia tenure review next fall, and her delivery in January.

But there is one softball league still playing, and today's first day of the East Village playoffs has a big-league postseason atmosphere. We are on the same schedule with the same weather as the major leaguers. Because we play during the daytime, there is an old-time feel to the games. And, as in my class, where everyone acts as though the Yankees–Red Sox playoff games are tantamount to the World Series, there is much talk of who is going to win it all.

The East Village Softball Association is also like the majors in that eight teams advance to the postseason. This week we will see if our d.b.a. team can make it to the division finals, where the Yankees and Red Sox are already. This is my last chance to win this season. Looking back, I can't help noticing that in the other leagues I played in, the champion was always able to defend its crown. The Hitmen hung on in the Sunday league, Irving Plaza won on Mondays, the firemen won on Tuesdays, and the Madison Square Garden stagehands romped on Thursdays.

Now it is up to d.b.a. to defend its title. Although we have to be considered the favorites, working through the probabilities is disheartening. Like most favorites in baseball postseasons, our chances of winning have to be reckoned at less than fifty-fifty. We should be able to win both series in the Western Division, though Cedar Tavern is much improved and could stop us. If we advance, Louie's Josie's team or commissioner Bart's Two Boots squad

EAST VILLAGE SOFTBALL ASSOCIATION, STANDINGS AT END OF REGULAR SEASON

| Western Division | | | | Eastern Division | | | |
|---|---|---|---|---|---|---|---|
| Team | W | L | GB | Team | W | L | GB |
| d.b.a. | 15 | 5 | — | Josie's | 16 | 5 | — |
| Cedar Tavern | 12 | 8 | 3 | Two Boots | 15 | 5 | 0.5 |
| Junno's | 12 | 9 | 3.5 | Welcome to the Johnsons | 11 | 9 | 4.5 |
| Aggravators | 9 | 11 | 6 | Niagara Fish | 10 | 11 | 6 |
| Bowery Ballroom | 5 | 13 | 9 | Nice Guy Eddie's | 10 | 11 | 6 |
| Starfoods | 0 | 7 | 8.5 | Agitators | 8 | 13 | 8 |

will have an even chance to beat us. We recently split a makeup doubleheader against Josie's, and another makeup game last week against Two Boots went poorly. With Billy in Arizona for his mother's operation, I was pitching. We lost embarrassingly, 9–3, in front of Robin's friends, visiting from Georgia, and a Japanese film crew doing a piece on Jackie Robinson. Like Josie's, Two Boots has done some recruiting since we beat them last spring to add to its already powerful lineup.

Still, we are the Yankees of this league, the team with the mystique, the team that others fear and loathe. They fear us because we are talented and win. They loathe us because we have so many players that play in leagues other than this one, and a few of us don't even live in Manhattan. They are probably also envious of our free beer and pizza, which is as close as amateur softballers come to having big salaries, not to mention the fact that the d.b.a. women are by far the league's most talented and beautiful. Like our competitors, we have made some improvements during the season, notably the addition of the home run threat Juan. But what has been keeping us a cut above the opposition is Billy, who is, thankfully, back from Arizona. When asked, Billy says his mother is "doing OK, thanks." Otherwise he is pretty quiet about it. I am glad to see him back and glad not to be pitching myself now that the games matter. Sated though we are by pizza, many of us—Billy, Krishy, Penny, Big Artie, Zeus, Tommy, Robin—are hungry to win, after having been denied in other leagues. Zeus is the Captain Ahab of the group, still seeking a championship after a year of jumping aboard new teams, taking command, and watching them sink. If he is going to win, it will be as a deckhand. What we all have left is a few weeks of softball and a chance to end the season on top.

On the d.b.a. team more than any other, however, there is tension between playing to win and playing for fun, if fun is understood to mean maximizing participation and rewarding seniority and dedication. The conflict is personified in our two managers. Miles, a trumpeter with an open face and ready smile, gets a lot of gigs at Hasidic weddings. He believes firmly that

THE CONFLICT WAS PERSONIFIED BY OUR CO-MANAGERS

everyone should play, especially teammates who, like him, have played all season and who, also like him, don't play in other leagues. When push came to shove during the regular season, he argued for giving preference to the d.b.a.–only players or whoever appeared first. And he collected statistics on the number of games each teammate played, providing a sweat-equity basis on which to make playing-time decisions during the playoffs. There is precedent in softball and in life for rewarding the diligent and the punctual, and Miles's approach is consistent with the idea that this coed league should be just for fun, something bar and restaurant workers do during their time off on summer days. But because most of the better players play in other leagues, his way didn't usually result in putting the best team on the field.

The other manager, the intense Billy, wants a championship, and badly, given all his near misses. He thinks that it's more fun and rewarding to win than to play everyone and risk losing, and he believes that the bulk of the team shares his vision. He argues that through the quality of their play the best players have earned the right to be out there in their optimum positions at crunch time. Everyone else will see action when and if it is possible. At worst, they can share in the partly vicarious glory of being a member of a championship team. In his view, playing in another league is a valid excuse for most of the players who missed games. In any case, thirteen of us played in at least eight games, so sweat equity isn't going to settle the issue. Miles has inadvertently strengthened Billy's hand by also distributing batting statistics for the team. These numbers, which include on-base percentages, demonstrate who has been helping the team at the plate and who hasn't. Also working against Miles's early-bird approach is the fact that so many teams in the league have become so serious about winning. Some have reconfigured themselves explicitly to beat d.b.a., the way the Red Sox made over their team to beat the Yankees. And it's not as if *any* of us work at the bar.

For most of the year team d.b.a. dodged the too-many-players problem. The league's erratic schedule, with games possible on any day of the week, produced conflicts with our players' work schedules as well as those of other softball leagues. But at this time of year there are no other leagues, and the playoff schedule is set in advance, so players with flexible jobs can clear the decks. Altogether thirteen of our players are here today for game one of a best-of-three series against the overmatched Aggravators. Only three are women, leaving ten men for seven spots. More than one of them is going to have his feelings hurt. Probably for the same reason that he has a stronger preference to win, Billy has the more dominant personality, and so the "best" team will start today's game.

Since the series with the Hitmen, I've adopted a new attitude. When I was doing as well as I have been in this league, I used to think that I couldn't keep it up. Who could? It was as if I had decided that my "true" on-base percentage—as the sabermetricians would call it—was about one-half, with slightly lower numbers expected for the leagues with better pitchers and fielders, and slightly higher numbers expected for leagues like this one. When my stats were above expectations I would hope only that I wouldn't get too unlucky and see them sink too far down. That was my attitude after my strong start with Pamela's Foxes this season.

Now I believe that there isn't any good reason I can't reach base almost every time. If Barry Bonds went by what was expected, he would be retired instead of rewriting the record books. Sure, he's lifted more weights than Schwarzenegger and uses the kind of dietary supplements and sports balms that add inches not only to the chest and forearms but also to the chin and forehead. All the same, it's not as if my true on-base percentage is known. I should always get a pitch to hit. All I need to do is hit it hard, and since I'm aiming up the middle or right side and not for the fences, it should usually drop in. I will take the walk unless I have a chance to break up the game—the lesson I learned in September. I think of my plate appearances now as being less like taking a shot from the field in basketball—where 50 percent is good—than shooting a free throw—all of which are makeable. When I face pitchers now, I find myself being alternately irked and amused at their pre-sumptuousness in even thinking about getting me out. In on-base percentage I led the team, and no doubt the league, by plenty. I went twenty-seven for thirty-seven with six extra-base hits and ten walks. In April I started the season musing about baseball history and baseball in Japan, lost in baseball novels and movies, applying sabermetric theory to every at bat, and here in October it's all come down to "See the ball, be the ball."

So I'm definitely going to be playing and batting leadoff. But I am setting myself up to be at least a little upset here. Players who hit well usually have a big voice in where they play. Managers will rarely risk alienating their hitting stars by placing them outside their favorite positions and will risk giving something up on the defensive end just to keep the peace. For me, however, that principle doesn't seem to apply. The stats say that I've been our best hitter, and I would like to play shortstop. What's more, I'm our best shortstop. But no matter how much I lobby, it's not going to happen. Billy and Miles want Zeus at shortstop. Otherwise, "He's just going to sulk," Billy tells me. I would have to go oh for an entire season to get my OBP down to where Zeus's is, but his reputation is so great that it doesn't matter. When it counts, they want his best effort at the plate—which, admittedly, can be formidable. Also, there are only three men here today who can play outfield, and I am one of them. So because of my defensive versatility, underdeveloped reputation, and sunny disposition, I will be exiled to the outfield for our playoff run.

It is a bright, sunny day, but with a crispness in the air, and left field, where I am stationed, is already a squinty sun field at one-thirty. After Billy sets them down, I come up, get ahead in the count, as almost always, and then reach base, waiting for a pitch down the middle and whistling it past the pitcher's head. We score three in the first, two in the second, three in the third, and three in the fourth before we *really* start hitting. Juan inside outs two homers toward the East River. Billy and Miles clear the bench and allow me to mop up in this 21–2 wipeout, which we play to the finish because in this league there is no mercy.

**WEDNESDAY, OCTOBER 15, EAST RIVER #7**

## *Bad News*

It's like Marx's dictum in reverse all over again. We finished off the Aggravators last week in game two, a much closer contest as only ten of our players showed up. For the Western Division finals, we drew Cedar Tavern, which has improved tremendously, having added several recognizable players from the Central Park leagues. In game one on Monday we were ready, with another fifteen players showing to the game, including my Machine teammate Tommy, who barely qualified for the playoffs. Just as in game one against the Aggravators, we put our best team on the field, went way ahead, and cleared the bench. We are to finish the Western Division finals series today, playing a doubleheader if necessary.

When I arrive for practice before the eleven o'clock game, Billy is already there, looking haggard. He has bad news, sad news. Yesterday his mother died. He is leaving for the airport at two o'clock and will be gone for two weeks. It quickly becomes apparent that Billy doesn't want to talk about it. It's too raw and painful, and in any case he's the strong and silent type.

The worry he is willing to voice concerns today's games. He's expecting a low turnout. Our teammates may be underestimating our opponent after the game-one blowout. Or maybe it's the weather. It rained last night, and even with the sun peeking out this morning, it remains cool and windy. Gusts are blowing up to sixty miles per hour, kicking up little leaf-and-litter twisters here and there. Or maybe guys who felt they didn't play enough in the one game are just skipping the next. Whatever the reason, we have only nine players at game time, and only Juan, who has a court date, was expected to be missing. Fortunately, the field needs work. Some Cedar guys are shoveling cloudy water from depressions near the batter's box and the rubber into a barrel and carting it off, while Billy and Miles fill the holes with dirt from a pile along the third-base line. The first pitch is held up past eleven-thirty, and in the meantime Penny appears. Still, if we have to play a second game today, it's going to be bad news for d.b.a. Billy will be gone, and I have "Baseball and Society" this afternoon. We need to win the first one.

We are the visitors. I lead off with a walk, Billy gets a hit, and I come home when Krishy and Zeus fly out, but that is all we get. Runs are scarce today, and a seesaw battle ensues. The game is tied in the fifth, and we have chance to break it open with runners on second and third and one out. Miles is due to bat, but he sends in Juan, fresh from his day in court, to pinch-hit. The Cedar manager objects, claiming that no one can bat until having played the field. This seems wrong—just Monday three of our guys pinch-hit in the blowout. Also, no rule could be more nonparticipatory and antibaseball. So of course it is on the books. Miles eventually steps up to the plate and pops to first. Soon, though, there is payback. For some reason Andrés is working the bases for game one, though with his poor eyesight he might as well flip a coin on any close play. In bottom of the fifth, he saves us a run by calling a runner out at first, whom Big Artie had tried to throw out from his back but who was safe by at least a step. In other circumstances Billy might let them have it—but not after Juan-gate.

It is still tied and already one-fifteen when we come to bat in the seventh. Both teams have the top of the order coming up, and because Billy and I won't be around for another game, in effect this inning is for the Western Division title. I have noticed that the umpire Andrés calls Blue, behind the plate today, seems afraid to call batters out on strikes. Billy has twice thrown what looked like strike three past Cedar batters only to have Blue call it a ball. Yet Blue seems willing to call strikes on questionable pitches, especially high ones, if they come early in the count. It is as if he were trying to avoid the anger of the pitcher most of the time but also to forestall the greater wrath of a batter sent back to the bench on strikes. The pitcher seems nervous and goes three and oh. I'm not even thinking of swinging, and I am on my way to first when Blue calls the next pitch, a questionable one, a strike. I give him a hard look as I walk back. The pitcher sends one down Broadway to fill the count, but the next one is outside, and I'm off to first before Blue can make a call. Billy steps in, treating his at bat as if it were his last of the year, which it likely is. He waits for his pitch and laces a single. The pitcher loses Krishy, leaving it up to Zeus, who has been appeased by Billy all season for such a situation. From third I am encouraging Zeus to get a hit and not hit a sacrifice fly, as he did in the first. Zeus must lead the tristate area in sac flies. He compromises by hitting a line drive that sails between the left and left-center fielders. It's a grand slam, it's the ball game, and d.b.a. is returning to the finals.

Billy is packing up his stuff and saying his good-byes when he pulls me aside. He seems worried about many things, but what he says is that he fears Miles won't put the best team on the field and that we will lose to Two Boots or Josie's, who are squaring off in the other divisional final. So far everyone has played, and we have won. But we won't have Billy calling the shots when we need him the most. Billy says that he will ask Miles to treat me as a manager. He's counting on me as his replacement to bring home the championship. More important, we won't have Billy's steady pitching arm to rely on. I will have to pitch.

I'm flattered at Billy's confidence in me. I started the season hoping that he would let me play on his team and that, as a rookie manager, I could turn around my hapless Performing Arts team. Now I'm charged with managing and pitching a team to the championship. It seems like a lot to handle. Although I've built up my credibility, I know I don't want to be in charge of making lineups and substitutions for d.b.a. And I don't know if I can pitch well enough to beat Two Boots or Josie's. Still, I want to win, and to win for Billy. I try to look as confident as possible. We shake hands and wish each other good luck.

## *"Only Recreational Softball"*

In anticipation of game one of the finals, I've been awake since dawn. I would almost be nostalgic about the early-morning anxiety—as it happens so rarely now—if I weren't feeling even more powerless than when I was running Pamela's Foxes. I head to the park far earlier than usual, biking along Fourth Street and crossing over the FDR on the Sixth Street overpass. On the path to the Tenth Street field my tires uncap the occasional acorn. My own head is bursting with worry. After his mother's funeral, Billy e-mailed Miles to ask him if I could serve as a manager and made several lineup suggestions, including making sure that Tommy, the sometime d.b.a. player, would be at the game. Yet Miles didn't get in touch with me.

I want to use the extra time to warm up for my big assignment, but Andrés, who has already drawn the bubble-dot baselines and is carefully misplacing the bases, has a different exercise in mind. Today is sunny and pleasant, but yesterday's intermittent rain left standing water in front of our first-base dugout. Andrés hands me a push broom. I carve out a makeshift canal system, channeling this filthy reservoir into the drain near our on-deck circle.

Miles arrives and makes no mention of Billy's message. We have our usual complement of women—who are key to our success. Imagine the American League team getting to use the DH in the World Series while the National League has to bat the pitcher—then multiply it by three. Robin will be at first, Gina in right field, and Uma, a personal trainer who specializes in triathlons and Iron Man events, behind the plate. We have nine men. Penny, Zeus, and Juan are starting in the infield, and Miles, Krishy, and Big Artie in the outfield. Starting on the bench is George, an Upper East Side former prep school boy and current production assistant. A lanky and angular lefty, he has the upright bearing and patrician nose of a young George Plimpton. His film just wrapped. With George is another Mike, whom we call Monk, a backup pitcher and a jazz composer. Tommy is either unavailable or Miles didn't call him. Miles tells Uma to warm me up.

Our opponent is Two Boots, same as last year. Louie's anti-d.b.a. crusade will have to wait until next year. In the rubber match of the Western Division series, the Josie's captain had been doubled up off second base after failing to tag on a fly, forcing extra innings, and Two Boots won it in the eighth. Commissioner Bart's Two Boots team has, however, suffered setbacks. In the first round, their pesky leadoff man/shortstop and their left fielder, a rangy power hitter, collided, and the left fielder broke his thumb separating the shortstop's shoulder. Unlike in baseball, there is no provision in softball for replacing injured players on playoff rosters. A team that sustains injuries must carry on as best it can. However, Bart, in his role as league commissioner, has renegotiated the rule with Miles. Bart has with him today a guy from Brooklyn with the excellent old-school name of Noodles, whom Penny recognizes as a star player from one of the many leagues he plays in. I go to complain to Miles about it, but he seems to be treating this like a pickup game. "Calm down," he tells me. "It's only recreational softball."

Miles is, however, taking the ceremonial aspects of the championship very seriously. He lines up both teams on the baselines as before the World Series, unsheathes his trumpet, and bleats out the national anthem in a sort of Miles Davis dirge. Miles is taking it so slowly that the Two Boots team starts clapping, hoping to summon the final notes, well before he arrives at the land of the free.

I head out to the rubber, taking with me my three main advantages as a pitcher. One is that I can always lob the ball over the plate. Behind in the count I force batters to hit their way on. Another is that I can field the position. A surprising number of balls go up the middle, and a pitcher with a good glove can help his cause. Third, in theory I know how to pitch—get ahead, mix them up, change speeds, pitch to batters' weaknesses. Working against me is my minimal repertoire. I have a fastball, a straight change, and a knuckleball. But my heater is both lukewarm and difficult for me to control, and my knuckleball is unorthodox. When I first started throwing it as a kid, I thought I was supposed to grip the ball with the knuckles, the way a palm ball is held in the palm. I later learned that a knuckleball was supposed to be released from the fingertips. As it turned out, I wasn't holding the ball with my knuckles, as I had thought, but with the outside of my fingernails. With this foolish grip I still somehow can keep the ball from spinning, but it doesn't move much and mainly looks funny.

Fortunately, I had a chance to pitch against Two Boots recently and know the players by tendency—except Noodles, who Penny tells me is a right-handed hitter with some pull pop. More important, during warm-ups I gained control over my fastball and was able to induce some movement out of my knuckler. All I want to do is to get the fastball in and over, change speeds, and

MILES TOOK THE CEREMONIAL ASPECTS SERIOUSLY

freak them out with the occasional knuckler. I am relying on Stan Musial's dictum that pitchers need only two pitches: "the one the batter's looking for and the one he ain't." Andrés is behind the plate, leaning on Uma. It is the sort of perfect autumn day on which World Series games used to be played, before television dictated that the Series become a nighttime event. There are about thirty spectators on the asphalt bleachers, mainly players from other teams, who are mainly rooting for us to lose, and our fan base, retired Puerto Rican men from the nearby projects who are also Yankee fans.

For all my confidence, warm-ups, and theory, I fall behind their leadoff man, the right fielder, a speedy, left-handed pull hitter who laces a nothing ball to right for a single. I get ahead of Noodles and try to bust him inside with a fastball, but he inside outs a hit to right anyway. As Billy would, I call for an extreme shift on Bart, a pronounced right-handed pull hitter. Big Artie abandons right center for short left, and Juan sets up behind second base. Bart pops up a changeup, and I'm breathing easier when their powerful cleanup batter also double-clutches on a change, lifting a short fly to right. Artie has a play but stops in his tracks. The ball drops, a run scores, and Two Boots has runners on first and second. Fearing a blowout before we bat, I gather myself to work on Stosh, who has moved from third to shortstop and has good pop to all fields. He is so closely identified with his thick mustache that even though he has shaved I still see it on his face. Which I want to kiss, as he one-hops a knuckleball right back to me. I wheel and fire to Penny, who relays to Juan to complete the double play.

No rest for the weary. I come up to bat facing Bart. His repertoire consists of a fastball, which has far more speed and movement than mine, and a nothing ball, which can't even count as a changeup since he telegraphs it. He might as well be placing the ball on a tee. But he is difficult to hit if he can locate his fastball. Bart starts off nervously too, missing high with a fastball and a meatball and then complaining to Andrés that I am ducking to get the calls. It seems to be an article of faith among pitchers that a bobbing batter intimidates umpires. He loses me. Krishy singles, and up steps Juan, who has exploited the short right-field fence for four playoff homers. This time he reaches only the top of the fence, sending me and Krishy home. Neither Zeus nor Penny can bring Juan in, but Robin shoots one between third and short for the third run.

The bottoms of both orders are retired easily. To start the third I retire their top two, and we swing the shift on Bart. Never one to give in, Bart turns on one and skies it to medium left just behind Artie, who makes no effort to make the play, thinking apparently that Miles is going to make it. But Miles is too deep. Bart trots into second. This brings up their cleanup hitter. He sends one high and deep to left. Miles's deep position is paying off. He is backpedaling—baseball body language for "I've got a bead on this one"—but at the last moment lunges backward, and the ball drops behind him. The game is tied. In our half, we load the bases for Artie with two outs, but he pops open a can o' corn.

I'm wondering what's up with him. He's let two fly balls drop and hasn't done a thing with the bat. In the summer, Artie and I had ventured to Brooklyn with Francesca, her sister Maddy, and shortstop Mike and rocked several tables of twentysomethings in Quizo, my Machine-teammate Matt's trivia game. Artie answered most of the questions. But since school began, I've seen Artie only during d.b.a. games and haven't had much chance to go back to the bar. Artie doesn't seem himself lately, popping up and not fielding well. He has gone from mainstay to substitute. Because he is my friend I'm taking his misplays personally, even if they weren't the most costly. I don't know what his problem might be—the eyeglasses?—but the finals is no place to work it out. I can't say that I'm unhappy when Miles replaces Artie in the fourth with George.

We rally. Gina, Krishy, and I all single, and Juan splashes one into the East River. I set them down again in the fifth and sixth, and single and score in our half to make it 8–3. The game is all but in the bag, as they have number nine coming up in the seventh, and I'm in a groove. As I head out to the rubber, Miles

BART SENT ONE DEEP, BUT KRISHY
RAN IT DOWN

pulls me aside. He wants Monk, our other pitcher, to pitch the last inning. I'm in such disbelief that I can barely argue. It is not that I think that I'm such a big star that I can't come out. And I'm fine with having Monk in the game. He can play outfield and hit. As far as I'm concerned he could've easily gone in for, say, Miles. But the championship is no time to bring in a new pitcher, especially one that can start wild and hasn't seen action since September. If Monk were to walk the two women, he would face the top of the order and trouble. It seems a little selfish on Miles's part. So many teammates want to win this championship. I was unable to bring in Mule to finish out a meaningless dog-day game because my team-mates didn't want him to harm our chances. Mainly, I'm worried about keeping my promise. I can almost hear Billy say, "We lost to Two Boots because you let Miles pull you out of the game?"

Missing the point, Miles is acting as though I were some toddler to whom he is explaining the concept of sharing. I want to tell Miles that if he feels I have to go he should bring in Juan or Zeus to pitch. But I can't now with Monk standing right there. Maybe this move is payback for Miles's having to play second fiddle to Billy all season. Maybe it is designed to put me in my place after what he may perceive as a coup attempt. Whatever, Miles is adamant and tries to calm me by telling me that it's "only recreational softball." I'm not sure I know what he means. But he's the manager, and I'm not about to pull a Dick move, so I join Big Artie on the bench to root. Both Two Boots women reach base. Monk pops up the leadoff man, but Noodles singles, driving in the fourth run and sending the tying run into the on-deck circle. Bart has a chance to make a game of it, and the outfield shifts over. He sends one deep to left center. But Krishy runs it down. The cleanup hitter also drives one long and deep. Krishy runs that down too.

We survive, but I'm neither happy nor even particularly relieved. If this is how we're going to play it, we will lose.

## Team Photo

I couldn't believe this was happening. We were going to lose the series over the phone. It was up to Two Boots where to play the next game, and Bart chose East River #1, the artificial-turf field for which I held a permit. It is symmetrical, with short distances to the foul poles to right and left field, but then the fences splay out obtusely toward infinity—or the Williamsburg Bridge. It's impossible to homer to left center or, more important, right center, where Juan has been exploiting the cozy layout of East River #7. But Bart's dead-pull power is a threat to yank cheap homers past the foul pole and onto the FDR Drive. Two Boots handled us easily there last month and also stopped Josie's there in the playoffs. Bart's latest proposal was to complete the series today. All his players will be available, but some won't be on Friday, when the series is scheduled to conclude. He also wanted to play the third game on East River #1. Miles agreed to everything. I was extra worried about pitching, thinking I would have to stake us to an insurmountable lead before Miles inevitably replaced me on the mound.

But agreeing with Bart was Miles's last act as manager. Billy and Miles have definitely solved the manager's playoff dilemma. Both skipped town. Miles had to fly to a gig in Little Rock. I e-mailed Billy to ask him what to do next, and he instructed me to take over and contact Tommy. It was hard to disagree. Tommy's good. Also, although sabermetrics has proved that major league players only rarely have a propensity to be clutch, the pros are surfing way out there on the tail of the normal curve of calmness, which is not true of amateur players. But Tommy is not afraid of big games. So I gave him a call. Tommy said he needed to make an appearance at his Brooklyn office but would love to play if he could sneak away.

This morning I was devising a lineup when I called Krishy to make sure he'd be showing up to the game. Krishy informed me that before Miles left he turned the managerial reins over to him. I was surprised at how relieved I was. In the preseason, if someone told me I would be pitching, batting leadoff, and managing a team for the championship, I would've asked him to pinch me. If I'd then been told that I was going to be deposed as manager and would accept it eagerly, I would've said he was crazy. But pitching and leading off is enough to think about, without worrying about getting everyone to the game and making up the lineup—and keeping my promise to Billy. Krishy's otherworldliness and thick skin make him the perfect playoff manager. He's savvy and legitimate too, having managed d.b.a. to the championship last year. Krishy had already called Tommy, who confirmed. Also, with Krishy as manager, the manager won't have any trouble producing Krishy.

For game two of the finals, the day is gray, cold, and windy. In the air there is something more biting than seasonal chill, a harbinger of the winter that we are all trying to stave off a little longer with our bats and balls. I apply sunscreen, mainly out of superstition, the retro fragrance of my lucky Coppertone SPF 45 redolent of childhood days at the beach. I bike to the field early, hoping someone will be there to warm me up. I want to get a feel for my fastball so I can get it over the plate and give the team a chance to win. When I roll up, only one of our players is here. Robin the fashion model, who stayed home last night to be ready today, is slipping on a head sleeve like the ones football players wear. She agrees to catch me.

Soon the field is filled. I retreat to the left-field foul territory and continue warming up there. Two Boots has exactly the same cast of characters and lineup as in game one. On our side, Miles is out, but we have in attendance Little Artie, a slightly built jazz trumpeter with hipster sideburns and an outfielder who sprays line drives. His sub status is largely due to his laid-back personality. When Tommy comes running up to the field near the end of batting practice, the Two Boots brains trust is visibly upset to see him. But what are they going to do? Contest a guy who is on our roster, appeared in five league games, grew up in Chelsea, and lives downtown, when they are playing a guy from Brooklyn who made his East Village debut two days ago? Or are they mad about Juan, who grew up in the projects overlooking the field? Aside from Tommy replacing Miles in left, Krishy has George starting in right in place of Big Artie. The powerful Two Boots third baseman comes over to our bench and says that his team is withholding their bats from the common pool in response to Juan's placing his bat off limits. "He's hit some bombs with that bat," he says, pointing to Juan's DeMarini. I would like to keep this as friendly as possible, hoping that Juan will give them access to his stick. But he shakes his head no. I can't blame him. The latest high-tech alloy bats never break, but they wear out. In each one there are indeed only so many hits, and Juan wants them for himself.

With Miles gone, there is no pregame pomp, and the weather has scared off all but the most intrepid fans. There are a couple of the Agitators, a guy from Cedar Tavern, and two women attached to Two Boots players huddled under blankets on the first-base bleachers. We have Juan's friend and neighbor Jorgy and a friend of Gina from work in our third-base dugout. I didn't tell anybody about the games, because when I had fans show up against Irving Plaza and the Hitmen, we lost every time.

Two Boots takes the field, and I work a full count from Bart. I foul one off, and then take ball four outside and low. I am well on my way to first when Andrés calls out, *"Strike three!"* The ball was so far off the plate that I could not have been more surprised had Andrés cried, "Eet ees a *foul* ball!" More out of habit than anger, I give it to him John McEnroe–style as I cross back in front of him: "There's no way that was a strike. You can't be serious." When I return to the bench, as if freshly graduated from lack-of-diplomacy school, Penny offers me the conventional advice that dropping the bat and heading to first before the umpire's call "forces" him to call a strike, blaming me for this bad call. His parents are academics, and maybe he is working something out, but I'm upset. I've heard this theory once too often. Even with this "strikeout," in the playoffs I'm batting twelve for sixteen, with four walks. Each time I took off for first as soon as I could tell the pitch was ball four. With my stats, my opinion should at last be deemed good enough. "That's totally wrong," I bark at him, before he can repeat the thought. "The man cannot see! He probably couldn't tell I was going to first."

I know from pitching that Andrés's missed calls are dispersed almost randomly—play long enough and, as in Russian roulette, you're certain to be blown away. If my protest to Andrés was pro forma, it's because I feel I owe him. Last year against Two Boots in the finals, with the game tied in the bottom of the seventh, I was facing the bottom of their order but walked the bases loaded and ran the count to three and one on the woman batting last. I dispatched a nothing ball down Broadway, but to my horror I had left it maybe a little high and tailing outside. I was already walking off the field in disgrace when Andrés bellowed, *"Strike two!"* I got the strikeout, Robin made a big play, the next guy flew out, and the rest is, well, likely to be forgotten, but we won.

I imagined all season that when I finally rebutted the left-too-early theory, it would be deeply satisfying. But it isn't at all, and my outburst has only provided me a warning sign that I'm too much on edge. The game is two minutes old, and I've already gone off on the nicest guy on any team and insulted an elderly man with a handicap doing his best for a minimal wage. The game continues, and Krishy loops a hit to left, then Juan smacks one deep to right center, bringing our bench to its feet. At Tenth Street this shot would've been river-bound, but here at Grand Street it one-hops the fence for a double. It doesn't matter because Zeus and Tommy also bang out hits. After Penny's sacrifice fly, we are up 3–0, and I offer my hand for slapping in partial apology, even though he knows I think it's way too early for the sac fly.

I head out to the rubber, which is painted on the artificial turf, and to my surprise and delight I find that my minimal repertoire is all present and accounted for. By shortening my stride and reducing my arm motion, I can throw the fastball for a strike almost every time, and locate it too. Even the fingernail knuckleball is swaying in the turbulence. I set down the first two easily. Zeus fields Bart's smash deep in the hole, but air mails the throw over Robin and into a soccer net that had been dragged off the field. I am halfway expecting Andrés, with his pronounced broadcasting skills, to shout, "*Gooooooal!*" It would serve Zeus right. But Blue the base umpire merely waves Bart to second, while Robin fishes out the ball. Whatever. The cleanup hitter lifts a long drive to Death Valley in left center that Tommy tracks down and brings to justice, pumping his fist.

In the top of the second I get back up to bat with two outs and Gina at first, but ground to second for an inning-killing force out. Earlier in the year I would have been suffering from a different sort of Tommy anxiety than the Two Boots bench, wondering whether his presence would turn me back into a Little Leaguer. But far from being the gun-wielding bully of my imagination, I know now that he devotes long hours to scrutinizing bad guys' financial records and crafting budgetary reports to prevent layoffs. He's the rare softball player for whom the pumped-up football approach works. All I can say is more power to him and Roger Clemens.

I have to stay focused on my pitching. Five, six, and seven go down one, two, three. In the third Krishy gets another hit, and Juan, Zeus, and Tommy follow suit. Robin drives in one run and Penny another on his second sac fly. It is 6–0 when I take the ball for the bottom of the third. I miss with two fastballs to the third baseman, who is batting eighth ahead of his wife and seems still irked about our not sharing our bats. Not wanting to start with the double walk, I switch him to a steady diet of meatballs. He lays into one and lines it to left center. It should be in Krishy's back pocket, but as I look back I see that he's been playing very shallow and has turned his back to the infield to chase this one. There is almost endless room out there, with the baseline of #2 a football field way, and the artificial turf, rubberized underneath, ensures a good roll. OK, one run—so what? I can't let it get to me, and don't, setting down the next three.

Well away from our bench Big Artie is lying on the ground in a fetal position. It looks as though he might be praying or crying. When I ask him what's up, I learn that he's stretching his back, and he's irked: "It's not right that someone who comes for a few games should play ahead of someone who has been to all the games." It's not clear if he's upset with Krishy, who has benched him, or with George or Tommy, who barely qualified for the postseason but got the call today. Little Artie is on the bench too, and may be thinking along the same lines. They both should be upset with me, as I encouraged Tommy to show up. I wonder if Big Artie's sore back is responsible for the recent drop-off in his play. He went down hard making a big play against Cedar, and he's the sort of guy that wouldn't mention it. Either way, I can't help thinking that he's right and feeling like a jerk for having been upset with him.

But I have to bat, again with two outs, and from on deck Krishy asks me, "Are you planning on getting a hit today?" I have played with him all season, but his delivery is so deadpan and his dark eyes so impassive that I still can't tell when is putting me on. I suspect not this time, since he is in charge and may feel I'm letting him down. I suppose if your OBP is .800, two outs in a row—one courtesy of Andrés—constitute a major batting slump. As I look at Krishy I think, "I would be tossing a no-hitter if you'd been playing the outfield instead of deep shortstop." But I'm grateful that he's taken over, freeing me to concentrate on matters at hand. Bart falls behind, and his 3–1 grapefruit slips out of his hand and passes the plate eye-high and a foot outside. Andrés does not weigh in on it, his failure to remark obviously meaning "ball." Nonetheless, I linger in the batter's box, then turn to look at him, and wait in mock solicitousness for his call. Getting no response, I look for Penny on the bench to see if he thinks that I'm standing here long enough. He smiles. Finally, Andrés, irritated, points to first, and I ceremoniously toss away the bat and head there, where Krishy, his mind probably focused on substitutions, strands me.

Andrés has replaced the original Clincher with a new one, as always, in the bottom of the fourth. The new ball will fly, and this is their chance to get back in the game. Noodles lines out, but Bart reaches when his grounder glances off third base and ricochets past Penny. But for me it's as if there is nothing to this pitching. When I can hit spots with the fastball, no matter how mediocre it is, I'm difficult to hit. And I've got it going on. They are sawing themselves off on the fastball, mis-hitting the knucklers, and lunging at the changes. Bart's freak hit is all they get with the new ball, and after four innings they have batted only three over the minimum.

In the fifth, the meat of our order is up, and I have asked them all to foul the ball out of play on the left side. I don't want to take any chances on a Two Boots comeback. After all, they chose the field, and as I know from Saturday

TOMMY'S DRIVE CHASED ZEUS TO THIRD

pickup games, for which I pay for everything, ball attrition is one of East River #1's key liabilities. No one ever chases a ball, no matter how new, onto the FDR. Juan, Zeus, and Tommy all agree to this clever plan, but when the time comes none of them remembers. More likely, none of them wants to hit a dead ball behind in the count. Juan singles, and Zeus, who has nothing but line drives in his bat today, sends Juan home. Tommy's drive chases Zeus to third. Everyone is getting into the act now, as Little Artie, who has replaced George, drives in the third run of the inning.

In the bottom of the fifth, Krishy sends Big Artie into the game, Tommy sitting down. Two Boots rallies, loading the bases with two outs on two hits and an error. Zeus, who has been steady since the first inning, gloves a hard-hit grounder and again misfires to first base. This time Robin goes up the line, risking collision with the runner, leaps and snags the ball, applies a sweep tag in midair, and wins another softball heart forever. In our half, from the on-deck circle I watch Gina stroke her second hit of the game. She has improved so much over the course of the season! I'm determined to take the ball out of the game and line a foul down the left side. But twice my drive clanks off the middle of the fence. Up two strikes in the count Bart tries to blow me away, but I inside out his heater to right—and join our hit parade. Bearing down, Bart retires Krishy and runs the count full on Juan, who is sitting on a ball to drive. Instead Bart unleashes his nastiest fastball ever and blows it by Juan. As they cross paths Zeus is giggling at Juan, who shrugs his shoulders and grins too. It is the kind of abuse that winners give one other. Zeus singles in Gina, and it's 10–1.

Now Krishy sends Monk into the game, but to the outfield instead of the rubber. Krishy is taking no chances, and I am going to be allowed to finish what I started. I'm not relieved so much as glad to know that I wasn't out of line on Monday. It's the obvious move. Big Artie shifts over to third base, as Penny takes a seat. We are going to win, and everyone is going to see significant playing time. I set down the first two batters on three pitches and get ahead of the next one—they are all just meat to me now—who sends a pop fly way over into the extensive foul territory on the left side, but Big Artie runs it down. It's great to see him make the play, even if it's overkill. The fight out of them, the Two Boots players don't even contest whether he might've been out of play. They will start the seventh with the bottom of the order. Two Boots needs a miracle.

My teammates are congratulating one another in our dugout. We pay only intermittent attention to our own batters and then only to jeer them. Our imminent victory is mood altering, like a time-release mixture of ecstasy and endorphins; euphoria and relief wash over us. Zeus is giddy. Even the Arties seem happy. One player just saying no to the drug of triumph is Krishy. "This game is really boring," he complains. This time he's kidding, I think. In the seventh, with one away, the Two Boots third baseman is upset again. He's wondering why, in this blowout, I'm sailing knuckleballs past his wife. "That's bullshit, man," he tells me. I had been pitching on autopilot, not taking into account the score. Shamed, I start serving cantaloupe. Two Boots scores twice, but then Bart lines to third, and Big Artie snags it and flips me the game ball. In the high-five line, the Two Boots players are sheepish, but with an undercurrent of disgruntlement over Tommy. They seem somehow to believe that this personnel move was both unfair and responsible for our victory, rather than its being legit and our having rocked them from here to Thanksgiving. They clear the field, and at long last I get to set up a team photo on the final day of the season. It can't be official, with so many of our players, including both managers, missing. But I want to do it anyway, if only for the pageantry. We gather at the rubber.

Despite our big victory and how well I've played, I feel as if something is missing. I can see now that I got myself far too caught up in the crossfire between Bart and Billy. Like Billy I want to win—and after all he's gone through I wanted to win for him. But I want to win a certain way—with our players concentrating, doing their best, and getting the most out of their talent. If the team is playing well, winning should just happen. Although unlike Miles I

WE GATHERED AT THE RUBBER

would reward those who have played the best with playoff starting positions, I have to agree that when it's all on the line it's bad form to turn to guys who haven't played much just to counter a team that is illegally reloading. There is a certain measure of grace in saying that no matter who is on the field for us, we will be good enough to kick your asses. Maybe that was the point of Miles's taking me out of the game on Monday. In any case, I realize that my desire to get Tommy to the game and my anger at Artie for not playing his best related to my own fears. I was afraid that I would let the team down by not pitching well enough and becoming the focus of the sort of anger I had directed at Artie, but in spades.

I wish we could start the game over and win it with both Arties in the starting lineup. Hell, Bart could decide which of our players would play and make out the batting order too, if he wanted. I know we would win again, and easily. I wish we could keep playing. I think momentarily about trying to call the teams back on the field. I would be happy to play out the needless third game, as they do in the Davis Cup. Or if that seemed unfair, we could mix up the teams—have a pickup game. Now that winter is on its way, opportunities to play softball will be scarce. Soon Francesca and I will have twins to handle. I don't know when I'll get to play again. And I'm just starting to understand this game!

My teammates pile into Tommy's and Penny's cars for the ride to d.b.a. and the victory party. I'm looking forward to calling Billy, and maybe I will drink my entire postgame beer—class or no class. But I'm on my bicycle and hang back after everyone has left. On field #2, just to the north of us, eight young Hasidic men have materialized. They are celebrating Sukkoth in an unorthodox way. They are playing softball, having shed dark coats and hats in favor of white shirtsleeves. Seeing their formal attire and old-fashioned facial hair, I feel as though I might be stepping back in time to the first days of baseball. They are oblivious to the chill and the championship drama only a hundred yards away. Right field is closed off. As I draw near, I try to identify their game. Is it pitcher's-hand out, work up, three o' cat, or a game they've invented on the spot? Everyone is playing. There are no umpires, no fans, no trophies on the line. I hop off the bike and walk right up to the diamond, thinking about asking if I can join them, wondering if they will ask me without my asking first. I flash back to the softball games I watched when I first came to New York. As the pitcher and batter square off, it's as if I were invisible.

# Hot Stove

**IN A LOT OF WAYS** the season played out as I dreamed it would. I made it as a player with Billy's team, the Machine. I went on a hitting tear, took over for Billy as the d.b.a. pitcher, and shut down Two Boots for the championship. I was voted playoff MVP by my teammates and received a plaque during the team's victory party at d.b.a. In the annals of athletic achievement I suppose that isn't much, but it's not bad for a former Little League benchwarmer. In the process I made a lot of friends—Cookie, Big Artie, shortstop Mike, Matt, Penny, Robin, Gina, and even the crusty Billy and the tortured Zeus. And I transformed the losing Sharkeys into the division champion Pamela's Foxes. Although we didn't win it all, we earned a massive trophy that no one wants, not our sponsor Mickey and definitely not Francesca, who has seen it more than most, as it gleams discordantly from our otherwise tasteful mantle.

In other ways things did not turn out anything like the way that I had expected. I began the season hoping to make right my failed Little League career. I thought I would find myself in a world where friendships flowed as easily as fellow feeling in Budweiser and Gatorade commercials. I also thought I would demonstrate to all, myself included, my profound understanding of both baseball and how to run a tiny organization. I began the season expecting to hand out Eddy Ball lessons like so many midterm exams, but I found myself time after time being schooled.

One thing I've learned is that it is impossible to redo childhood failures. I never made it in Little League, and despite the hundred-odd hits I accumulated this year, I never will. By looking backward, I found myself spending much of the softball season playing not to win or for fun, but to avoid being treated like a mascot again. We've all heard the chestnut that just because you're par-

221

anoid, it doesn't mean that they aren't out to get you. I've learned that even when people are sometimes against you, a paranoid response doesn't do any good. As for failures, the only thing to do is learn from them and move on. I've removed the Little League photo from my dresser, put it in the drawer, and replaced it with the MVP plaque.

Proving things to other people isn't all that it's cracked up to be either. I've spent several seasons trying to show Zeus that I can play, and he may never see my value. I could have left the Machine on what seemed to Billy and my teammates like a personal high note, but it would have been a sour one to me. I had to prove things to myself. I know now that I can play, and in any of these leagues.

I also found out that softball isn't its own perfect little world, a laboratory in which to test pet ideas without having to file paperwork with the human-subjects review committee. Adults won't eagerly adopt unconventional ways of thinking, especially where softball is concerned. What they've learned in their years of playing matters to them. Far from being edifying, my professor-baseball demonstrations often freaked out my teammates and made them play worse. If my teammates think the batting order matters, then it does. I should've known better because there's an old sociological law, stated by the University of Chicago's W. I. Thomas, that says that if people define situations as real, they are real in their consequences. The law borders on tautology, but after decades of teaching and repetition, baseball situations are difficult to redefine. In-your-face stunts like the ones I pulled are likely to backfire—the way Bill James was caricatured in the press as championing "closer by committee"—and will discredit other valuable moves.

My success with Pamela's likely had less to do with analyses than with close observation, the standard, disparaged scouting skills. I used the data I had, but there just weren't enough to draw detailed conclusions. If I was forced to rely on my deceiving eyes, at least I had some sabermetric hypotheses about what to look for. Analysts will someday soon figure out defense in baseball and whittle down the errors in their projections. In softball, there is never going to be enough information or analytic attention to advance beyond the sort of hypotheses I generated. Because most of the players in softball are on the fat part of the bell curve of talent and personality characteristics, sabermetric findings based on major leaguers's performance about the small variations in pitchers' ability to get outs on balls in play, defensive efficiency, and even "clutchness" are not likely applicable to softball. And in softball, as in assisted reproduction, no one is interested enough to collect detailed statistics. Like the earliest baseball games and players, softball will remain shrouded in mystery.

I've also found that it's not worth contesting every little misconception. You have to pick your fights. Although I may never understand the logic behind it, from now on I will strive to do as my teammates advise: duck under a questionably high pitch, because this bid at intimidating the umpire always works and makes him call it a ball, but never leave for first base early on an obvious ball four, because that always backfires and results in a called strike. I still believe in patience and that it's key to walk. But I learned—when I failed to try to win the game against the Hitmen—that there are limits to this and any policy. At some point, you have to swing the bat.

I made some new friends, but the way it worked was nothing like on TV, where after the game everyone relaxes with a cold one and cracks one another up recounting misplays. There is no easy way to make friends anywhere; in softball, as in academic departments, there are going to be conflicts over goals and the allocation of scarce resources. Still, it's heartening to know that despite the squabbles everyone will be back out on the field after the first thaw.

But competitive recreational softball is as organizationally volatile as the earliest days of baseball, when teams formed, disbanded, and reconfigured yearly. Casey of the Hitmen persuaded Billy to give the Lower Manhattan Softball League one more try and not to convert it into a coed league. So next year the Machine will return but with a retooled roster. Billy finally pulled the plug on the irascible Dick, and Superman, the catcher Billy benched during the playoffs, has joined the Hitmen. At least they will have someone on the team we all know well. The championship d.b.a. team broke up over the dispute about its purpose. The d.b.a. owner wanted to ensure that anyone working at the bar could play on the team. So Billy is forming his own team in the East Village Softball Association, turning his back on free beer and pizza. Miles will be leading a kinder, gentler, more representative, and better-fed d.b.a. team against him.

Papi, Dog, and Q quit Pamela's Foxes to team up with Q's best friend Tanner; their team, P's & Q's, will shift into the Performing Arts Softball League, replacing the defunct Mickey Mantle's, and become our rivals. I didn't have the heart or nerve to ask Mickey to sponsor us again. Pamela's Global is tanking; not even New York is ready for Middle Eastern hip-hop. But I didn't want the team to go the way of the Pilots or the Motor Kings either. I'm planning to call the team Pamela's Global Foxes and partially sponsor it myself without telling anyone. The itinerant slugger Zeus has agreed to rejoin the team, and I have my eye on some pickup-game players who may be ready for Central Park. My skin is thicker, and I've moved along the learning curve, but I hope that Billy or Krishy will take a bigger role in running the Foxes.

In the matter of responsibility, too, this season made me realize that you have to be selective. I began last season eager to run the NYU sociology department, recruiting new colleagues while reassuring old ones, to run and revamp my softball team, and to reorganize a long-standing pickup game and eliminate the more disagreeable of its antique rules. By the end of the season I was almost prepared to seize the reins of team d.b.a. in order to lead my championship-starved teammates to nirvana and to ease Billy's pain. But it was too much work for too little fun.

The most important members of any of my teams arrived on January 24, when Francesca gave birth to our twins, Gregory and Luisa. They were so tiny that at first I was afraid to pick them up. That didn't last long. Our having twins meant something like having a baby of my own. Gregory doesn't breastfeed, so it's been my responsibility all February to keep him alive. It has been nothing but marathon feeding and diapering sessions, but that's taught me something too. It's made me wonder why I was forfeiting sleep over trivial matters like who would become chair of my department, what to say in class, or how to construct a lineup. The babies—with not so much as a hair between them yet—like to stare at my shiny softball hardware, so for now at least Francesca is letting me keep it. Sadly, all my game-used jerseys have been boxed up, along with most of our other possessions that are not baby-related.

Francesca and I are both on leave. Francesca is determined to finish her book on narrative by the fall, when she will be reviewed for tenure again by an ad hoc committee. In the meantime we are listening to overtures to relocate to the University of California or the University of Arizona. She sometimes calls me "Meat" as I had hoped, but not in the way I'd imagined, as in, "Isn't it about time to empty the Diaper Genie, Meat?"

Now that I can start for all my softball teams and have been invited to join others, I don't know how much I'll be able to play this season. But whenever I'm out there, I will try to win and try to have fun. I began the season thinking that these goals were completely compatible and know now that they aren't. I won often, and often it was great fun—sometimes even big league fun. I've also won and felt bored, miserable, angry, vengeful, or merely relieved. I've lost and found it exhilarating. I don't know any better now how much conflict there is between winning and having fun or even whether I will ever know. But if I ever figure it out, I look forward to digging out my best sweater and telling Ken Burns all about it.

## *Bibliography and Acknowledgments*

The material for *Professor Baseball* was collected over several seasons of softball in New York City. It is a study in what Loïc Wacquant would call "observant participation," as no statements were solicited and everything was recorded as it was played. See his *Body and Soul: Notebooks of an Apprentice Boxer* (New York: Oxford University Press, 2004). I performed the roles I did, as player and coach, because I was invited to do so. I sought to gain the respect of my teammates, but much like any other player I complained about how I was being deployed, and much like any other manager I was the object of complaints. The notes and photos I took form the basis of the book. Because I played with a lot of performers and writers, some of whom have their own softball-related screenplays, it was not viewed as odd to be taking notes and photographs or referring to my journal. Although the players and umpires were acting in public, I employ pseudonyms for them and some of the teams involved to protect their privacy. Friends and family are named. A strong case for using names in ethnographic writing is made by Mitchell Duneier in *Sidewalk* (New York: Farrar, Straus and Giroux, 1999), 347–52. There are no composite characters, and every incident happened as portrayed. In a very few instances I incorporated memorable moments from games not otherwise recounted into those narrated here. You could look it up (or at least some of it; Performing Arts Softball League data are archived at http://www.esportsdesk.com).

The book also refers and alludes to literatures on sociology and baseball, as well as films. Nineteenth-century and recent classics of social theory referred to in the text include the following: Karl Marx, "The Eighteenth Brumaire of Louis Bonaparte," in *The Marx-Engels Reader*, edited by Robert C. Tucker, 2nd ed., pp. 594–617 (originally 1852; New York: Norton, 1978). Emile Durkheim, "The Normal and the Pathological," in *The Rules of Sociological Method* (1895;

New York: Free Press, 1966). Max Weber, "The Types of Legitimate Domination," in *Economy and Society*, edited by Guenther Roth and Claus Wittich (1925; Berkeley: University of California Press, 1978). W. I. Thomas and Dorothy S. Thomas, *The Child in America* (New York: Knopf, 1928). George Herbert Mead, *Mind, Self, and Society*, edited by Charles W. Morris (1934; Chicago: University of Chicago Press, 1962). Albert O. Hirschman, *Exit, Voice and Loyalty: Responses to Decline in Firms, Organizations, and States* (Cambridge, MA: Harvard University Press, 1970). Pierre Bourdieu, "Sport and Social Class," *Social Science Information* 17 (1978): 819–40. The Bourdieu article has spawned an entire sociological literature on sport. I thank Max Weber for making possible my career as a sociologist.

More recent and notable sociological studies of baseball and socialization and identity formation mentioned or relied upon in the text include Gary Alan Fine, *With the Boys: Little League Baseball and Preadolescent Culture* (Chicago: University of Chicago Press, 1987), and Michael S. Kimmel, "Baseball and the Reconstruction of American Masculinity, 1880–1920," in *Sport, Men, and the Gender Order: Critical Feminist Perspectives*, edited by Don Sabo and Michael Messner (Champaign, IL: Human Kinetics Press, 1989). For an institutional approach to fandom and sports cultures in historical and comparative perspective, see Andrei S. Markovits and Steven L. Hellerman, *Offside: Soccer and American Exceptionalism* (Princeton, NJ: Princeton University Press, 2001). On narrative conventions in historiography, see Hayden White, *Metahistory* (Baltimore: Johns Hopkins University Press, 1973). See also Francesca Polletta, *It Was Like a Fever: Storytelling in Protest and Politics* (Chicago: University of Chicago Press, 2006).

Several passages also refer to the history of baseball, and these relied especially on the following: Harold Seymour, *Baseball: The Early Years* (New York: Oxford University Press, 1960). Warren Goldstein, *Playing for Keeps: A History of Early Baseball* (Ithaca, NY: Cornell University Press, 1989). Benjamin Rader, *Baseball: A History of America's Game* (Urbana: University of Illinois Press, 2002), which includes an extensive bibliography on the historiography of baseball and many biographies of players and discusses issues regarding professional baseball in comparative and historical perspective. On baseball in Japan, see Robert Whiting, *You Gotta Have Wa* (New York: Vintage, 1989) and *The Samurai Way of Baseball: The Impact of Ichiro and the New Wave from Japan* (New York: Warner Books, 2004). See also Sadaharu Oh, *Sadaharu Oh! A Zen Way of Baseball* (New York: Times Books, 1984). On the Black Sox scandal, see Eliot Asinof, *Eight Men Out: The Black Sox and the 1919 World Series* (New York: Henry Holt, 2000). For the Negro Leagues and the integration of major league baseball, see Jules Tygiel, *Baseball's Great Experiment: Jackie Robinson and His Legacy* (New York: Oxford University Press, 1997), and Neil Lanctot, *Negro League Baseball: The Rise and Ruin of a Black Institution* (Philadelphia: University of Pennsylvania Press, 2004).

Some great novels have had baseball as their subject or backdrop. Of those referred to in the text, the top ten, listed in order of publication, are as follows (list in order of greatness available upon request): Ring Lardner, *You Know Me Al: A Busher's Letters* (1916; New York: Macmillan, 1960). Bernard Malamud, *The Natural* (1952; New York: Farrar, Straus and Giroux, 2003). Mark Harris, *The Southpaw* (1953; Lincoln, NE: Bison Books, 2003). Mark Harris, *Bang the Drum Slowly* (1956; Lincoln, NE: Bison Books, 2003). Robert Coover, *The Universal Baseball Association, Inc., J. Henry Waugh, Prop.* (New York: Random House, 1968). Phillip Roth, *The Great American Novel* (New York: Holt, Rinehart and Winston, 1973). William Brashler, *Bingo Long Traveling All-Stars and Motor Kings* (New York: Harper and Row, 1973). W. P. Kinsella, *Shoeless Joe* (Boston: Houghton Mifflin, 1982). Eric Rolfe Greenberg, *The Celebrant* (New York: Everest House, 1983). Don DeLillo, *Underworld* (New York: Scribners, 1997). I want to express special appreciation to Mark Harris, as the depiction of Francesca in the book—so, so much material to choose from—is modeled in part on Harris's depiction of his character Henry Wiggen's girlfriend/wife Holly, who in turn was apparently based on Harris's wife Josephine. Also, apologies to Harris for, among other things, "Bang the Drum for the Kid from Greenwich Village."

John R. Tunis's baseball novels for the underage set, published in the 1940s and still current in the late 1960s, are quite dark by today's standards. See, for instance, *The Kid from Tomkinsville* (1940; San Diego: Harcourt Brace Jovanovich, 1987), which ends with the rookie, whose freak injury has already forced him off the mound and into the outfield, crashing into a wall, and possibly dead; *Keystone Kids* (1943; San Diego: Harcourt Brace Jovanovich, 1990), in which a rookie earns the respect of his anti-Semitic teammates by singling out one and threatening to beat the bejesus out of him; and *Young Razzle* (New York: Morrow, 1949), whose rookie hero's rise to stardom is fueled by his resentment of his famous big-league, deadbeat dad. For the dark side of sports fandom, see Tunis's incomparable *Yea! Wildcats!* (1944; San Diego: Harcourt Brace Jovanovich, 1989), which gives new meaning to Hoosier hysteria when a high school basketball team's heartbreaking loss in the state playdowns leads seemingly inevitably to the town's forming a lynch mob.

Feature films on baseball tend to be less impressive and much lighter in tone than the novels, especially since the late 1970s. Some key exceptions, as mentioned or alluded to in the text, include this top six, listed in descending order of greatness: *Eight Men Out* (directed by John Sayles, 1988); *Bang the Drum Slowly* (John D. Hancock, 1973), in which Robert De Niro puts on the least plausible display of ball playing by an actor in a feature film since Anthony Perkins in *Fear Strikes Out*; *Bull Durham* (1988) and *Cobb* (1994), both directed by Ron Shelton; *A League of Their Own* (Penny Marshall, 1992); and *Field of Dreams* (Phil Alden Robinson, 1989). Honorable mentions, also referred to in the text, go to *The Bad News Bears* (Michael Ritchie, 1976), *The Natural* (Barry Levinson, 1984), and *The Bingo Long Traveling All-Stars and Motor Kings* (John Badham, 1976). Perfectly anodyne recent baseball-related films include *The Rookie* (John Lee Hancock, 2002) and *For the Love of the Game* (Sam Raimi, 1999). Other films mentioned in the text include *The Godfather, Part Two* (Francis Ford Coppola, 1974), *The Freshman* (Andrew Bergman, 1990), *Adaptation* (Spike Jonze, 2002), *Breaking Away* (Peter Yates, 1979), *Easy Rider* (Dennis Hopper, 1969), and the highly influential and unfortunate *Rocky* (John Avildsen, 1976). In Ken Burns's essential nine-part documentary *Baseball* (1994), numerous scholars, writers, and other luminaries appear, including Mario Cuomo and the late George Plimpton, whose contributions are referred to in the book.

Baseball has also incited a kind of novelistic journalism that is frequently invoked in the text. The poet laureate of baseball writing and the imaginary ballpark companion of all literary wannabes following baseball is Roger Angell, the author of several compilations of pieces that ran initially in the *New Yorker*, including *The Summer Game* (New York: Viking, 1972), *Late Innings: A Baseball Companion* (New York: Simon & Schuster, 1978), *Season Ticket: A Baseball Companion* (Boston: Houghton Mifflin, 1988), *Five Seasons: A Baseball Companion* (Lincoln: University of Nebraska Press, 2004), and *Once More around the Park: A Baseball Reader* (Chicago: Ivan R. Dee, 2001). His thoughts about baseball and time appear on the last pages of *The Summer Game*. Other notable writers with work in this genre include Robert Creamer, David Halberstam, Roger Kahn, Thomas Boswell, Daniel Okrent, George Plimpton, and Pat Jordan.

Because high-profile journalism on baseball has the literary quality of baseball fiction, the two genres are often placed side by side in readers. See, for example, *The Baseball Reader: Favorites from the Fireside Books of Baseball*, edited by Charles Einstein (New York: Lippincott & Crowell, 1980). John Updike's 1961 piece "Hub Fans Bid Kid Adieu," along with many other classics, appears in *Baseball: A Literary Anthology*, edited by Nicholas Dawidoff (New York: Library of America, 2002). Given a much harder time than he deserves was the late A. Bartlett Giamatti, whose writings on baseball are insightful and frequently poetic. See his "The Green Fields of the Mind" in the Dawidoff reader and, for more, *A Great and Glorious Game: Baseball Writings of A. Bartlett Giamatti*, edited by Kenneth S. Robson (Chapel Hill, NC: Algonquin Books, 1998).

The finest first-person accounts of seasons by major league ballplayers include these classics: Jim Bouton, *Ball Four: My Life and Hard Times Throwing the Knuckleball in the Big Leagues* (New York: World, 1970); Jim Brosnan, *The Long Season* (New York: Dell, 1960) and *Pennant Race* (New York: Harper, 1962); and Sparky Lyle and Peter Golenbock, *The Bronx Zoo: The Astonishing Inside Story of the 1978 World Champion New York Yankees* (New York: Crown, 1979). I thank Jim Bouton for his inspiration by example, with apologies for "Big League Fun," and for his willingness to wedge into his schedule a talk to my class. Even though I had him put on a free clinic, it is in no way his fault that I still can't get my knuckler to do much more than wobble.

Although quantitative baseball analysts have forced their way into major league front offices, the genre of writing dubbed by Bill James as "sabermetrics" is still segregated from baseball journalism and nonfiction. This literature has been truly Jamesian in that the bulk of its practitioners imitate his style, which encases rigorous thinking and extensive data analyses in playful, nonacademic prose. For some central works in sabermetrics, see Bill James, *Baseball Abstract* (self-published 1977–1981, then by Ballantine as *The Bill James Baseball Abstract*, 1982–1988); John Thorn and Pete Palmer, *The Hidden Game of Baseball* (New York: Doubleday, 1985); Bill James, *The New Bill James Historical Baseball Abstract* (New York: Free Press, 2001); and the Baseball Prospectus Team of Experts, *Baseball between the Numbers: Why Everything You Know about the Game Is Wrong* (New York: Basic Books, 2006). Two Web sites that make new advances in baseball analysis daily (and publish baseball annuals) are Baseball Prospectus (http://www.baseballprospectus.com), whose Nate Silver among others is much appreciated, and Hardball Times (http://www.hardballtimes.com). For a history of baseball-analytical ideas by way of their innovators, see Alan Schwarz, *The Numbers Game: Baseball's Lifelong Fascination with Statistics* (New York: Thomas Dunne Books, 2004). For a recent prominent think-journalism book, discussed in the text, on the application of sabermetric ideas by major leaguers and the controversy that has ensued, see Michael Lewis, *Moneyball* (New York: Norton, 2003). I thank him for the 2004 paperback's lyrical, fever-dream afterword, which I recommend for all authors everywhere who have ever fantasized about inflicting payback on narrow-minded critics.

For a comprehensive and entertaining glossary of baseball terms and the ways they have worked their way into common parlance, see Paul Dickson, *The New Dickson Baseball Dictionary* (New York: Harcourt Brace & Company, 1999). And, Paul, for the next edition please look into "twist."

I owe a debt of appreciation to all my teammates in the various New York City softball leagues and especially to all the Pamela's Cantina Foxes for their season of magic and forbearance. I also thank Angel Lebron, Ted Smits, Ken Mahadeo, Spencer MacLeish, Jeff Lyons, and especially Juan Parra and Jimmy Maresca for letting me play for their teams. A special shout-out goes to teammate Matt Wasowski, who read the entire manuscript, provided excellent commentary ("cut, cut"), and induced his mother, Isobel Wasowski, to read and edit the manuscript as well ("cut out Matt") at the friends-and-family rate. I thank teammates Paul Weinstein, Mark Golubow, Judd Cady, Snowdon Parlette, and Mark Gasper for many stimulating discussions about baseball and life. And I thank Ozzie Guillen and the 2005 Chicago White Sox for ending my lifetime of fan misery. I wish only that I was in New York for it. I had no chance to crow about it to my doormen or teammates after taking years' worth of shit. But with the team's dreamlike sweep though the postseason, I was able to reignite the argument with Francesca over total domination.

I thank Douglas A. Mitchell of the University of Chicago Press for his belief in the book and his reading and encouragement. All writers should be so lucky as to get a chance to work with Doug. I thank Timothy McGovern for his able steering of the book through the editorial process and Peter Cavagnaro and Levi Stahl for their marketing savvy. I thank Joel Score for his keen eye and supple editing. I also thank my agent Betty Anne Crawford of Books Crossing Borders for her readings, enthusiasm, and energy, and I hope she can make *Professor Baseball* number one in Japan.

I thank Douglas Harper and John D. Skrentny for their extensive expert readings and criticisms of the manuscript for the Press. I thank Doug also for his perceptive, image-by-image critique of the photos. My great appreciation goes out, too, to the many friends and colleagues who read and commented on the manuscript, especially Kim Blanton, Robert Zussman, and Jim Jasper ("Jim"). I thank Jeff Goodwin ("Jeff"), Sarah Rosenfield ("Sarah"), Robb Bloom ("Robb"), Joe Jackson ("Joey"—yes, that's his name), Maddalena Polletta ("Maddy"), Pedro Diez, Gabriella Polletta, and Gregory Polletta for their friendship and support. I thank my sister Marybeth Amenta ("Marybeth") for her slick camera work during the playoff game with the Hitmen, and my brother Chuck for making me a White Sox fan. I thank my brother Francis and my sister Kerry Garesche ("Kerry") and their families for being there for me. I thank my mother Mary for turning Chuck into a White Sox fan and my father Charles for transmitting his love of sports. Gregory Charles Amenta and Luisa Jean Amenta ("rice-grain fetuses") helped me realign my priorities.

It is impossible to thank adequately Francesca Polletta ("Francesca"). She read through so many partial and entirely too long "complete" drafts and listened to so many half-baked ideas for the book that she probably merits an as-told-to author's credit. And by the way, on the second review she did indeed get tenure at Columbia University, as she very well should have the first time. If you are keeping score at home, chalk up another one for redemption.